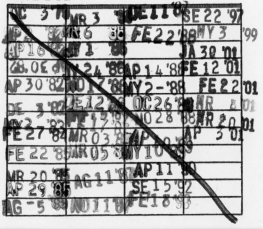

THE POLITICS OF ELECTORAL COLLEGE REFORM

THE POLITICS OF
ELECTORAL COLLEGE REFORM

by Lawrence D. Longley and Alan G. Braun

with a Foreword by U.S. Senator Birch Bayh

Second Edition

NEW HAVEN AND LONDON, YALE UNIVERSITY PRESS, 1975

Library of Congress catalog card number: 72-75202
ISBN: 0-300-02587-9 (cloth); 0-300-01588-7 (paper).

Designed by Sally Sullivan
and set in IBM Selectric Press Roman type.
Printed in the United States of America by
The Colonial Press
Clinton, Massachusetts

Published in Great Britain, Europe, and Africa by
Yale University Press, Ltd., London.
Distributed in Latin America by Kaiman & Polon,
Inc., New York City; in India by UBS Publishers'
Distributors Pvt., Ltd., Delhi; in Japan by John
Weatherhill, Inc., Tokyo.

Contents

Foreword by Senator Birch Bayh   vii

Acknowledgments   xi

Preface to the Second Edition   xiii

1. The Electoral College System in Two Elections   1
   The Election of 1960   1
   The Election of 1968   7
   Problems of the Electoral College System   18

2. The Creation and Operation of the Electoral College   22
   The Birth of the Electoral College System   23
   Changes in the Electoral College System   28
   The Electoral College System Misbehaving   32

3. The Multiple Roads to Electoral College Reform   42
   The Automatic Plan   43
   The Proportional Plan   49
   The District Plan   57
   The Direct Vote Plan   64
   Hybrids and Other Plans   69

4. Assessment: The Case for the Direct Vote Plan   74
   Criteria for Evaluation   74
   Proposals with Less Support   76
   The Direct Vote Plan   82

5. Direct Vote: A Goal Nearly Reached   127
   Obstacles to Constitutional Change   127
   Activities during the 1960s   131
   1969 and House Action   137
   1970 and Senate Action   156
   Prospects   175

Appendix A. 1970 State Populations and 1972–80
   Electoral College Apportionments   177

Appendix B. Recent Empirical Research on the
   Electoral College   179

Notes 181

Index 215

Foreword

Direct popular election of the president is the only system that is truly democratic, truly equitable, and can truly reflect the will of people.

On the other hand, we know only too well the defects of our present electoral college system. The 1968 election highlighted most graphically one of these problems, that of the independent elector. It is true that the electoral college was originally designed as a select assembly of independent electors, but that notion soon became obsolete with the rise of the party system. Yet the prospect of unknown electors auctioning off the presidency to the highest bidder remains all too real and frightening. That is the lesson of 1968, when the present electoral system brought us to the brink of constitutional crisis. A shift of only 42,000 popular votes in three states would have denied any candidate an electoral majority. It would have given the third-party candidate, with his 46 independent electoral votes, the balance of power.

Of course we could avoid this danger simply by eliminating the independence of the elector. But eliminating the independent role of the elector is not a cure-all for what ails our present electoral machinery. The elector, in fact, is merely a symptom of more fundamental flaws in our system of electing the president. We desperately need to overhaul the electoral college system itself.

First, it assigns to each state a minimum of 3 electoral votes, regardless of population and voter turnout. Second, the present system awards all of a state's electoral votes to the winner of the state popular vote, whether his margin is 1 vote or 1 million votes, thus canceling out all of the popular votes cast for the losing candidate in a state. Third, it provides for a patently undemocratic method for choosing a president in the event that no candidate receives an electoral majority—by an election in the Congress, with each state entitled to 1 vote.

One of the major difficulties of the present electoral system—

the so-called winner-take-all rule—is not even a constitutional provision. In effect, millions of voters are disfranchised if they vote for the losing candidate in their state because the full voting power of the state—its electoral vote—is awarded to the candidate they opposed.

The unit rule discourages the minority party in traditionally one-party states. Simply stated, where there is no hope of carrying the statewide popular vote, the size of the voter turnout for the likely loser is meaningless. This necessarily leads to the atrophying of the party structure in many states. In sum, the unit rule has the unhealthy political effect of both maintaining weak second parties and discouraging voting.

Many have concluded that the present system favors one citizen over another, one region over another, or one group over another. Any such argument presents a fundamental question of national fairness. The president represents every American, regardless of region or state, and he should be elected by all Americans, fairly and equitably. Every vote should count the same, urban or rural, black or white, rich or poor, North, South, East or West. Any system that favors one citizen over another or one state over another is inherently inconsistent with the most fundamental concept of a democratic society.

Despite their seriousness, these defects in the electoral college system are not so dangerous as the most fundamental flaw: the fact that the present electoral vote system cannot guarantee that the candidate with the most popular votes will be elected. In 1948, to give only one example, a shift of less than 30,000 votes in three states would have made Governor Dewey the president—despite President Truman's immense margin of more than 2 million popular votes. This dangerous prospect, more than anything else, condemns the present system as a faulty device for recording the sentiment of American voters.

How can we possibly justify the continued use of such a patchwork of inequity and chance? In this book we have the benefit of a comprehensive and carefully researched study of the electoral college and proposed reform legislation. The authors offer a thoughtful analysis of the myths and realities surrounding the arguments for various reform proposals.

As chairman of the Subcommittee on Constitutional Amendments, I have conducted hearings and studied testimony on electoral reform for over five years. Direct popular election is the only real reform. It guarantees that the man who receives the most votes is elected president. It counts every vote equally, and it provides the people themselves with the right to make the choice directly.

In an examination of the prospects for change to a direct vote, the authors ask why it has proved so difficult to obtain reform of the present widely condemned system. Supporters of reform legislation have had to face this question repeatedly. Although the struggle for reform has been difficult and sometimes bitter, I, for one, intend to continue it. We already have widespread support for direct popular election in the Congress. The measure was approved by the House of Representatives in September 1969 by a vote of 338 to 70. And during Senate debate the following year we came within a handful of votes of breaking the filibuster that prevented a vote. I believe that only the extreme time pressures at the end of the session kept us from bringing direct popular election to a vote.

It is especially important that a coalition of nationwide support be maintained. That is why I warmly welcome this thought-provoking and needed edition.

BIRCH BAYH
United States Senator

Acknowledgments

Many persons have been of assistance in the preparation of this book, but no one more than John Yunker, a Lawrence University student who worked closely with one of the authors for a period of months under a National Science Foundation COSIP Faculty-Student Grant to Lawrence University. His invaluable contribution to the research on which this book is based is acknowledged with deep appreciation—and cited in too few places.

Other Lawrence students found themselves involved in this project at various points in their academic studies, among them being: Chris Bowers, Jeff Fox, Beth Fravell, Betsy Georg, Paul Hartwig, Tom Hosmanek, Doug Kohrt, Jim Lewis, Mike McKenzie, Mark Roudane, Andrew Saxe, Marilyn Taylor, and Phil York. Their insatiable tendency to raise questions and challenge assumptions helped keep this book off several reefs.

Appreciation is also due to Professors Minoo Adenwalla, William Boardman, William Bremer, James Dana, Chong-Do Hah, and Jules LaRocque of Lawrence University, as well as Professors John F. Banzhaf III of George Washington University, Steven J. Brams of New York University, Max S. Power of the University of Victoria, and Carleton Sterling of Rutgers University, and most of all Neal R. Peirce of the *National Journal*, all of whom assisted and advised at various points during this project.

For interview time, background information, and general help in the research conducted by both authors specifically in Washington, D.C., thanks are given to: John F. Banzhaf III, Jason Berman, Doug Bennet, Jr., Donald Channell, David Clanton, Myron P. Curzan, Ken Davis, Bess Dick, Joseph J. Fanelli, Charles Ferris, Malcolm Hawk, Jack Lewis, Dan Leach, Clark MacGregor, David Osterhort, Neal R. Peirce, Richard Scammon, Robert Smith, Dorothy Stimpson, and Benjamin L. Zelenko.

Mrs. Edward Lorge, Jr., typist for the book, proved very skilled at coping with essentially illegible handwriting under pressures of time. Special appreciation is indisputably due to Mrs. Marian Ash and Mrs. Judy Yogman of Yale University Press, who guided this book through the editorial and production stages of publication with unfailing grace, courtesy, and, most of all, intelligence.

Finally, one author—the other being unmarried—would like to thank his wife, Jane Longley, for giving up her husband to the study of the electoral college—an absence little made up for by his recitation of facts about it when at home.

Preface to the Second Edition

In the three years since publication of the first edition of this book, efforts toward reform of the electoral college have stalled while scholarship concerning the effects of the electoral college system has proliferated.

The reform drive of the late 1960s culminated in stunning victory for electoral college reform in the House of Representatives in 1969 but frustrating defeat in the Senate in 1970. These events, described in detail in chapter 5 of this book, had the effect of profoundly discouraging supporters of electoral college reform and also led to the dismemberment of the powerful coalition of diverse interests that supported reform in 1969 and 1970. As we noted in 1972 and repeat in this edition: ". . . electoral reform, if it is to be again advanced, must travel the same route as before—of committee hearings, struggles for committee votes, floor consideration, and agonies in getting a final affirmative vote—and this in both Houses. Certainly, discouragement over facing this prospect again is sufficient to shake even the most committed direct vote advocate."

The presidential election of 1972 seemingly did little to heighten any sense of urgency concerning reform of the electoral college. Neither condition associated with likely electoral college deadlock was present—a third party strong enough regionally to capture a number of electoral votes or the two major parties so evenly matched as to negate the usual multiplier effect by which the electoral college majority far exceeds the popular vote plurality. The candidate preferred by 61 percent of American voters received total of 520 out of 538 electoral votes, or 97 percent. The multiplier effect was, in fact, exceedingly strong in 1972 at a close to record 36 percent. The electoral college seemed to be performing the role often attributed to it by its defenders: strengthening a popular vote winner's mandate.

In the light of the post-Watergate era, some harsh second thoughts might seem, however, to be in order. Is such an artificial magnification of the electoral verdict desirable? To what extent does such an expansion of a president's mandate heighten his sense of omnipotence and supremacy? Can the evolution of the Nixonian imperial presidency be traced, to some degree, to the electoral college's magnification of electoral outcomes in both 1968 and 1972?

Another feature of the 1972 election was the appearance, for the fourth time in the last five elections, of a "faithless elector." Republican presidential elector Roger MacBride of Virginia decided, after election day, not to vote for Richard Nixon, as the nearly one million Republican voters in Virginia had assumed he would (or at least any who did not assume they were voting directly for Nixon for president). Instead, MacBride cast his vote in December 1973 for virtually unknown Libertarian party candidate John Hospers, director of the School of Philosophy of the University of Southern California.

Despite these interesting events, the 1972 election did not give new impetus to reform. The reform bills regularly introduced in each new Congress gathered little support, and the September 26 and 27, 1973, hearings on electoral college reform conducted by the Subcommittee on Constitutional Amendments of the Senate Judiciary Committee were largely ignored by both press and public.

The result of this stalling of reform efforts during the first half of the 1970s is that, as we express it in the final lines of this edition, "... the 1976 and possibly subsequent elections will be held under the traditional electoral college system, modified only by Maine's use of the district plan. As a result, a presidential election may yet provide the American people and their political leaders with tragic evidence of the potentially disastrous shortcomings of the present system. At that point, the politics of electoral college reform will become lively again."

Given this state of inactivity concerning electoral college reform, what has happened in terms of professional scholarship since the first edition? Here the picture is more encouraging. In the past few years, new empirically based research focusing on the effects of the system has appeared and stimulated further study. Panel sessions at professional conferences have given rise to correspondence among scholars and debates in professional journals. This literature is significant not only because of its marked methodological and theoretical diversity, but also because of the compatibility and complementarity of many of the major findings. A new appendix, "Recent Empirical Research on the Electoral College," lists a number of these works. The reader is urged to consult this literature for in-depth studies of many of the points and findings only alluded to in the book.

Finally, let us briefly describe how this new edition of our book differs (and, we hope, builds upon) the earlier version. Besides the customary and always necessary correction of minor errors and clarification of obscure points, we have also incorporated data from the 1972 presidential election throughout the book. This is especially visible in our discussion of how the electoral college has worked (and threatened not to work) in recent elections; tables and figures have been revised where appropriate. Several points made elsewhere in the book have also been modified in light of the 1972 election, most notably the argument in chapter 3 that there is a bias in favor of the Republican party inherent in the district plan; this theory now appears questionable in light of new analysis of the presidential vote by congressional districts in 1972.

Certainly the most substantial change in this edition, however, comes in chapter 4, where entirely new data are presented evaluating the biases of the present electoral college system and various reform proposals. Not only the result of a refinement of the techniques utilized in the first edition for evaluating the electoral college, the findings presented here are also based, for the first time, on the population totals and electoral college apportionments of the 1970s, which apply to the presidential elections of 1972, 1976, and 1980. We conclude that the electoral college is an institution that operates with noteworthy inequity. While its biases are not cumulative and unidirectional, they are significant and introduce a complex element of citizen inequality into the American political system. Yet the politics of electoral college reform has resulted in this curious institution continuing, for at least a while, to be the means by which we elect our presidents.

Appleton, Wisconsin   L. D. L.
Minneapolis, Minnesota   A. G. B.
March 30, 1975

1. The Electoral College System in Two Elections

*Every boy and girl should go to college and if they
can't afford Yale or Harvard, why, Electoral is just as
good, if you work.*

*The guys at the bar poor-mouth Electoral somethin'
awful. Wasn't they mixed up in a basketball scandal
or somethin'?*

Man-on-the-street interviews

*I think that if the man who wins the popular vote is
denied the Presidency, the man who gets the Presidency
would have very great difficulty in governing.*

Richard M. Nixon during the 1968 campaign

There are many ways of approaching the study of how the electoral college works, some abstract, some descriptive in detail, and many more formal and legalistic. The method used here is to examine the operation of the electoral college system in specific instances, namely, the presidential elections of 1960 and 1968. These two contests are of special interest in terms of electoral reform; in fact, the 1967 assessment by Neal R. Peirce, that "the 1960 election summed up the evils of the Electoral College in our time," is equally true for both the 1960 and 1968 elections.[1]

The Election of 1960

On November 8, 1960, almost seventy million Americans—a record number—went to the polls to cast their ballots for the various candidates of their choice. The voters cast their ballots directly for their preferred candidates in 437 House, 33 Senate, 29 gubernatorial, and thousands of state and local elections. The voters also participated indirectly in the election of the only truly national officers, the president and vice president of the United States. In accordance with the provisions of the

1

Constitution and various state constitutions and statutes, the American people cast their ballots for from three to forty-five potential presidential electors. Each state was allowed the number of electors corresponding to "the whole Number of Senators and Representatives to which the States may be entitled in the Congress."[2] Thus, each state was guaranteed a minimum of 3 votes in the electoral college, regardless of the size of the state population or the voter turnout.[3]

The American voters did not cast their ballots for the candidate of their choice; they voted for slates of candidates for the position of presidential elector—generally unknown individuals who had worked diligently for their parties and had secured their nominations through a wide variety of selection methods. Undoubtedly few citizens could later remember the names of the electors for whom they voted—if they had ever known them. For most voters, the act of voting entailed not a decision about presidential electors, but a choice between two presidential candidates—Richard M. Nixon and John F. Kennedy.[4]

The election turned out to be a virtual standoff. In popular votes, Nixon and Kennedy both received slightly over 49 percent, with the remainder almost all going to unpledged elector slates in Mississippi and Alabama. Their popular vote difference was 118,000 (margin for Kennedy) or 58,181 (margin for Nixon), depending on how you count some of the votes in Alabama cast for both unpledged and Kennedy-pledged electors.[5] The former figure—a Kennedy margin of 118,000—was the one widely reported on election night by the wire services, which announced that Kennedy, with a margin over Nixon of but .2 percent, had amassed an electoral vote count of 303, 34 more than the needed majority of 269,[6] and 56.4 percent of the total.

This magnification of electoral vote strength over popular vote strength was a classic example of the *multiplier effect* turning thin or nonexistent pluralities into resounding electoral vote majorities.[7] In terms of popular vote results, Kennedy's margin—even forgetting for the moment the question of how to count the Alabama votes—seems almost nonexistent; in terms of electoral vote results, his margin appears secure.[8] How secure, in fact, was this electoral verdict?

There are two different ways of asking this question: How likely was it that the popular vote winner would also be the electoral vote winner, and how likely was it that a candidate would receive the needed electoral college absolute majority of 269 votes? In regard to the first question, Charles W. Bischoff of the Department of Economics of M.I.T. conducted a computer analysis of past popular vote-electoral vote relationships and concluded that in an election with a margin as small as in 1960, there is no better than a fifty-fifty chance that the popular and electoral vote results will agree as to the winner. When the margin of one candidate over the other is 500,000 votes, the chance of his not leading the electoral vote is still one out of three; with a margin of 1 to 1.5 million, there is one out of four chances of his not being the electoral vote winner; and a margin of 2 million still leaves him one chance out of eight of losing the electoral vote.[9] That the Kennedy margin in popular votes (assuming for the moment that there was one) agreed with the electoral vote verdict was, therefore, both coincidental and fortunate.

The second question—How secure was the existence of an electoral vote majority that would avoid an electoral college deadlock?—can be answered through an examination of the state-by-state popular vote totals, keeping in mind the importance of the *unit rule*, which confers all of a state's electoral votes upon the plurality winner. A number of possibilities exist, but probably the most striking is that a shift of only 8,971 popular votes from Kennedy to Nixon in the two states of Illinois and Missouri[10] would have resulted in an electoral college deadlock in 1960 with neither candidate having an electoral vote majority. A shift of 11,424 votes in the five states of Illinois, Missouri, New Mexico, Hawaii, and Nevada[11] would have resulted in an electoral college majority for Nixon.[12] The Kennedy victory was actually built on quite a flimsy base.

Thus far, we have discussed the electoral results of the 1960 election on the assumption that the popular vote totals were accurately and fairly reported. It can be easily seen, however, that the incentive for vote manipulation is enormous when a few thousand votes can change a state's entire electoral vote. It is not surprising, then, that charges were made of fraud in 1960—especially since two large states carried by Kennedy by extremely small margins—Illinois and Texas—happen also to share a reputation for occasional carelessness in vote counting. In fact, if the electoral votes of Illinois alone had been withheld from the Democrats, Kennedy's electoral vote total would have shrunk to 273, only 4 more than the needed majority. In this case, it was thought possible that four southern electors might bolt Kennedy—either by voting for someone like Senator Harry F. Byrd of Virginia or merely by abstaining on the single ballot, thus precipitating an electoral college deadlock, resulting in selection of the president by the House of Representatives. In his book *Six Crises*, Nixon recounts how he received a phone call from President Eisenhower the day after the election suggesting that he check out early reports of vote fraud in Illinois and Texas. In subsequent days other friends also urged him to question these returns. Nixon finally decided not to provoke a possible constitutional crisis, he writes, because such an action would create major problems in the orderly transfer of responsibilities to the new administration, give rise to great bitterness, and set a bad example for foreign countries.[13]

One feature of the election results of 1960 was the election, in Mississippi and Alabama, of fourteen unpledged presidential electors. This was the first time since the birth of political parties in America that voters had consciously put their faith in the wisdom and veracity of the men who serve as electors. Actually these men were not entirely independent thinkers—failing in their prime objective of deadlocking the electoral college, they all decided to give their votes to Senator Byrd when the electoral college met in the various state capitals on December 19. In this singular resolution, they were joined by a Nixon-pledged elector, Henry D. Irwin of Oklahoma, giving to the noncandidate Byrd—who had received no popular votes—15 electoral votes, or just under 3 percent of all the electoral votes.[14] While the hopes that the unpledged elector strategy would deadlock the electoral college and then wring concessions from the two major parties failed, the threat was explicit.

The peculiar problem of determining the popular vote in the case of Alabama arises directly from the election in that state of six unpledged Democratic electors along with the five Democratic electors pledged to Kennedy. Different totals were recorded for each of the elector candidates, with the highest vote for a Kennedy elector being 318,303 and the highest vote for an unpledged elector being 324,050. The technique used by the wire services on election night was both simple and erroneous—it credited Kennedy in Alabama with the highest vote received by *any* Democratic elector—thus 324,050 votes, the count received by an unpledged elector! This resulted in a reported national Kennedy margin over Nixon of 118,000 votes.

Congressional Quarterly, under the leadership of Neal Peirce, its political editor at that time, subsequently developed another method for counting these votes, which seems somewhat fairer. This was to credit Kennedy in Alabama with the votes received by any Kennedy-pledged elector—thus 318,303 votes. This results in a slightly smaller national Kennedy margin over Nixon of 112,827 votes. This measure, however, along with the preceding technique, is subject to a most serious criticism—it counts the 300,000-plus votes of Alabama twice—as votes for Kennedy (318,303) and as votes for unpledged electors (324,050).

As a means of meeting this problem, *Congressional Quarterly* developed a third measure—one that does not double the votes cast in Alabama. This is to take the highest vote received by any Democratic elector—324,050 for an unpledged elector—and divide it in proportion to the types of elector actually chosen: five-elevenths to Kennedy corresponding to his five electors, and six-elevenths to a category of *unpledged-elector slate* corresponding to the six unpledged electors. This latter technique, seemingly the fairest of all three, credits Kennedy with only 147,295 votes from Alabama and results in a Nixon national popular lead of 58,181 votes![15] Tom Wicker of the *New York*

Times accurately describes the muddle generated by the Alabama returns when he writes:

> Nobody knows to this day, or ever will, whom the American people really elected President in 1960. Under the prevailing system, John F. Kennedy was inaugurated, but it is not at all clear that this was really the will of the people or, if so, by what means and margin that will was expressed.[16]

Besides the basic indeterminability of the popular vote results, another unusual occurrence imposed itself between the popular vote and the election of the president. This was the postelection plan, concocted by Lea Harris of Montgomery, Alabama, to urge that Republican electors (who knew that Nixon had lost the election) and southern Democratic electors (who presumably could not stand Kennedy) join together to deadlock the electoral college and force a true conservative president upon the nation—Senators Byrd or Goldwater being mentioned. Telegrams were sent to all Republican electors soon after election day by Henry Irwin, stating:

> I am Oklahoma Republican elector. The Republican electors cannot deny the election to Kennedy. Sufficient conservative Democratic electors available to deny labor Socialist nominee. Would you consider Byrd President, Goldwater Vice President, or wire any acceptable substitute. All replies strict confidence.[17]

Although the forty-odd replies Irwin received were somewhat discouraging or evasive, he still decided to follow his own plan, at least individually, and consequently, on December 19, he voted for Senator Byrd for president and Senator Goldwater for vice president. The great conservative plot of 1960 fizzled and flopped but still left a dark hint of what might happen sometime in the future—especially if the electoral vote margin were close. A Henry Irwin, then, might conceivably have enormous potential for influencing the choice of the president.[18]

A final question that should be asked is: If an electoral college deadlock had occurred in 1960—whether caused by a closeness of popular votes, unpledged electors, or defecting electors —would it have made any difference in the eventual outcome? The question of the contingent election procedure will be dealt with in greater detail in regard to the 1968 election, but suffice it here to note that, in 1961, voting by the House of Representatives through the constitutionally prescribed one vote per state method would not necessarily have resulted in Kennedy being elected. On the contrary, the House elected in November 1960, which would have been called upon, starting on January 6, 1961, to choose the president from among the three top candidates—Nixon, Kennedy, and Byrd—had twenty-three state delegations controlled by northern and border-state Democrats, six controlled by Deep South Democrats, seventeen controlled by Republicans, and four tied—thus losing their votes. Since twenty-six states are needed for a president to be elected, it is probable that the House would have been unable or slow to decide the presidency as the constitutionally prescribed inauguration day of January 20 grew closer and that the votes of the Deep South delegations would have proved decisive, thus allowing them to play a key role in the determination of the president.[19]

What, then, are the electoral college evils illustrated by the 1960 election? They are (1) the distortion of popular results when translated into electoral votes, (2) the possibility that a relatively few votes in key states could swing large blocs of electoral votes and thus an election, (3) the resulting incentive for fraud in those same states, (4) the ability of unpledged (or third-party) political movements to deadlock the electoral college if the two-party race is close enough, (5) the indeterminability of popular vote preferences when transferred into both pledged and unpledged electoral votes, (6) the danger of the faithless elector—especially when working in contact with others and when an election is close, and (7) the uncertainty and possible deals attendant upon a House contingent election.

The Election of 1968

The presidential election of 1968 was different from that of 1960 in one fundamental respect: for the first time in American history, there was a slate of elector candidates pledged to each of three contenders in all of the fifty states. Clearly the operations of the electoral college system in this election were to be both complex and uncertain.

A feature of the electoral college system of special significance for this election is that in each state a plurality of votes determines the entire electoral vote for that state—assuming, of course, the electors vote as pledged. This plurality need not be a majority, or of any particular size, but just the largest number of votes received by any single slate of electors. The results of this feature can be clearly seen in the state-by-state returns in the 1968 election. North Carolina, South Carolina, and Tennessee all exhibited similar patterns of one candidate—Nixon—receiving 100 percent of the state's electoral votes by obtaining only 39.5 percent, 38.1 percent, and 37.8 percent, respectively, of the popular vote. Although Nixon did carry seventeen of his thirty-two states with less than a majority of the votes cast, these three-way divisions did not always help him.[20] In Arkansas, for example, Nixon and Hubert Humphrey together split slightly over 61 percent of the popular vote, while Wallace, with 38 percent, received 100 percent of that state's electoral votes.

Of course, in most states outside the South, Wallace was not likely to receive a plurality—although to do so, he might need as little as 34 percent of the popular vote. His real impact came through his ability to draw off votes from the two major parties and possibly tilt a large state's bloc of 26 or 40 or 43 electoral votes one way or the other. In other words, it was the magnifying tendency of the unit rule, with its *winner-take-all* feature, that constituted Wallace's impact outside the South.

The Wallace candidacy, however, had another, more important goal than just carrying a few border and Deep South states or determining which of the major two parties would carry Michigan or California. The main goal of the Wallace campaign was to deadlock the electoral college through ensuring that neither Nixon nor Humphrey would have an electoral vote majority on election day. To accomplish this, two conditions would have to be present: (1) Wallace would have to receive a considerable number of electoral votes from both the Deep South and the border states, and (2) Nixon and Humphrey would have to divide the remaining electoral votes approximately evenly. If these two conditions occurred, Wallace would be in an excellent position to bargain, threaten, bluff, or cause general confusion as the electoral college system underwent crisis.

One major advantage that the Wallace movement had was that it was a *regionally based* rather than a *nationally distributed* third party. This is of great importance because of the unit rule feature of the electoral college, which denies all electoral votes to the second- or third-place candidate in each state. In order to receive any electoral votes—and thus to meet the first condition stated above—a third party must be powerful enough to run first in some state and thus receive electoral votes. The classic example of this difference between regionally based and nationally oriented third parties, which is inherent in the unit rule, is found in the election of 1948 when Senator Strom Thurmond and former Vice President Henry A. Wallace ran as candidates of the States' Rights and Progressive parties respectively; each received slightly over 1.1 million votes—about 2.4 percent of the popular vote total. Senator Thurmond carried four states and received 39 electoral votes, 7.3 percent of the electoral vote total or an inflation of almost three times over his popular vote strength. Henry Wallace, on the other hand, had his more than 1 million votes spread throughout the country and thus received no electoral votes at all. The electoral college system is quite clear in its bias: it favors third parties with a sectional orientation, and it discriminates against those with a national orientation.[21]

That George Wallace would receive some electoral votes in 1968 seemed certain. The question, then, was how many states would he carry—and, therefore, how many electoral votes would he get, and, consequently, how much of a margin would one of the two major-party candidates have to have over the other to avoid an electoral college deadlock?

These two questions are closely related, with the necessary margin between the two major-party candidates directly dependent upon the number of states that Wallace—or any third-party candidate—would remove from the pool of available states. The work of Professor Bischoff discussed earlier in this chapter illustrates this well and can be summarized in terms of three possibilities:

1. If Wallace should carry eleven states[22] (almost all of the South) for 128 electoral votes, one of the major-party candidates would have to get 270 of the remaining 410 electoral votes, or 66 percent of those left, in order to avoid an electoral college deadlock. Because of the multiplier effect turning narrow popular margins into large electoral vote margins, this probably could be accomplished if the candidate led the other candidate by an average of 4 to 5 percent in the popular vote in the non-Wallace states.
2. If Wallace should carry five states[23] (the Deep South) for 47 electoral votes, one of the major-party candidates would have to get 270 of the remaining 491 elector votes, or 55 percent of those left, in order to avoid an electoral college deadlock. This probably could be accomplished if that candidate led the other candidate by an average of 2 percent in the popular vote in the non-Wallace states.
3. If Wallace should carry two states (Mississippi and Alabama) for 17 electoral votes, one of the major-party candidates would have to get 270 of the remaining 521 electoral votes, or 52 percent of those left, in order to avoid an electoral college deadlock. This probably could be accomplished if that candidate led the other candidate by an average of 1 percent in the popular vote in the non-Wallace states.[24]

These relationships were very real during the 1968 election. During late August and into September, Wallace was being credited with about 21 percent of the popular vote and up to 128 electoral votes. In order to avoid a deadlock, the leading candidate—without doubt Nixon in this case—would need a margin over Humphrey of 4 to 5 percent, which Nixon clearly enjoyed throughout the period.

As election day approached, Wallace's popular vote strength and, more important, his electoral vote strength had shrunk, while Humphrey's popular and electoral vote strength had rebounded—not a coincidental relationship. The danger here was that Wallace, while falling back to a hard-core base of about 45 or 47 electoral votes, might retain sufficient strength—given an electoral-vote standoff between Nixon and Humphrey—to deadlock the electoral college.

The results on election day, November 5, 1968, finally laid these fears to rest for the next four years. Wallace, with a national popular vote of 13.5 percent, received 45 electoral votes from five states of the Deep South,[25] a low 8.4 percent of the total electoral vote. While Nixon, with a popular vote of 43.4 percent, led Humphrey by only .7 percent nationally,[26] the vicissitudes of the electoral college resulted in Nixon receiving 302 electoral votes, or 56 percent of the total—a seeming comfortable 32 electoral votes over the 270 required.[27]

The security of the 1968 election night decision is, however, subject to the same type of examination earlier conducted on the 1960 decision. In this case also, we find that shifts by relatively small groups of voters could have altered the results.[28] If 53,034 votes for Nixon in New Jersey, Missouri, and New Hampshire had shifted at the last minute to Humphrey,[29] Nixon would then have had 269 electoral votes, 1 less than the needed majority, Humphrey, 224, and Wallace, 45.

One possibility could have affected the preceding analysis—a faithless elector who would cast his vote for president contrary to expectations. In fact, the 1968 election, like the 1960 election, did give rise to such an individual—the fifth in the history of the electoral college and the fourth in the postwar elections to vote clearly contrary to the expectations of those who had elected him. Not as colorful as Henry Irwin, the 1960 defecting elector, the 1968 individual was Dr. Lloyd W. Bailey of North Carolina, a Nixon elector. A member of the John Birch Society, Dr. Bailey finally decided that he could not vote for Nixon because of some of his early appointments of presidential advisers and his decision to ask Chief Justice Earl Warren to continue on the Court for an additional six months. When the electoral college met on December 16, Dr. Bailey, therefore, gave his electoral vote to Wallace, thus increasing Wallace's final count to 46 electoral votes.[30]

The danger shown here is less in the action of one isolated individual—although voters of a state might wonder what their vote is really worth in such a situation—than in the possibility of electors deviating from their pledges on a multiple basis should an electoral vote majority rest on 1 or 2 votes—a very real possibility in both 1960 and 1968. One thing is certain: if Nixon had lost the three close states previously mentioned and thus had had only 269 electoral votes, 1 short of a majority, it would not have been Dr. Bailey who would have saved the day. He was a Nixon-pledged elector—and, in fact, if he had still switched, Nixon's revised total would then have been 268, two short of a majority.

The final, but major question to ask about the 1968 election is: What if the results of the election had been an undecided electoral college deadlock? What would have been the likely series of events and results? To answer these questions, we have to look rather closely at some possibilities inherent in the electoral college system.

It is important to realize that the absence of an electoral vote majority on election day, November 5, would not necessarily ensure a deadlocked electoral college when it met on December 16 in the various state capitals. First, there would be what has been termed "the legitimacy of the popular vote majority"[31] — the demand that the electoral college choose the winner in terms of the popular vote. These pressures would undoubtedly be exceptionally strong if the winner of the popular vote had fallen just a few votes shy of an electoral college majority. Along these lines, James Michener, the president of the 1968 Pennsylvania electoral college, tells how he had resolved that if this were the case, with Nixon leading, he would seek to swing enough electoral votes to Nixon so as to decide the election in the electoral college. He reports that he was both pleased and surprised to discover, on December 16, that Thomas Minehart, the Pennsylvania Democratic state chairman, had had the same resolve.[32]

Besides the pressures to conform to the popular vote verdict, another factor that would have affected the activity during this time was the knowledge of the lineup of the new House and the assessment, in advance, of contingent election prospects there. Certainly Nixon, knowing that the new House contained only nineteen delegations controlled by Republicans, might see little reason not to give Humphrey an electoral vote majority on December 16 through releasing some of his electors before then—especially if Humphrey had led in the popular vote. If, however, Nixon had led in popular votes but Humphrey had the probable edge in contingent House voting, major-party accommodation would then seem far less likely. This latter situation was the most likely one during most of the campaign and was, in fact, the actual result, with one addition: an electoral college majority for Nixon.[33]

If the two major parties had been unable to stave off a Wallace-forced deadlock, what then would have been the consequences? We suggest three likely scenarios that might have followed. The first two relate to voting in the electoral college itself and assume that one or two faithless electors were not sufficient to make a majority. Given a deadlock, a first possibility is that one or the other major party candidate could make a deal with Wallace and/or his electors individually.[34] This could give rise to "the spectre of the highest office in the Nation being given to the highest bidder."[35] However, it might be relatively unlikely, if only because of the disastrous consequences of the almost inevitable disclosure—such a deal would involve too many people to be kept secret; and it is unlikely that Wallace would wish to do so—a king-maker enjoys real advantage from his actions only if he is recognized as being one. Given leaks about such arrangements, a major-party nominee would suffer the stigma of having bought the presidency by a deal, face possible threat of impeachment if the nonenforcement of existing laws were part of the understanding, and very likely find at least a few of his own electors in revolt and threatening to block the deal by abstaining on December 16.[36] This would be a very effective action on their part, since the needed majority of 270 electoral votes remains the same no matter how many electors might abstain.

A second scenario would involve a clever ploy by Wallace. Without attempting to extract any implicit or explicit promises or understandings, he would throw his bloc of electors one way or another while hinting at such promises and understandings. While seemingly fantastic, this strategy could have had enormous benefits to Wallace in terms of prestige, and, in fact, now appears to have been precisely the tactic Wallace would have followed.[37] By this action, Wallace could avoid the difficulties of trying to influence House members, who would certainly prove less pliable than his own electors, and could enjoy the benefits for the next four years of being the man who had made the president. The beneficiary of Wallace's generosity, on the other hand, would have received the presidency, but along with it, he would have reaped a harvest of bitterness, mistrust, and anger.

The third scenario assumes that the election was not settled through explicit or implicit deals, by means of a Wallace switch, or through the actions of a few electors willing to abandon their pledges in order to avoid a deadlock. In this case, the electoral college meetings on December 16 would result in a deadlock, with no candidate receiving 270 electoral votes, and the action would now shift to the newly elected House of Representatives meeting at noon on January 6, 1969, only fourteen days before the constitutionally scheduled inauguration of the new president.[38]

The House of Representatives contingent procedure, which would be utilized, is a relic of the compromises of the writing of the Constitution and is clearly the most widely condemned aspect of the constitutional provisions for electing the president. Used previously only in 1801 and 1825,[39] the necessity to adapt its provisions to the election of a twentieth-century president would be likely to cause massive confusion and uncertainty and threaten the basic legitimacy of the man who finally survives it to claim the presidency.[40]

The Twelfth Amendment to the Constitution specifies that if no candidate has received a majority in the electoral college,

> then from the persons having the highest numbers not exceeding three on the list of those voted for as President, the House of Representatives shall choose . . . , by ballot, the President. But in choosing the President, the votes shall be taken by States, the representation from each state having one vote . . . and a majority of all the States shall be necessary to a choice.

Therefore, each of the fifty states would be entitled to 1 vote with a majority of 26 required for election. The District of Columbia would have no vote. Delegations that were evenly split would lose their votes, but the necessary majority of 26 votes would still hold. Massive inequalities would be present in the House voting. In terms of 1960 census data, by following the one-state–one-vote arrangement, 76 House members from twenty-six states with a population of 30.7 million could theoretically outvote 359 members from twenty-four states with a population of 148.6 million.[41] Beyond these problems of equity, however, lurks an even more serious problem—what if the House itself deadlocks and cannot agree on a president?

It was commonly assumed and widely reported on election night that, as a result of the 1968 congressional elections, the House that would have been faced with acting, if the electoral college had deadlocked in 1968, would have elected Humphrey. Twenty-six state delegations were controlled by Democrats, nineteen by Republicans, and five were evenly divided and consequently would cast no vote.[42] However, this belief is based on one very questionable assumption: that each representative would have voted along party lines. A closer analysis shows that the complexity of the election in the House would have been much greater.

The first complicating factor is that in many cases, House delegations that were split, and thus could cast no vote, or that had a narrow majority for one party or another, could be swung through the actions of a single House member seeking to express his independence or maverick tendencies, raise his price, or just seek mammoth publicity.

This problem, however, pales in comparison with another: How would the House delegations from the five Deep South states carried by Wallace with percentages up to 66 percent vote? While at least normally Democratic and thus counted in the twenty-six state total, the representatives from these states would likely feel compelled to recognize and support Wallace in the House voting. On the other hand, if they broke party rank and failed to support the Democratic nominee at this critical moment, they would be subject to terrible retribution including loss of patronage, party seniority, and committee chairmanships. The dilemma of these congressmen would be intense, and its resolution uncertain, although a likely pattern would be to support Wallace for a couple of ballots and then to switch to Humphrey. The problem here, then, would not be manipulation by Wallace, for his direct control over these unhappy congressmen would be comparatively weak, but whether sufficient Democratic leadership pressure would lead to an eventual Democratic House majority.[43]

One last factor in the actual 1968 election might have given rise to severe problems in reaching a twenty-six state majority— and possibly have resulted in a House deadlock. This factor was the 1968 election-time pledges of a number of congressmen— mainly southern Democrats in Wallace- or Nixon-leaning districts—that if elected, and if the election came to the House, they would not automatically vote for Humphrey, but would vote however their district had voted for president. In many states, this pledge would not have made a difference, but in several it would.

Among at least thirty candidates for the House of Representatives who had made such pledges prior to the election[44] were all six men who were elected to the House from South Carolina. All six were Democrats, but three of their districts went for Nixon, two for Wallace, and one for Humphrey.[45] If these candidates had honored their pledges, South Carolina's vote would have gone to Nixon, despite its solid Democratic representation.

The Virginia delegation would have been evenly divided between Republicans and Democrats. However, two Democratic representatives, David E. Satterfield III and John O. Marsh, Jr., had made the pledge; their districts were carried by Nixon. A third Virginia Democrat, W. C. Daniel, would have been pledged to Wallace. Thus Virginia's vote might have gone to Nixon.[46] Finally, Nevada's lone congressman, Walter S. Baring, a Democrat, would have been publicly pledged to cast his state's vote for Nixon.[47]

The results of these publicly recorded pledges, alone, would be—assuming complete party loyalty otherwise, and no Wallace defections—a House vote not of 26 to 19 and 5 states split, but 24 to 22 and 4 states split. No majority of twenty-six states would have been immediately forthcoming, and political chaos could have resulted as the nation approached inauguration day.[48]

The 1968 election did not put the electoral college system to its greatest test; Richard Nixon did receive a majority of the electoral votes, and the nation was spared the opportunity of observing the dark nooks and crannies of the contingent election procedure in action. This election, however, illustrates many of the features of the electoral college system: (1) the uncertainty of state winner-take-all results with a three-way split of popular votes, (2) the incentive given to regional third parties and the handicaps conferred upon nationally based third parties, (3) the likelihood of electoral college deadlock if a third-party movement coincides with an evenness of major party strength, (4) the possibilities that shifts of relatively few votes could deadlock an election, (5) the dangers of one or a few faithless electors affecting the electoral college results, (6) the opportunity for a third-party candidate to throw his electors one way or the other, with or without a deal, and (7) the likelihood of uncertainty, confusion, and even deadlock in the House contingent selection of the president.

Problems of the Electoral College System

The electoral college seems to be an institution in which familiarity breeds contempt. Breakdowns of Gallup surveys on the electoral college system show that the more educated a person is—and thus more likely to be familiar with what the electoral college really is—the more likely he is to favor its abolition.[49]

In the course of examining how the electoral college system worked—and threatened not to work—in the two elections of 1960 and 1968, we have become familiar with many features of the electoral college system subject to criticism. It is the purpose of this section briefly to integrate these various features into five basic problems of the electoral college system, which have provided the impetus for electoral college reform efforts. These five basic problems are:

1. the faithless elector
2. the unit rule concerning a state's electoral vote
3. the constant two electoral votes per state
4. the contingency election procedure
5. the uncertainty that the winner will win

The first problem, that of the faithless elector, arises since the electoral college body is not the assembly of wise and learned elders assumed by its creators, but is rather a state-by-state collection of political hacks and fat cats. Neither in the quality of the electors nor in law is there any assurance that the electors will vote as expected. Pledges, apparently unenforceable by law, and party and personal loyalty seem to be the only guarantees of electoral voting consistent with the will of a state's electorate. The problem of the faithless elector is neither theoretical nor unimportant. Defecting electors in four of the past five elections have illustrated its realities, and the possibility of such action on a multiple basis in the case of an electoral vote majority resting on one or two votes proves its potential importance.

The second problem, the unit rule or the winner-take-all custom, is a universal, extraconstitutional innovation that completely disenfranchises those voters who cast their ballots for a candidate who fails to win the state's plurality.[50] As Senator Thomas Hart Benton of Missouri noted in 1824,

> To lose their votes is the fate of all minorities, and it is their duty to submit; but this is not a case of votes lost, but of votes taken away, added to those of the majority, and given to a person to whom the minority is opposed.[51]

Besides this transfer of votes feature, the unit rule also gives rise to three additional results. First, the unit rule encourages low voter participation in all but the truly competitive, swing states.

> The minority voters do not bother to go to the polls because they know that their votes cannot be effective. Their indifference is shared by the majority voters; these stay home because they know their votes are not needed.[52]

A second result of the unit rule is the placing of a premium on fraud and accident.

> In a state where the division of parties is approximately equal, great effects will result from small causes. Stormy weather may keep rural voters from the polls; local issues may bring out voters in some particular districts in unusual numbers; any of the thousand casualties of political fortune may determine the column in which a state's electoral vote will be found.[53]

A final consequence of the unit rule is somewhat more complex and will be subject to mathematical treatment in chapter four. Simply stated for now, the unit voting of state electors tends to magnify tremendously the relative voting power of residents of the larger states, since each of their voters may, by his vote, decide not just one vote, but how 41 or 45 electoral votes are cast—if electors are faithful.

The third problem of the electoral college system has its basis in the apportionment of electoral votes among the states. The constitutional formula is simple: 1 vote per state per senator and representative. A significant distortion from equality appears here because of the *constant two* electoral votes, regardless of population, which correspond to the senators. Because of this, inhabitants of the very small states are advantaged to the extent that they control 3 electoral votes (one for each senator and one for the representative), while their population might otherwise entitle them to but 1 or 2 votes. This is weighting by states, not by populations; however, the importance of this feature is greatly outweighed, as we shall see in chapter four, by the previously mentioned unit rule.

The fourth problem of the electoral college system, the contingent election procedure, is probably the most complex—and probably also the most dangerous in terms of the stability of the political system. This is the requirement that if no candidate receives an absolute majority of the electoral vote—in recent years, 270—the election is thrown into the House of Representatives for voting among the top three candidates. Two questions have been asked: Is such an electoral college deadlock likely to occur in terms of contemporary politics? And would the consequences likely be disastrous? The answer advanced to both questions has been a cautious yes.

One final, crucial problem of the electoral college system must still be mentioned—under the present electoral college system, there is no assurance—and in some recent elections, not even a better than even chance—that the winner of the presidential election in popular votes will be the winner of the election in electoral votes. Three times in our history,[54] the candidate with the most number of votes has failed to receive the presidency.[55]

The problem of the winner losing and the loser winning in a democratic political system is a profound one. Professor Paul Freund of Harvard Law School aptly summed up this problem when he testified:

The one objective that any democratic electoral system must achieve is to avoid the election of a candidate who secures fewer popular votes than an opposing candidate. The electoral college system offers no assurance of this, and in fact three times in our history the election went to a candidate other than the winner in the popular count. It has been said that this record is a good one, showing that in 93 percent of our elections the popular winner was the actual winner. This is like boasting that 93 percent of the planes leaving Washington airport arrive at their destination.[56]

The possibility that a candidate receiving a plurality of the popular vote might be defeated in the election of the president has its basis in the other four problems of the electoral college system. The constant two in the apportionment of electoral votes leaves room for popular vote-electoral vote reversals when the fifty-one imperfect approximations are combined in the electoral college. The unit rule system distorts the relationship between popular and electoral votes and makes it possible for a candidate to lose heavily in several states while winning by small pluralities in others and still be elected president. The independence of electors gives 538 citizens the freedom to violate the will of millions. The contingent election scheme makes it possible for a few men, operating in a supercharged political environment, to choose a president without regard to the popular vote of the people.

In what seems today to be a rather ironic statement in *The Federalist*, Alexander Hamilton said,

> The mode of appointment of the Chief Magistrate of the United States is almost the only part of the system, of any consequence, which has escaped without severe censure. . . . I . . . hesitate not to affirm that if the manner of it be not perfect, it is at least excellent.[57]

No perfect election system is, as yet, known to man. The electoral college system, however, is far from perfect and hardly appears to be excellent.

2. The Creation and Operation of the Electoral College

The Electoral College was neither an exercise in applied Platonism nor an experiment in indirect government based on elitist distrust of the masses. It was merely a jerry-rigged improvisation which has subsequently been endowed with a high theoretical content.

John P. Roche

I can return to private life with the consciousness that I shall receive from posterity the credit of having been elected to the highest position in the gift of the people, without any of the cares and responsibilities of the office.

Samuel J. Tilden, following the awarding of disputed electoral votes to Rutherford B. Hayes in 1877

A recurring theme in discussions about the electoral college is "the intentions of the founding fathers" concerning the manner of the election of the president. It is entirely possible, of course, to deny the relevance of these considerations to an assessment of the adequacy, in terms of today's needs, of the electoral college. The problem with this position, however, is that much of the debate over the electoral college, and its place in the constitutional framework of the American political system, utilizes references to, and draws support from, concepts of how the electoral college evolved out of the Constitutional Convention of 1787. Whether or not the intentions of these radical reformers of nearly two hundred years ago are really relevant today is less important than the fact that in political debate over the electoral college these intentions are given weight and significance. It should also be kept in mind that these same men devised many arrangements that have withstood the tests of close to two centuries. It is not at all inappropriate—and

22

actually rather illuminating—to consider how this group of intelligent and well-meaning men sought to create a mechanism for selecting their nation's leader that would similarly stand the test of time.

The Birth of the Electoral College System

The Constitutional Convention, which met in Philadelphia from May 25 to September 17 of 1787, was beset with massive tensions and rivalries as it sought to draft a new constitution. With profound differences of opinion existing on such questions as the degree of centralized power for the new federal government, the type of special recognition small states would be given, the division of powers among the different branches of government, and the extent to which sectional interests would be protected, the delegates to the convention found themselves engaged in the most difficult of political negotiations in their attempts to achieve consensus—a task so difficult and demanding of their political astuteness as to cause John Dickinson of Delaware to cry out "Experience must be our guide. Reason may mislead us."[1]

During the summer of 1787 successive crises had threatened to destroy the work of the convention as delegates fell to bitter quarreling over regional and big-state—small-state differences. The most profound and dangerous of these conflicts had been between large-state and small-state plans for representation in the new congress, with proponents of the Virginia Plan, which provided for congressional representation to be based on population, locked in battle with supporters of the New Jersey Plan, which established equal congressional representation for each state. This deadlock had finally been broken on July 16 through acceptance of the Connecticut Plan—"The Great Compromise"—which provided for one house of Congress to be based on population and the other on equality of states. As the Constitutional Convention moved, in late August, to determine the means by which the president would be elected, there was little wish to see the conflicts and tensions that had plagued the preceding months of the convention renewed.

On August 31 a Committee of Eleven was commissioned to study various possible methods for the election of the president and to work out a plan on which the delegates could agree. The task of the committee was a formidable one. In the preceding months several different schemes had been advanced, including election by Congress and direct election by the people. Although congressional election of the president had been tentatively approved by the Constitutional Convention on four occasions during the summer, there existed strong opposition to this plan on the grounds that this would make the chief executive subservient to Congress and unable to develop an independent leadership capacity.[2] The other proposal, that of direct election by the people, had strong support from some of the leaders at the convention, including James Madison of Virginia, Gouverneur Morris of Pennsylvania, and James Wilson, also of Pennsylvania—all three of whom, not very surprisingly, were from large, populous states. Strong objections to direct vote were raised on various grounds, among them being: (1) the lack of awareness and knowledge of candidates by the people, with unforeseen consequences resulting from the scattering of votes by the electorates in the various states among favorite sons they knew best;[3] (2) the loss in relative influence of the South because of its large nonvoting slave population; (3) the dislike, on the part of small, less populous states, of too open an admission of an inferior role in the choice of the president; and (4) the fear of many that direct election of the president would consolidate too much power and influence in one person.[4] With the convention striving for delegate consensus on its proposed constitution, these strenuous objections to both the congressional-election and direct-vote plans meant that some alternate plan would have to be found.

As early as June 2 James Wilson had suggested, as a possible compromise, an *intermediate election* plan involving an electoral college, and during the summer this alternative developed as "the second choice of many delegates though it was the first choice of few."[5] When the Committee of Eleven met in the first few days of September, they turned to this compromise in order to avoid further deadlock and conflict.

On September 4 the committee reported its recommendations for presidential election by a college of electors based on congressional apportionment[6] (thus indirectly reflecting the Connecticut compromise of the preceding month), with the provision that if no candidate received a majority of the votes of the electors, the final selection would be by the United States Senate, choosing from among the top five contenders. With the subsequent change to contingent election by the House rather than the Senate[7]—but with the equality of states maintained through 1 vote per state—this was the plan adopted by the Constitutional Convention on September 7, 1787, after only brief debate. The electoral college method of selecting the president was the subject of little attention and discussion during the ratification debates following the convention, leading to Hamilton's earlier cited observation about its excellence, if not perfection.

The Constitutional Convention of 1787 created out of disagreement a system with broad, if somewhat artificial, support.

What really moved the delegates to accept the electoral system, with little enthusiasm and no unanimity of conviction, were certain practical considerations, dictated not by political ideals but by the social realities of the time—realities that no longer exist.[8]

Among these realities were: (1) the pressure on the delegates at the Constitutional Convention to reach agreement, (2) the lack of immediate concern about the operation of the electoral college, and (3) a major—and soon to be disproved—assumption about the dispersion of support for various presidential candidates.

The first of these realities has previously been discussed in terms of the overriding desire on the part of the delegates not to reopen the deep wounds of the first three months of the Constitutional Convention—divisions that had been papered over by the Great Compromise on congressional representation. When plans were advanced concerning the selection of the president that gave promise of renewing conflict, the delegates sought alternatives. As Neal Peirce puts it,

The most basic reason that the electoral college was invented was that the Convention was deadlocked on simpler schemes like direct election and choice by Congress, and thus invented a system that could be "sold" in the immediate context of 1787.[9]

Another commentator on this period, John Roche, puts it even more pointedly:

The vital aspect of the electoral college was that it got the Convention over the hurdle and protected everybody's interests. The future was left to cope with the problem of what to do with this Rube Goldberg mechanism.[10]

A second reason why the electoral college plan quickly gained support lay in the belief held by most delegates that any problems that might arise in this method of electing the president would not be immediate: they all knew that George Washington was going to be chosen president no matter what the system. With regard to this, Felix Morley suggests that "without this assured initial unanimity, it is probable that the electoral system would have been more closely scrutinized, with better anticipation of the troubles that lay ahead."[11] Being the practical men they were, the delegates sought to put off until a later time what could be postponed and considered then.

A third and particularly important reason for the support the electoral college system received had to do with the arrangements themselves. There was a general belief "that once Washington had finished his tenure as President, the electors would cease to provide majorities and the Chief Executive would usually be chosen in the House."[12] The assumption was that the electors chosen would, in effect, nominate a number of prominent individuals, with no one man—because of diverse state and regional interests—usually receiving the specified absolute majority of electoral votes. At times a George Washington might be the unanimous electoral choice, but, as George Mason of Virginia argued, nineteen times out of twenty, the final choice of president from the top contenders would be made not by the electoral college itself, but by the House of Representatives, voting by states with 1 vote per state. This conception of the electoral arrangements envisioned a mechanism for the selection of the president somewhat similar to today's national nominating conventions and general election procedure, except in their view the electoral college would serve the nominating function and the House the electing function. Implicit in the agreement on the electoral college system was this assumption about how it would work in practice—an assumption that was not to be borne out by events.

The key to acceptance of this two-stage plan for presidential selection lay in the different character of electoral college and House contingent voting. The electoral college, reflecting in a rough way the population of states, would favor the big states at the cost of the small states—or more accurately, populations rather than individual states. When the contingent House procedure went into effect—as it most often would—the voting would be 1 vote per state delegation, thus representing individual states regardless of population. This mechanism was a compromise between the principle of population and that of state interest. As James Madison later described the electoral college, it was "the result of compromise between the larger and smaller states, giving to the latter the advantage of selecting a President from the candidates, in consideration of the former in selecting the candidates from the people."[13]

One of the most common statements about the development of the electoral college is that the pattern of apportionment of electors was due to a large-state–small-state compromise. This is, in fact, only partly true in that the apportionment did reflect the Connecticut compromise about congressional representation; however, this feature of the electoral college was due more to expediency than to philosophy. The major large-state –small-state compromise lay in the linkage of electoral college nomination with House election where each state would have only 1 vote. By itself, the electoral college was not conceived to be a bulwark of small-states' rights; rather, if anything, it was seen as favoring large states—or at least the principle of population.[14]

Changes in the Electoral College System

The electoral college system has moved through a series of evolutionary developments during its long and often painful existence. With the exception of the essentially mechanical changes contained in the Twelfth Amendment, ratified in 1824, these modifications—often massive in impact—have come about through custom, state law, and political necessity, but not by formal constitutional change. These developments, however, have greatly altered the electoral college over the years. As John P. Feerick points out, "The system which emerged in practice is not the system contemplated by the founding fathers."[15]

Two of the most important of these changes both resulted from the rise of political parties out of legislative caucuses about the time of the 1796 election. As these political organizations developed, they began to aggregate national support for their candidates and to recruit electors pledged to them, thus making obsolete both the concept of the free elector who would vote for well-thought-of individuals and "the electoral college nominates, the House selects" balance previously anticipated.

With national politics emerging out of the era of Washington in dualistic patterns, no party or voter could allow electors to play the role of statesmen—the political stakes were too high. Thus was born the role of the elector as a faceless component of a state-by-state counting device, with predictability rather than wisdom the desired virtue. As a Senate select committee reported in 1826, electors are "usually selected for their devotion to party, their popular manner, and a supposed talent for electioneering."[16] Today, the necessary qualifications of these gentlemen are even less exacting—as one well-known 1968 elector reported: "My finest credentials were that each year I contributed what money I could to the party."[17] In most states even the formal fiction of elector selection has been forsaken: thirty-two states and the District of Columbia do not even indicate on the ballot the names of the electors at stake in a presidential election.[18] The body of individuals who are selected every four years to constitute the nation's electoral college are today not only without honor and prestige, they are also largely unknown.

As a direct result of the demise of the free elector even before three national elections had been held, there arose the curious phenomenon of the faithless elector—an elector who votes for president contrary to expectations based on his pledge or statement or on the assumption that he will support the candidate of the party whose designation as elector he has accepted. The first faithless elector was Samuel Miles, a 1796 Federalist elector in Pennsylvania, who declined to vote for Adams, the Federalist candidate, and instead cast his vote for Jefferson. Even at this early point in the evolution of the electoral college, this was rather shocking, leading one outraged Federalist to exclaim in the *United States Gazette*, 'What, do I chuse Samuel Miles to determine for me whether John Adams or Thomas Jefferson shall be President? No! I chuse him to *act*, not to *think*."[19]

Elector Miles established a pattern and opportunity that has been followed by remarkably few later electors. Between 1820 and 1972, 16,321 electoral votes have been cast for president. Of these only 6 votes can be said to have been cast indisputably "against instructions"—one each in 1820, 1948, 1956, 1960, 1968, and 1972.[20] That there has been so little a degree of political independence of these men is certainly due more to their character than to effective legal restrictions—only sixteen states have laws requiring electors to vote according to their pledges, and these laws themselves are of doubtful constitutionality.[21] The electoral college, then, has changed drastically from that conceived by the founding fathers—in place of a body of statesmen, we have a collection of political nonentities whose actions are justified only to the extent to which they put aside personal values and deliberations and vote automatically in accord with strict party regularity.

A second major change in the electoral college system has been previously mentioned as also resulting from the emergence of national political parties. With political parties aggregating support for candidates on a national basis, the electoral college has become not the nomination agency with the House acting as the selection agency—as had been assumed—but rather the final point of decision itself. The House procedure has become, conversely, not an integral part of the presidential selection process, but an emergency step to be taken when normal procedures break down—as in 1800 and 1824. The assumption of the founding fathers, which had been so important in the acceptance of the electoral college plan, has thus been made obsolete by events, while the remnant of the original selection structure—the House contingent procedure—remains, with its inherent chaotic possibilities.[22]

The third major change, besides the development of the bound elector and the emergence of the electoral college as the usual final point of decision, was the development of the popular election of electors. The Constitution gives the states complete freedom concerning the means of elector selection, and in the early elections practices varied widely, including variations on popular election and state legislative selection of electors, and often changed for a particular state from election to election. Massachusetts, always in the forefront of political manipulations, changed its system for choosing electors seven different times during the first ten national elections. Political advantage, rather than abstract philosophical principle, was the dominant force in these changes. Over the decades, however, the expansion of the electorate, the popularization of democratic ideals, and unfortunate experiences with legislative politics (such as in the case of New York, where a legislative deadlock resulted in the selection of no electors from that state in the 1789 election), combined to create an uneven, uncertain, but inevitable movement to popular selection of electors. Many political leaders found that once popular participation in elector selection had been instituted for one election (often for partisan ends), it was politically difficult to take it away. The last state to resist these trends was South Carolina, which adopted popular selection of electors only after the Civil War.[23]

The fourth change in the electoral college system also arose essentially from political expediency—this was the trend toward deciding all of a state's electoral votes on a unit rule, or winner-take-all basis. Generally, division of a state's electoral votes was supported by whatever party was momentarily in eclipse in a state, while the dominant party favored a winner-take-all arrangement. Not very surprisingly, the latter's view usually prevailed. In addition to such internal political pressures favoring a unit rule approach, an additional factor tended to force states toward this method. As other states adopted unit rule selection procedures, it became apparent to state leaders that their state must follow swiftly in order to maintain its relative political position. If another state was going to be able to deliver an entire slate of electoral votes, their state must be able to do so also.[24] Thus, again, political necessity created another substantial extraconstitutional deviation from the arrangements of the founding fathers.

The fifth change in the electoral college system was the direct result of an oversight of the creators of the electoral system, and, unlike the other changes, led to a formal constitutional change in the electoral college system. In 1800 the presidential and vice presidential Democratic nominees, Jefferson and Burr, both received an identical number of electoral votes, 73, since the Constitution stipulated that each elector would cast 2 equal votes, undistinguished as to president and vice president. The original plan was that the strongest candidate would thus become president and the next strongest vice president. This had happened, in fact, in 1796, although the leader, Adams, and the runner-up, Jefferson, were of different parties and were strong personal enemies. With national political parties developing an ability to enforce party regularity and elector faithfulness, the original system seemed likely to continue to produce hostile presidents and vice presidents at best, and ties between the same party's presidential and vice presidential candidates at worst—as happened in 1800.

Never a man to lose an opportunity (he has often been labeled "the man who could not wait"), Burr made no effort to step aside for his running mate, and the House of Representatives was called upon, in 1801, to make one of the most agonizing decisions it has ever faced. After thirty-six ballots between February 11 and 17, marked by the most disreputable deals and maneuvers, Jefferson was elected, partially due to help from his ancient antagonist Hamilton, who hated only Burr more. The sourness and sordidness of this episode led directly to the adoption of the Twelfth Amendment, which, essentially, changed the electoral college system only in requiring separate votes by the electors for president and vice president.[25]

The founding fathers showed great wisdom in many of the features of the new Constitution they created in Philadelphia in 1787. In the case of the electoral college system, however, it is difficult to attribute such virtue to them, for this institution never worked as intended by its creators. That the basic electoral college system has existed until today is due not to the wisdom of its creators, but to a combination of adaptation and chance.

The Electoral College System Misbehaving

Rather than examining the electoral college system through a chronological review of the forty-seven presidential elections that have been held through 1972, this section will instead examine these elections and the operation of the electoral college system in terms of four categories:

1. elections in which there was an electoral college reversal of the popular vote winner
2. elections in which there was an electoral college deadlock and use of the House contingent procedure

3. elections in which the president-elect did not have a majority of popular votes
4. elections in which minor vote shifts could have changed the outcome

There have been two, or possibly three, elections where the electoral college itself (as opposed to the House contingent feature, as in 1824) resulted in the candidate with the most popular votes losing (see table 1). The first of these elections, 1876, was a peculiar case in that the electoral college majority for the popular vote loser was based on a partisan verdict at best, and on fraud at worst.

Initially, it was assumed that Tilden, with a 250,000-vote

TABLE 1
Electoral College Reversal of Popular Vote Winners[a]

Year	Candidates and Popular Vote Results			Electoral College Results		
1876[b]	Tilden (D.)	4,287,670	50.9%	Tilden (D.)	184	50%
	Hayes (R.)	4,035,924	47.9%	Hayes (R.)	185	50%
	Tilden popular vote margin of 251,746			*Hayes* winner with electoral vote margin of 1		
1888	Cleveland (D.)	5,540,365	48.6%	Cleveland (D.)	168	45%
	Harrison (R.)	5,445,269	47.8%	Harrison (R.)	233	55%
	Cleveland popular vote margin of 95,096			*Harrison* winner with electoral vote margin of 65		
1960	Nixon (R.)	34,108,157	49.3%	Nixon (R.)	219	41%
	Kennedy (D.)	34,049,976	49.2%	Kennedy (D.)	303	59%
	Nixon popular vote margin of 58,181			*Kennedy* winner with electoral vote margin of 84		

Source: Adapted from Peirce, *The People's President*, pp. 302-07.

Note: The popular vote totals for 1960 used here are computed by the third method discussed in chapter 1, which consists of crediting Kennedy with five-elevenths of Alabama's Democratic votes and the unpledged elector slate with six-elevenths. See p. 5.

[a]The election of 1824 also resulted in a reversal of the popular vote winner, but through use of the House contingent procedure.
[b]The electoral vote results in 1876 were arrived at by a bipartisan election commission, voting along party lines, which awarded 20 disputed electoral votes to Hayes.

margin over Hayes, would enjoy a comfortable electoral college margin of 39 votes. The day after the election, however, it became apparent that if close races in South Carolina, Flordia, and Louisiana could be swung to the Republican side, thus switching 20 electoral votes, Hayes would become president by a single vote. Republican reconstruction state governments in each of these states eagerly cooperated in activities that found "agents of both parties using illegal and corrupt tactics to achieve their ends."[26] The conflict was intensified by the realization that the certification of just 1 Tilden electoral vote from among the 20 under challenge would suffice to elect him.

The dispute finally resulted in duplicate returns from each of the three states—one certifying Hayes electors, the other Tilden electors. Congress, called upon to decide this fiercely partisan dispute, established a bipartisan election commission made up of seven Republicans and seven Democrats together with an additional member to be drawn from the United States Supreme Court. It was understood that the crucially important swing member would be Justice David Davis, an appointee of Lincoln, who was widely respected for both his fairness and his nonpartisanship. With him on the commission it appeared likely that at least one of the disputed votes would be awarded to Tilden, thus making the Democrat president.

In probably one of the greatest blunders in American political history, the Illinois Democratic party undid all these plans and destroyed the prospects of the Democratic candidate for president. Within hours of congressional passage of the legislation establishing the election commission, news arrived in Washington that the Illinois legislature, under Democratic control, had the day before named Justice Davis to a vacancy in the United States Senate.[27] With Davis suddenly unable to serve, a substitute had to be found on the Court. He was Justice Bradley, a reputedly independent-leaning Republican. As a member of the commission, however, Justice Bradley did not exhibit any such independent traits—he joined with the seven other Republicans to constitute an 8-vote majority awarding the disputed electoral votes to Hayes, the Republican, in every case.[28]

The result of these events was even more sordid: potential Democratic objections to the commission's recommendations were muted through a Republican deal with southern Democrats, a major element of which involved the carrying out of previously indicated decisions to remove the remaining federal troops from the South in return for acquiescence in the commission's decisions. This deal—the Compromise of 1877—became one crucial element of a new willingness to give the South carte blanche to go its own way in its own affairs, including the development of its own peculiar institutions, such as Jim Crow segregation. The cost of Hayes's electoral college victory, then, was tremendous in terms of subsequent history—a cost still being paid today.

The election of 1888 has none of the complexities of the previous election. Very simply, in 1888 the winner in popular votes lost the election, while the candidate who ran second in popular votes won. This came about because of the distortions inherent both in the electoral college apportionment of votes among the states and in its winner-take-all feature. Specifically, in this election Harrison, the electoral vote winner, carried a number of large states, such as New York, Ohio, and Pennsylvania, by relatively small margins, while Cleveland carried a number of states, particularly in the South, by very large margins. Harrison's slender margins were turned into solid, large blocs of electoral votes, while Cleveland's large margins in his states were wasted in carrying states he could have carried with far fewer votes. Not one to be daunted by losing a victory, Cleveland ran again four years later and defeated Harrison, this time, in both the popular vote and the electoral college.

The election of 1960 has been fully discussed in chapter 1. Suffice it here to say that the third method of counting Alabama's votes—a perfectly reasonable and possibly even preferable method—results in a Nixon national plurality in that year. As mentioned in chapter 1 Nixon chose not to press this claim because of the complexities of explanation and the likelihood of appearing to be a bad loser.

Table 2 shows the two elections in which there has been a

TABLE 2
Electoral College Deadlock and Use of House Contingent Procedure[a]

Year	Candidates and Popular Vote Results		Electoral College Results	House Result
1800	Jefferson (D.)	not available	73	*Jefferson* winner with
	Burr (D.)	not available	73	10 states to 4 for Burr
	Adams (Fed.)	not available	65	after 36 ballots
	Pinchney (Fed.)	not available	64	
	Jay	not available	1	
1824	Adams (D.)	115,696 31.9%	84	*Adams* winner with 13
	Jackson (D.)	152,933 42.2%	99	states to 7 for Jackson
	Crawford (D.)	46,979 13.0%	41	and 4 for Crawford on
	Clay (D.)	47,136 13.0%	37	the first ballot
	Jackson popular vote margin of 37,237			

Source: Adapted from Peirce, *The People's President*, pp. 302-07.

[a]The Senate contingent procedure for selection of the vice president in case of no electoral college majority has been used only once, in 1837, after Democratic electors from Virginia refused to vote for the Democratic vice presidential nominee, Richard M. Johnson. He was subsequently elected by the Senate by a vote of 33 to 16.

resort to the House contingent procedure. The election of 1800 and the subsequent House action in 1801 were sufficiently painful as to lead to the Twelfth Amendment, ratified in 1804. The election of 1824 similarly both strained and stained the political system. Without going into great detail, it can be observed that one crucial component of Adams's House victory over Jackson, the popular vote and electoral vote leader, was the helpful support of Speaker of the House Clay, who had run fourth in electoral votes (although third in popular votes), and was, therefore, eliminated from House consideration, which was limited to the top three contenders.[29] Clay busied himself lining up support for Adams—support that proved both crucial and sufficient. Adams, probably not by coincidence, later appointed Clay secretary of state; this was not, however, to be the only price Adams would have to pay for his "victory." The charges and controversies resulting from the House victory of Adams were to haunt him throughout his single term and to be a decisive issue against him in his rematch with Jackson in 1828—which Adams lost.

In prophetic words written in 1823, Thomas Jefferson wrote:

I have even considered the Constitutional mode of election ultimately by the legislature voting by states as the most dangerous blot on our Constitution, and one which some unlucky chance will some day hit.[30]

Chance did hit it within the year, with the dreaded fearful consequences. That chance has missed it in the nearly 150 years since 1824 is fortunate, but, as we shall see, not assured.

Table 3 presents a category of elections that probably cannot be generally termed as ones in which the electoral college misbehaved. In these fifteen cases no candidate received a popular vote majority (although in every instance except 1860, at least one candidate received over 40 percent, Lincoln falling .2 percent below that figure), while in eleven of these cases, there was an electoral college majority for the leading vote getter. In a twelfth case, 1824, an electoral college deadlock resulted in a House contingent selection of the second strongest candidate. The remaining three elections, 1876, 1888, and possibly 1960, each had an electoral college majority—but for the loser in popular votes.

Table 3 not only summarizes the frequent tendency of voters not to give a clear majority to any one candidate; it also illustrates the feature of the electoral college that usually compensates for these nonmajorities—the multiplier effect. In the fifteen elections here examined, the popular vote leader had an average electoral college percentage 9.7 points greater than his popular vote percentage, thus in most cases producing an electoral college majority.

The final table in this section, table 4, introduces the concept of the *hairbreadth election*—one where a minor vote shift could have changed the outcome. Twenty-one such elections and twenty-four possibilities are examined—55 percent of the elections for which popular vote totals are available. It is very important to note the qualification at the end of this table that

TABLE 3
Presidents Elected without a Majority of Popular Votes

Year	Candidates and Popular Vote Results			Electoral College Results	
1824[a][b]	Adams (D.)	115,696	31.9%	84	32%
	Jackson (D.)	152,933	42.2%	99	38%
	Crawford (D.)	46,979	13.0%	41	16%
	Clay (D.)	47,136	13.0%	37	14%
1844	Polk (D.)	1,339,368	49.6%	170	62%
	Clay (W.)	1,300,687	48.1%	105	38%
	Birney (L.)	62,197	2.3%	–	–
1848	Taylor (W.)	1,362,101	47.3%	163	57%
	Cass (D.)	1,222,674	42.5%	127	43%
	Van Buren (F.S.)	291,616	10.1%	–	–
	Smith (L.)	2,733	0.1%	–	–
1856	Buchanan (D.)	1,839,237	45.6%	174	59%
	Fremont (R.)	1,341,028	33.3%	114	39%
	Fillmore (W.)	849,872	21.1%	8	3%
	Smith (L.R.)	484	–	–	–
1860	Lincoln (R.)	1,867,198	39.8%	180	59%
	Douglas (D.)	1,379,434	29.4%	12	4%
	Breckinridge (D.)	854,248	18.2%	72	24%
	Bell (C.U.)	591,658	12.6%	39	13%
	Smith	172	–	–	–
1876[a]	Hayes (R.)	4,035,924	47.9%	185	50%
	Tilden (D.)	4,287,670	50.9%	184	50%
	Others	94,935	1.1%	–	–
1880	Garfield (R.)	4,454,433	48.3%	214	58%
	Hancock (D.)	4,444,976	48.2%	155	42%
	Weaver (G.)	308,649	3.4%	–	–
	Others	11,409	0.1%	–	–
1884	Cleveland (D.)	4,875,971	48.5%	219	55%
	Blaine (R.)	4,852,234	48.3%	182	45%
	Butler (G.)	175,066	1.7%	–	–
	St. John (P.)	150,957	1.5%	–	–
1888[a]	Harrison (R.)	5,445,269	47.8%	233	58%
	Cleveland (D.)	5,540,365	48.6%	168	42%
	Fisk (P.)	250,122	2.2%	–	–
	Others	154,083	1.4%	–	–
1892	Cleveland (D.)	5,556,982	46.0%	277	62%
	Harrison (R.)	5,191,466	43.0%	145	33%
	Weaver (P.O.)	1,029,960	8.5%	22	5%
	Others	292,672	2.4%	–	–

TABLE 3 *(continued)*

Year	Candidates and Popular Vote Results			Electoral College Results	
1912	Wilson (D.)	6,301,254	41.9%	435	82%
	Roosevelt (P.R.)	4,127,788	27.4%	88	17%
	Taft (R.)	3,485,831	23.2%	8	2%
	Debs (S.)	901,255	6.0%	–	–
	Others	238,934	1.6%	–	–
1916	Wilson (D.)	9,131,511	49.3%	277	52%
	Hughes (R.)	8,548,935	46.1%	254	48%
	Benson (S.)	585,974	3.2%	–	–
	Others	269,812	1.5%	–	–
1948	Truman (D.)	24,179,345	49.6%	303	57%
	Dewey (R.)	21,991,291	45.1%	189	36%
	Thurmond (S.R.)	1,176,125	2.4%	39	7%
	Wallace (P.R.)	1,157,326	2.4%	–	–
	Others	289,739	0.6%	–	–
1960[c]	Kennedy (D.)	34,220,984	49.5%	303	56%
	Nixon (R.)	34,108,157	49.3%	219	41%
	Unpledged Elector Slates	638,822	0.9%	15	3%
	Others	188,559	0.3%	–	–
1968	Nixon (R.)	31,785,480	43.4%	301	56%
	Humphrey (D.)	31,275,165	42.7%	191	36%
	Wallace (A.I.P.)	9,906,473	13.5%	46	9%
	Others	244,444	0.3%	–	–

Source: Adapted from Peirce, *The People's President*, pp. 302-07.

Note: Number of times a president was elected without a majority of popular votes is 15, or 39 percent of the elections for which popular vote totals are available.

[a]Election where the winner did not have the most number of popular votes as well as lacked a majority of popular votes.

[b]Adams was elected president in 1825 through use of the House contingent procedure, although he lacked both a popular vote majority and a plurality.

[c]Depending on the calculation of returns from Alabama, this election may be one where the winner did not have the most number of popular votes as well as lacked a majority of electoral votes. The popular vote totals used here are computed by the second method discussed in chapter 1, which consists of crediting Kennedy with all of the popular votes received by the most popular of his pledged Alabama electors. See p. 5.

TABLE 4
Hairbreadth Elections

Year	Shift Needed	In What States	Outcome
1828	11,517	Ohio, Ky., N.Y., La., Ind.	Other candidate elected
1836	14,061	N.Y.	Electoral college deadlock
1840	8,386	N.Y., Pa., Maine, N.J.	Other candidate elected
1844	2,555	N.Y.	Other candidate elected
1848	3,227	Ga., Md., Del.	Other candidate elected
1856	17,427	Ind., Ill., Del.	Electoral college deadlock
1860	18,050	Calif., Oreg., Ill., Ind.	Electoral college deadlock
	25,069	N.Y.	Electoral college deadlock
1864	38,111	N.Y., Pa., Ind., Wis., Md., Conn., Oreg.	Other candidate elected
1868	29,862	Pa., Ind., N.C., Ala., Conn., Calif., Nev.	Other candidate elected
1876	116	S.C.	Other candidate elected
1880	10,517	N.Y.	Other candidate elected
1884	575	N.Y.	Other candidate elected
1888	7,189	N.Y.	Other candidate elected
1892	37,364	N.Y., Ind., Wis., N.J., Calif.	Other candidate elected
1896	20,296	Ind., Ky., Calif., W.Va., Oreg., Del.	Other candidate elected
1900	74,755	Ohio, Ind., Kans., Nebr., Md., Utah, Wyo.	Other candidate elected
1908	75,041	Ohio, Mo., Ind., Kans., W.Va., Del., Mont., Md.	Other candidate elected
1916	1,983	Calif.	Other candidate elected
1948	12,487	Calif., Ohio	Electoral college deadlock
	29,294	Calif., Ohio, Ill.	Other candidate elected
1960	8,971	Ill., Mo.	Electoral college deadlock
	11,424	Ill., Mo., N.Mex., Hawaii, Nev.	Other candidate elected
1968	53,034	N.J., Mo., N.H.	Electoral college deadlock

Source: Adapted from Peirce, *The People's President*, pp. 317-21.

Note: Number of hairbreadth elections is 21, or 55% of the elections for which popular vote totals are available. An important qualification to keep in mind concerning this table is that shifts in voting patterns are seldom isolated in individual states, but are usually part of regional or national trends. The changes that would have accomplished the electoral results outlined here would have most likely been part of national or regional shifts not limited to just a few states. Or, expressed differently, to swing these key states, there would likely have to be vote switching of considerably greater magnitude than the minimum shown here. This table does serve, however, as a demonstration of the relative closeness of many elections, as an illustration of how mighty results can come from relatively small voting shifts, and as evidence of the real potential for electoral college crisis in many of our past elections.

these shifts needed are theoretical minimums, extremely un-likely to occur in precisely these quantities in just these states. The figures do, however, provide a relative measure of closeness more realistic than popular vote margins, which do not take into account the crucial factor of the distribution of votes in the separate states. In these terms it can be seen that whole series of elections have been extremely close, such as 1836-68 (with one exception), 1876-1900 (with one exception)—or alternatively, the entire period of 1836-1916 (with only five exceptions) and 1960-68 (with one exception). Only in the era from 1920 to 1956 (with the exception of 1948) has there been a general absence of hairbreadth elections.

It has been previously argued that the electoral college system has continued to exist for close to two centuries through a combination of adaptation and chance. This element of chance is graphically illustrated in table 4; in light of the number of hairbreadth elections here examined, the fact that only two elections have produced an electoral college deadlock and only two or three have resulted in an electoral college result other than for the popular vote leader seems remarkable indeed.

3. The Multiple Roads to Electoral College Reform

*The cause of electoral reform seems to be endangered
by two age-old threats—the unwillingness of reformers
to agree on a single system and the insistence of some
that they could reform the system for their own
partisan advantage.*

Neal R. Peirce

*The road to reform in the method of choosing the
Presidents and Vice Presidents of the United States
is littered with the wrecks of previous attempts.*

Arthur Krock

Electoral college reform proposals date back to January 6,
1797, when Representative William L. Smith of South Carolina
introduced the first resolution to amend the presidential election provisions of the Constitution. Since this initial proposal,
constitutional amendments concerning the electoral college have
been offered in nearly every session of Congress—more, it is
claimed, than for any other single part of the Constitution.[1] In
spite of a history nearly as old as the Constitution itself, the
various attempts to change or modify the electoral college feature of presidential elections have, in every case thus far, ultimately failed—with the sole excpetion of the limited changes
incorporated in the Twelfth Amendment adopted in 1804. As a
result the electoral college functions today within essentially
the same constitutional framework as when it was first created
nearly two hundred years ago.

The question that arises, then, is why, at the end of almost
two centuries of experience with the electoral college marked
by recurring and insistent criticism and objections to many of
its features, and especially after several recent near electoral
misfires with possible disastrous consequences, has it proven so
difficult to obtain reform for a system so widely condemned in
whole or in part?

One formidable obstacle to electoral reform has been the number and variety of reform proposals—a diversity that provides grist for the analyst, but little unity to electoral college reform efforts. One count finds at least 513 different proposals for change introduced in the United States Congress through 1966.[2] While many of these amendments were repetitious or contained only variations (and some others were also quite bizarre), at least four distinctly different kinds of proposals have been repeatedly introduced. These we shall call the *automatic plan*, the *proportional plan*, the *district plan*, and the *direct vote plan*. This multiplicity of proposals has been one major factor that has inhibited the reform movement and made impossible the development of the broad national support for a single plan necessary for its enactment as a constitutional amendment. Only in the last two years of the 1960s was there any sign of a consensus emerging for one of the proposals—the direct vote plan—and even that agreement proved insufficient to overcome all the structural and political obstacles to electoral college reform.[3]

In this chapter, we will be examining in some detail the multiple roads to electoral reform—as well as a few lesser paths—in terms of their key provisions, their moments of potency in the past, the possible results of various presidential elections under them and the major arguments that have been arrayed in support of or in opposition to them.

The Automatic Plan

The most modest of the various reform proposals for the electoral college, the automatic plan, directs its attention primarily to one defect of the electoral college system, and secondly to another. The primary defect the automatic plan would remedy is the possibility of a faithless elector. This problem is much greater than the historical record would indicate, for, as argued in chapter 1, the likelihood of electors so acting on a multiple basis is greatest in the case of an extremely close electoral vote count with the needed majority resting on a margin of only 2 or 3 votes. In addition to this potential danger, there is the additional problem that the ability of a presidential elector to vote contrary to the wishes and expectations of those who elected him—usually without ever knowing who he was or even that he existed—seems to fly in the face of a basic sense of voter equity. Therefore, the automatic plan would eliminate the office of elector while, however, retaining all other aspects of the existing electoral college's allocation and counting of votes.

Perhaps the only aspect of the electoral college system that has come under more universal contemporary criticism than the existence of individual electors is the House contingent procedure for electing the president. The dangers and possibilities for constitutional crisis inherent in the procedure have been previously discussed; it is, therefore, not very surprising that most automatic plans also modify this procedure so as to provide for selection of the president by a joint session of both the House and Senate, with voting in this composite body being on an individual, equal basis.

Table 5 outlines the major provisions of the automatic plan, as well as three other major reform proposals. As can be seen, the automatic plan essentially is a "housekeeping plan" designed to take care of a couple of rough edges of the electoral college system—the possibility of a faithless elector and the dangers of the House contingent election procedure—while not changing the basic system itself in any fundamental way. In terms of the five problems of the electoral college system outlined in chapter 1, the automatic plan eliminates the faithless elector and provides for a more equitable contingent election procedure. It would not, however, modify the unit rule voting nor the constant two electoral votes per state. Most important, it would not change the possibility of the winner in popular votes not winning in electoral votes.[4]

The automatic plan has been a popular proposal since Jefferson's 1801 support, and was first introduced in Congress by Representative Charles Haynes of Georgia in 1826. Leading advocates of it in the twentieth century have included Senator George W. Norris of Nebraska during the 1920s and 1930s,

TABLE 5
Major Provisions of Four Reform Plans

	Automatic Plan	Proportional Plan	District Plan	Direct Vote Plan
1. Individual electors retained?	No	No	Varies	No
2. Unit Vote retained?	Yes	No	Partially	No
3. Constant two electoral votes per state retained?	Yes	Yes	Yes	No
4. Present House contingent procedure retained?	Usually Not	No	Usually Not	No
5. Possibility that winner of popular vote might not win election retained?	Yes	Yes	Yes	Yes—with joint session contingent. No—with runoff contingent.

Senator Homer Ferguson of Michigan in 1950 (as a counter to the proportional plan then being considered, the Lodge-Gossett plan), Senator John F. Kennedy of Massachusetts in 1956 (as a counter to the district plan then being considered, the Mundt-Coudert plan), President Lyndon B. Johnson in messages of 1965 and 1966, Senator Birch Bayh in 1965 and early 1966 (until his switch to the direct vote plan on May 18, 1966), Attorney-General Nicholas Katzenbach during much of the late 1960s, and Senator Sam Ervin, Jr., of North Carolina in the late 1960s (as a counter to the direct vote plan then being considered).[5] The automatic plan has often been supported, it can be seen, by those who essentially wish to head off a more sweeping reform that they oppose. Often caught in the middle between those who desire another plan and those whose primary wish is to block that other plan, the automatic plan has proved to be the stepchild of electoral college reform: a potential second choice of many, but one enthusiastically loved by few.

The possible results of various presidential elections under this plan can be assessed with some degree of confidence. Since the automatic plan would not change the allocations or counting of electoral votes but only the possibility of a faithless elector, the results and confusions of 1876 and 1888, as well as the electoral college deadlocks of 1824 and 1800, presumably would have still occurred under it. The election of 1960, however, is an uncertain case. Unpledged electors would be impossible under the automatic plan, and there is no way of assessing what the preferences of those voters in Alabama and Mississippi who voted for unpledged electors would have been had the choice been limited to only Nixon and Kennedy. It is, therefore, impossible to say whether 1960 might have been, under the automatic plan, an election where the winner in popular votes would have become the loser of the election.

The impact of the joint session of Congress modification of the present House contingent procedure is very difficult to assess. The congressional politics of the two early elections of 1800 and 1824 are too complex for any degree of analysis about likely outcomes under a joint session procedure; however, it can be noted that selection by a joint session procedure, with equal votes for all members, would in no way either then or now increase the likelihood that the winner in popular votes will be the winner of the election. Rather, it seems likely that whatever party dominates the 535-member composite body—if any does—will elect its candidate regardless of the popular vote results. What the joint session procedure changes are the gross inequities of House voting by states. It does not change the possibility that the joint session may choose the popular vote loser, or for that matter, that the joint session may have great problems electing anyone president as inauguration day approaches.[6]

The arguments that have been advanced for and against the automatic plan as in the case of all the reform plans—are themselves complex, ambiguous, and often contradictory. We will try to make some sense out of this confusion through an analytical summary of the major claims, both pro and con, for each plan. In this chapter, unlike the next, critical judgment on these often polemical statements will be withheld in favor of a succinct summary of the arguments themselves.

Arguments for the Automatic Plan

This reform would deal with the two most flagrant defects of the electoral college system—the faithless elector and the House contingent election of the president—while not otherwise disturbing the traditional and well-tested electoral college system. Therefore, many of the arguments for and against the automatic plan revolve around assessments of the adequacy of the present electoral college system. In favor of this system, it has been said that the present electoral college has stood the test of time well, with only one election (1888) of the thirty-seven for which popular vote totals are available resulting in an undisputed reversal of the popular vote winner because of the electoral college. "Although imperfect, . . . the Electoral College has at least been excellent,"[7] and, in the words of Falkland, "when it is not necessary to change, it is necessary not to change."[8]

The present electoral college system is a bulwark of federalism because of the constant two allocation of electoral votes and a vital support for the two-party system because of the winner-take-all procedure. The automatic plan would preserve these features of the electoral college system.

The automatic plan would preserve the voting advantage conferred by the present electoral college on inhabitants of small states, large states, swing states, the South, metropolitan areas, minority groups—especially black voters, and/or urban, ethnic voters.

The automatic plan, like the present electoral college, "counts by states, focuses the closeness of the race on one or a few states . . . and insulates recounts and other difficulties within those states."[9] Specifically, fraud is isolated in specific states and not allowed to affect more than one state's vote.

Because of the multiplier effect "the electoral vote system adds a further dimension of legitimacy to the popular vote mandate."[10] This source of stability would be lost in a plan that divides electoral votes within a state or abolishes electoral votes altogether.

The automatic plan—like the present electoral college—recognizes and preserves the separate and independent electoral base of president and Congress.

The automatic plan is a minimal compromise reform plan that formalizes the electoral process in a way many believe it already to be. There is a lack of agreement in favor of other plans.

Arguments against the Automatic Plan

The electoral college today "represents little more than an archaic and undemocratic counting device."[11] There is no reason to maintain remnants of it in a reformed electoral system, as the automatic plan would.

Under the automatic plan, the inequitable allocation of a constant two electoral votes to each state, regardless of population, would be maintained. The electoral vote total under this reform would reflect national popular vote results in an inherently distorted manner.

The winner-take-all feature of the electoral college would be retained in the automatic plan—in fact, for the first time, written into the Constitution.

The automatic plan—like the present electoral college—would allow the winner of the presidency in popular votes to lose in electoral votes.

The automatic plan—like the present electoral college—would allow large blocs of electoral votes to be decided by slender margins of popular votes, thus inviting fraud and magnifying the consequences of accidental circumstances such as bad weather on election day. The rewards for fraud, in fact, are magnified under either the automatic plan or the existing electoral college.

The automatic plan would maintain an intermediate counting system not based equitably on current population (because of the ten-year lag between censuses), nor on census population (because of the constant two electoral votes given each state), nor on the number of votes actually cast. It fails a basic test of equality.

A joint session of Congress contingent procedure would mean that in case of an electoral deadlock, there could be an extended period of catastrophic uncertainty as to who will be president as a result of what congressional deals. The man finally chosen president by this procedure would by no means necessarily be the popular vote leader.

The automatic plan is an extremely limited reform whose major effect would be to preclude other necessary electoral reforms. As Viscount John Morley puts it in his essay "On Compromise," "The small reform may become the enemy of the great one."[12] Its modesty is not worth the labor and risk of a constitutional amendment.

The Proportional Plan

Unlike the automatic plan, which has as its primary focus the individual elector, the proportional plan has as its concern the unit rule, winner-take-all aspect of the electoral college system. The proportional plan deals with this very simply: the electoral vote allotted to each state (including, of course, the constant two) is divided in proportion to the popular vote in that state to the nearest one-thousandth of an electoral vote.

Since individual electors are difficult to divide into one-thousands, the proportional plan also incorporates the automatic casting of electoral votes and frequently adds a joint session of Congress contingent procedure in the event that no candidate receives 40 percent of the electoral vote. This last change is crucial, for the primary result of the proportional plan is the total elimination of the multiplier effect of the electoral vote percentage exceeding the popular vote percentage because of the winner-take-all feature. The result is that in many elections, under the proportional plan, the electoral vote percentage of the leading candidate would fall below 50 percent. Without a lowering of the required percentage to 40 percent, a resort to contingent procedures could thereby be a quite frequent occurrence.

It is very important to note what this plan would leave unchanged—the constant two electoral votes for every state. As will be argued in the next chapter, the retention of this small-state advantage while eliminating the large-state advantage of the unit rule converts the proportional plan (and the district plan to a slightly lesser extent) into a mechanism strongly and systematically favoring small states. Through proportional division of electoral votes and elimination of the office of elector, the electoral college is left with no purpose or existence except that of being an imperfect counting device with a systematic built-in bias favoring voters residing in the smaller states.

The history of the proportional plan is quite long and dates back to its first introduction in Congress by Representative William T. Lawrence of New York on December 11, 1848. Although it has not been introduced as frequently as other major reform proposals, it has come the closest to being approved by Congress. The proportional system was embodied in the Lodge-Gossett resolution (sponsored by Senator Henry Cabot Lodge of Massachusetts and Representative Ed Gossett of Texas), which was introduced in both houses of Congress in 1948. It reached the Senate floor early in 1950 and was approved by that body on February 1 of that year by a 64 to 27 vote, 3 more than the required two-thirds majority. Later in the same year, however, the House defeated the measure 210 to 134. The debate in the House centered around the fear that the plan would greatly disadvantage the Republican party because of the Democrats' strong hold on the South.[13]

Since 1950 the proportional plan has had occasional spurts of popularity centering around its seeming fairness in dividing electoral votes among candidates, and has been, in recent years, an occasional second-choice preference for those desiring the direct vote plan. Perhaps because of this, the proportional plan also sometimes has been advanced by those hostile to the direct vote alternative as a means of weakening direct vote strength. Its intrinsic popularity today was perhaps best caught in an exchange at the 1969 House Judiciary Committee Hearings on Electoral College Reform between Chairman Emanuel Celler and witness Neal Peirce:

> *The Chairman:* Could you comment on the suggestion made by the President with reference to the proportional method?
>
> *Mr. Peirce:* I think it is an idea whose time came and went.[14]

The analysis of possible results of past presidential elections under this plan is not too difficult to calculate, but potentially quite misleading. This is because any attempt to show what would have happened in a past election had it been conducted under another electoral system assumes that such factors as political strategies and voter motivations would remain constant under the different plans. This assumption is, of course, in opposition to most of the arguments made concerning the reform of the present electoral college system, which asserts that such factors as voter turnout and campaign strategies will indeed change to some degree under the various proposed reforms (except for perhaps the automatic plan). What analysis of past elections does show is not what would have actually happened, but what some of the various possibilities are under the various plans.[15]

Keeping in mind these limitations, it is illuminating to discover that the record of the proportional plan in elections of the nineteenth century might have been no better than that of the actual electoral college. While the present electoral college reversed the popular vote results in the elections of 1876 and 1888, the proportional plan would have done the same in the elections of 1880 and 1896—and, possibly, also in 1900. James A. Garfield (R.), the 9,000-vote leader in 1880, would have been defeated by Winfield S. Hancock (D.) by 6.8 electoral votes. In 1896, under the proportional plan, William J. Bryan (D.) would likewise have defeated the popular vote leader,

William McKinley (R.), who had a margin of close to 7,000 votes, by almost 6 electoral votes. The outcome of the election of 1900 is uncertain but might also have resulted in a victory for the popular vote loser—Bryan. Only in the election of 1888 would the proportional plan have improved upon the actual electoral college. Under the proportional plan the popular vote winner Grover Cleveland (D.) would have won with 202.9 electoral votes over Benjamin Harrison, with 185.8.[16]

One interesting fact stands out from these four elections: in each instance the Democratic candidate for president would have benefited under the proportional plan relative to the actual electoral college. In one classic analysis of past elections, political scientist Ruth Silva found that in sixteen of the eighteen elections between 1880 and 1948, the Democratic candidate would have had an advantage under the proportional plan in comparison with the existing electoral college—in one case by as much as 7.217 percentage points. The average Democratic advantage in the eighteen elections, Silva found, was 3.006 percent, while the average Republican disadvantage was 2.879 percent.[17] This bias extending over a sixty-eight-year span was largely due to the existence of the solid Democratic South, where large margins for Democratic candidates would, under the proportional plan, not be wasted as in the existing electoral college. In addition, the South also had a long history of low voter participation in elections, making electoral votes in the South "cheaper" in terms of popular votes actually cast—and thus cheaper in terms of Democratic votes. In 1948, for example, 1 electoral vote could have been determined, under the proportional plan, by an average of 40,260 votes in the eleven-state South, but required 107,840 votes in the thirty-seven other states.[18] With the proportional plan appearing, at least historically, to have a built-in Democratic and southern bias, it is not surprising that the Lodge-Gossett plan of 1950 failed to pass.

A closer examination of seven recent elections under the proportional and other plans is possible because of data calculated by the Library of Congress Legislative Reference Service.[19]   Figure 1

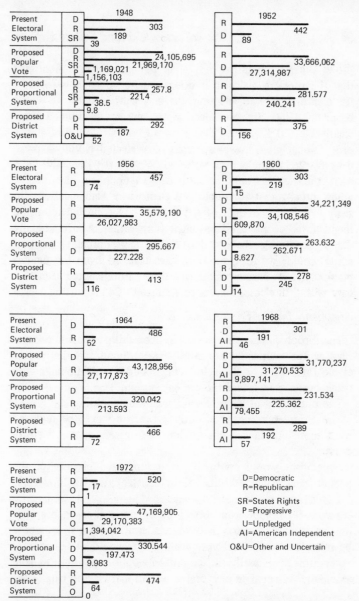

		1948			1952
Present Electoral System	D	303	R	442	
	R	189	D	89	
	SR	39			

Figure 1 *Presidential Elections: Comparative Result under Present and Proposed Systems*

Source: United States Chamber of Commerce. Data from Legislative Reference Service, Library of Congress, in U.S., Congress, House, House Judiciary Committee, *Hearings on Electoral College Reform,* 91st Cong., 1st sess., February and March 1969, p. 973. The 1972 election data were supplied by the Library of Congress especially for this book.

shows these comparative results in bar graph form. Assuming that the proportional plan in effect required only 40 percent of the electoral vote for election, the only shift in outcome would occur in 1960. In that election the present electoral college clearly elected Kennedy, the supposed popular vote leader. The proportional plan, however, might have elected Nixon as president by 263.632 electoral votes to 262.671 for Kennedy; however, the result would actually depend upon the decision of votes actually cast for unpledged electors in Alabama and Mississippi.[20] If about half of these votes had gone to Nixon, he might have become president eight years earlier than he actually did. It should also be noted from this table that the same outcome would, without question, have resulted from the district plan: under it, Nixon would have had an undisputed 1960 victory with 278 electoral votes to Kennedy's 245.

Arguments for the Proportional Plan

The proportional plan would reflect faithfully the popular support for each candidate in each state. As a result the national electoral vote totals would correspond to the popular vote totals better than under the present system.

The outmoded office of elector would be abolished.

The House contingent election procedure would be replaced by a more equitable joint session of Congress contingent procedure.

Federalism would continue to be supported because of the proportional plan's retention of the constant two electoral votes for each state, no matter how small.

Two-party competition would be encouraged in each state—especially where a party is weak—since all popular votes would be reflected in electoral vote results. This would also encourage voter turnout generally since a citizen would know that his vote would be reflected in electoral votes, no matter who carries the state.

Votes cast for minor-party candidates would be reflected in electoral vote results.

The results of fraud and accidental circumstances would be lessened, since small margins would not determine large blocs of electoral votes.

The proportional plan would eliminate any extraordinary power that organized minorities in large urbanized states may have under the existing system, since they would no longer be able to swing large blocs of electoral votes by small margins.

The proportional plan—at least in its proportional aspect—is easily comprehended.

The proportional plan is a compromise between the present electoral college and a direct vote plan in that proportional divisions of electoral votes are provided, but in an electoral college framework based on weighted states.

Arguments against the Proportional Plan

Under the proportional plan, the inequitable allotment of a constant two electoral votes to each state, regardless of population, would be maintained. The electoral vote totals, under this reform, would reflect national popular vote results in an inherently distorted manner.

Under the proportional plan, a winner of the presidency in popular votes could lose in electoral votes.

The proportional plan would have an undesirable impact upon the president elected, since it "would deflate his victory margin and along with it his decisive mandate to govern."[21]

The proportional plan would allow for election of a president with as little as 40 percent of the electoral vote (and conceivably even less in popular votes). Because of the elimination of the winner-take-all feature, and consequently the multiplier effect, such results would be quite likely under the proportional plan. In addition, because of the absence of the multiplier effect, the electoral college's choice of a candidate other than the popular vote leader would be more likely under the proportional plan than under the present electoral college.

Because of the elimination of the winner-take-all system of determining each state's electoral votes, minor parties would flourish and be rewarded for their activities by fragments of electoral votes. This would undermine the established two-party system.

The proportional plan would confer a marked advantage upon the smallest states because of the retention of the constant two. The proportional plan is not an equitable compromise between the present electoral college and a direct vote plan, but rather is "the most extreme 'reform' of all." The major consequence of the proportional plan "would be to confer an additional political bonus upon states already overrepresented in positions of Congressional power."[22] It would transform an electoral system with countervailing features favoring small states (the constant two) and large states (the winner-take-all) into a "reformed" system with a single, unidirectional bias favoring small states.

The proportional plan would eliminate any extraordinary power that organized minorities in large urban states may have, since they would no longer be able to swing large blocs of electoral votes. The influence of these groups would decrease even more, since the proportional plan sharply favors small states where these interests are underrepresented.

The proportional plan would maintain an intermediate counting system not based equitably on current population, nor on census population, nor on the number of votes actually cast. It fails a basic test of equality.

The proportional plan, with its basic feature of proportional division of inequitably determined blocs of electoral votes, is not a plan easily comprehended.

The proportional plan would divide the "solid, hard numbers of the old electoral college."[23]

A joint session of Congress contingent procedure would mean that in case of an electoral deadlock (quite possible under the proportional plan—even with a 40 percent requirement—because of the elimination of the multiplier effect), there could be an extended period of catastrophic uncertainty as to who will be president as a result of what congressional deals. The man finally chosen president by this procedure would not necessarily be the popular vote leader.

The District Plan

This approach to reform of the electoral college has a long history dating back to a proposal made by Representative John Nicholas of Virginia on March 14, 1800, and has the distinction of being the only currently advocated reform proposal that has actually been used by some states, during the early history of the electoral college. District plans have varied widely in their specific provisions. However, the plan that has been given the most consideration in the last two decades is the so-called Mundt, or Mundt-Coudert plan, which was repeatedly introduced during the 1950s and 1960s by Senator Karl Mundt, Republican of South Dakota and during the 1950s by Representative Frederic R. Coudert, Jr., Republican of New York.

This reform of the electoral college system would retain individual electors (although constitutionally bind them),[24] retain the constant two electoral votes per state, change to a joint session of Congress contingent procedure, and retain the possibility that the winner in popular votes might not win the election. Its chief result would be to divide a state's electoral votes, although not as thoroughly as under the proportional plan. In each state, the two electoral votes corresponding to the two senators would be decided by the statewide vote, with the plurality winner receiving both votes. The remaining electoral votes would be determined through a district-by-district counting of votes, in other words, a series of miniature winner-takes-all elections involving 480 different district and state electoral units.[25] The unit rule, then, would be eliminated only to a limited degree, and not at all for the very smallest states. In the case of a state with the minimum of 3 electoral votes, those 3 votes would always constitute an unified bloc, since the single district results would also be the statewide results. In the case of a state with 4 electoral votes—such as Mundt's South Dakota—the maximum division of electoral votes would be 75 percent to 25 percent, since at least one of the two district results would have to agree with the statewide results.[26] The unit rule is also preserved, for every state, in the statewide two votes, and the miniature winner-take-all feature incorporated in the district elections.

The district plan had its chief moment of glory, in recent decades, in the form of the Mundt-Coudert plan of the 1950's. The result of years of effort by backers of this plan, together with backers of the Lodge-Gossett plan (the proportional plan), resulted, in 1956, in a shotgun marriage in the form of the "Daniels substitute," which would give each state a choice between the proportional and district plans for casting its electoral vote. This startling idea was approved by the Senate by a vote of 48 to 37, on March 27, 1956, as a substitute for a pending proportional plan, but was eventually dropped when it became evident that it lacked the necessary two-thirds vote for final passage as a constitutional amendment.[27]

The analysis of possible results under the district plan is greatly complicated by the limitations of congressional district election data for many past presidential elections. However, an examination of the seven recent elections summarized in figure 1 is illuminating. Except in 1948, in each election the second- and third-place candidate in electoral votes would have done better under the district plan than under the electoral college and would have done worse under either than under the proportional plan. In other words, the district plan represents state-by-state minority preferences better than the present system, but less well than the proportional plan.

Inherent in the district plan, however, is a great unevenness of representation of these state-by-state minorities. In 1968, under the existing system, Nixon with a very thin margin of 223,326 votes in California out of an over 7-million-vote total, received all 40 of that state's electoral votes. If the election had been held on a district basis, however, Nixon would have received 23 electoral votes to 17 for Humphrey.[28] The proportional plan results would have been even closer: 19.127 for Nixon, 17.895 for Humphrey, and 2.687 for Wallace (who would have received no electoral votes under the two other plans).[29]

Results under the district plan may differ from the popular vote, however, in result as well as in degree. If the 1960 election had been held under the district plan, it would have given an undisputed electoral college verdict to Nixon in spite of a questionable or undeterminable popular vote margin.[30] How would this have happened? An examination of some particular state voting patterns will help to answer this question.

In 1960 Kennedy carried Missouri with 50.3 percent of the popular vote, yet, under the district plan, he would have lost that state by 7 electoral votes to 6. He carried the four districts including Saint Louis and Kansas City by large margins sufficient to narrowly carry the state as a whole, for a total of 6 electoral votes. However, in the seven districts outside the two major metropolitan areas Kennedy lost each by relatively thin margins, thus losing 7 electoral votes.

Likewise, in two other states in 1960, Illinois and Michigan, thin popular vote statewide leads for Kennedy would have been turned by the district plan into electoral vote leads for Nixon. One way of calculating the national impact of this phenomenon is to look at the number of congressional districts each candidate would have carried under the district plan, excluding in this total the statewide electoral votes they also would have won. As shown in table 6, in 1960 Kennedy carried 196 congressional districts and Nixon 227, this despite a virtual deadheat in popular votes. This happened because of a greater geographical concentration of Democratic votes, which means a greater number of votes wasted in districts already carried for the candidate. In the districts carried by Kennedy in 1960, there was an average margin of 20.7 percentage points above the needed plurality; in the Nixon districts, this average margin was but 13.8 percentage points.[31] It was because of this greater waste of votes in districts already decided for Kennedy that the district plan would have greatly favored Nixon in 1960.

Whether this Republican advantage under the district plan is a short-range bias peculiar to this one election or whether there is a more durable tendency for Democratic presidential votes to be more geographically concentrated in congressional districts than are Republican votes is a crucial question. Table 6 reports comparable data for four recent national presidential elections.

TABLE 6
Geographic Concentration of Presidential Votes
in Congressional Districts

Election	Number of Congressional Districts Carried		Average Margin, in Percentage Points, above Plurality Needed to Carry District
1960[a]	Kennedy (D.)	196	20.7
	Nixon (R.)	227	13.8
	Unpledged Electors	11	18.4
1964[b]	Johnson (D.)	371	28.3
	Goldwater (R.)	60	21.7
1968[c]	Humphrey (D.)	161	21.4
	Nixon (R.)	226	14.1
	Wallace (A.I.P.)	48	23.2
1972[d]	McGovern (D.)	58	22.3
	Nixon (R.)	378	30.3

Sources: Congressional Quarterly Inc., *Congressional Quarterly Almanac: 1960* (Washington, D.C.: Congressional Quarterly, 1961), pp. 1033-75; *Congressional Quarterly Weekly Report*, March 26, 1965, pp. 465-512; *Congressional Quarterly Weekly Report*, June 6, 1969, pp. 885-921; and *Congressional Quarterly Weekly Report*, February 23, 1974, pp. 441-81. The district vote figures reported by *Congressional Quarterly* for the 1972 election, and used here, differ slightly from those supplied by the Library of Congress (see figure 1, page 53) by awarding one additional congressional district to Nixon in both Ohio and Texas.

[a]The analysis of presidential election results by congressional districts for 1960 excludes the single at-large congressional district in Connecticut, which also had local districts, and excludes one of the two at-large congressional districts in New Mexico and North Dakota.
[b]The analysis of presidential election results by congressional districts for 1964 excludes the single at-large congressional district in Maryland, Ohio, and Texas, each of which also had local districts, and excludes one of the two at-large congressional districts in Hawaii and New Mexico. It includes the District of Columbia presidential election results as a congressional district.
[c]The analysis of presidential election results by congressional districts for 1968 excludes one of the two at-large congressional districts in Hawaii and includes the District of Columbia as a congressional district.
[d]The analysis of presidential election results by congressional districts for 1972 includes the District of Columbia as a congressional district.

In two cases the Democratic candidate had an average margin in percentage points in those districts that he carried considerably in excess of the comparable Republican margin in Republican-carried districts. In 1964 and 1972, when the Republican candidate carried some Deep South districts by *margins* in excess of 60 percentage points, the Republican excess margin approached or exceeded the Democratic figure. In the other two instances, the Democratic figure was close to half again as large as the Republican figure. On the basis of this limited analysis, it is unclear that there is a contemporary tendency for Democratic presidential votes to be more geographically concentrated in congressional districts than Republican presidential votes. The district plan, however, introduces distinct short-term partisan biases into the electoral process—in addition to its other shortcomings.

Arguments for the District Plan

The district plan would allow for the division of electoral votes within a state to the degree that presidential candidate strength differs in different districts within the state. As a result the national electoral vote totals would correspond to the popular vote totals somewhat better than under the present system.

The problem of the faithless elector would be solved either by requiring an elector to cast his vote as anticipated or by abolishing the office of elector.

The House contingent election procedure would be replaced by a more equitable joint session of Congress contingent procedure.

Federalism would continue to be supported because of the district plan's retention of the constant two electoral votes for each state, no matter how small.

Two-party competition would be encouraged in those states where each party has a chance of carrying at least one district.

The district plan would, to a degree, encourage minor parties and reflect their popular votes in electoral votes—but only those minor parties capable of carrying electoral districts.

The district plan would lessen any extraordinary power that organized minorities in large urbanized states may have under the existing system, since they would no longer be able to swing large blocs of electoral votes except in the unlikely case that they are distributed in large numbers in all of a state's districts.

The results of fraud and accidental circumstances would be localized in individual districts.

The district plan is the only currently advocated electoral reform plan that has actually been used by some states, during the early history of the electoral college. By adopting the district plan, we would be returning to a well-tested, historic system.

Through making the election of the president more resemble the election of Congress, harmony between the two branches would be heightened.

Arguments against the District Plan

The district plan would, to a degree, reduce the multiplier effect of electoral votes exceeding popular vote totals. As a result, electoral college deadlock or choice of a candidate other than the popular vote leader would be made more likely under the district plan than under the present electoral college.

There is no reason to retain the outmoded office of elector, as some versions of the district plan do.

A joint session of Congress contingent procedure would mean that in case of an electoral college deadlock (which is made quite likely because of the district plan's weakening of the multiplier effect), there could be an extended period of catastrophic uncertainty as to who would be president as a result of what congressional deals. The man finally chosen president by this procedure would not necessarily be the popular vote leader.

Under the district plan, the inequitable allocation of a constant two electoral votes to each state, regardless of population, would be maintained. The electoral vote totals, under this reform, would reflect national popular vote results in an inherently distorted manner.

Under the district plan, a winner of the presidency in popular votes could lose in electoral votes.

Two-party competition would be encouraged only in those

districts that are seen as marginal or swing—where two-party competition is probably already strong. In other districts there would be little added incentive for the development of two-party competition under the district plan.

The district plan would introduce at least a short-range, distinct partisan bias favoring Republican presidential candidates over Democratic candidates.

Because of the partial elimination of the winner-take-all system of determining electoral votes, minor parties, to some degree, would be encouraged and rewarded for their activities with electoral votes when they can carry electoral districts. This would undermine the existing two-party system.

The district plan would, to some degree, confer an advantage upon the smaller states because of the retention of the constant two and partial elimination of the winner-take-all feature.

The district plan would lessen any extraordinary power that organized minorities in large urbanized states may have under the existing system, since they would no longer be able to swing large blocs of electoral votes—except in the unlikely case that they are distributed in large numbers in all of a state's districts. Instead, under the district plan, minority group voters would be concentrated in a relatively small number of geographic districts and, consequently, would be relatively disadvantaged.

The effect of fraud and accidental circumstances would be magnified in swing or marginal districts where shifts of relatively small numbers of votes could determine entire blocs of electoral votes.

The district plan maintains an intermediate counting system not based equitably on current population, nor on census population, nor on the number of votes actually cast. It fails a basic test of equality.

The inequities of a winner-take-all system would be retained in the district plan—but on a district rather than state basis.

The district plan, with its basic feature of district determination of individual electoral votes together with statewide determination of 2 electoral votes, is not easily comprehended.

Political, ethnic, or ideological gerrymandering would be

almost inevitable in the presidential electoral districts—even if they were drawn numerically equal. This would be especially true if existing congressional districts were not used, but special presidential districts created.

The district plan "would drastically localize presidential elections" in a sort of miniature federalism within states not justified by history or political tradition. It would introduce "a newly effective political geography, the geography of local districts."[32]

The district plan would greatly change the character of the presidency by making that office the counterpart of Congress. The separation of powers, which rests on a diversity of political bases, would be dangerously weakened by the district plan.

The Direct Vote Plan

The fourth of the major proposals for electoral reform is noteworthy because it alone totally abolishes the mechanism of an electoral college—and along with it each of the five problems associated with it. This reform is easiest to grasp not in comparison with the existing system, which would be eliminated, but in terms of the single-member constituency form of elections widely used in the American political system. In essence, the direct vote plan would elect the president in the same manner as state governors, United States Senators, and members of the House of Representatives are elected—in a popular direct vote by all the eligible voters in the constituency. Neither states, electors, nor any other counting mechanism would play an intermediary role in this electoral reform. Specifically, individual electors, the unit rule, the constant two, the present House contingent procedure, and the possibility that the winner in popular votes might not win the election would be eliminated—at least in the plan widely advocated and supported in the late 1960s with a runoff contingent feature.

It is on this last aspect of the direct plan that most controversy about it has centered, as will be discussed in the next two chapters. As this reform evolved and periodically reappeared since it was first proposed on the floor of the Senate on March

20, 1816, by Senator Abner Lacock of Pennsylvania,[33] it often contained some type of modification of the existing contingent feature such as a joint session of Congress procedure. It was with this provision that the direct vote plan acquired its most dramatic and important recent sponsor on May 18, 1966— Senator Bayh, chairman of the Constitutional Amendments Subcommittee of the Senate Judiciary Committee. Bayh, who announced that he was abandoning his earlier support of the administration's automatic plan in favor of the direct vote plan, was to emerge in the next few years as the most tireless and persistent promoter the direct vote plan had ever enjoyed—in addition to being the first chairman of an appropriate committee to support that reform.[34]

Early in 1967 a blue-ribbon study commission of the American Bar Association (ABA) issued a widely publicized report on electoral reform, which was quickly ratified by the ABA's House of Delegates in February of that year.

The commission's evaluation of the existing electoral system was harsh: "The electoral college method of electing a President of the United States is archaic, undemocratic, complex, ambiguous, indirect, and dangerous."[35] In its report, the commission strongly supported the direct vote plan, but with a runoff between the two top candidates if no candidates received 40 percent of the national popular vote. This would, it was argued, largely deter possible splinter parties because of the elimination of the possibilities of throwing the election into a joint session of Congress, with the resulting uncertainties, deals, and intrigues. In light of this formidable support, the direct vote plan being advocated by Senator Bayh and others was quickly modified so as to incorporate this run-off provision—a feature that was, however, to prove the Achilles' heel of the direct vote plan.

Chapter 5 will continue this story of the direct vote plan's emergence as *the* electoral college reform plan (the major book on the electoral college published during the 1960s has as the title as its last chapter, "Today's Alternative: Direct Vote or the Status Quo").[36]

It is probably more misleading to examine past elections

under this plan as if such factors as voter turnout and campaign strategy were unchanged, than for any of the other reform plans, for the changes anticipated (or claimed) as resulting from this reform are greatest in precisely these areas. Thus, to note that with a 40 percent popular vote requirement, only one election, that of 1860, would have been forced to a runoff, does not at all prove that had the plan actually been in effect, there would not have been many more runoff elections. All that we can say is it has been a very rare occurrence in our history under the present electoral system for no candidate to receive well over 40 percent of the popular vote. The important question, however, of whether the direct vote plan with runoff might encourage the proliferation of parties sufficient to create a recurring pattern of runoff elections, will be reserved for consideration in chapter 4. What can be most clearly said about the direct vote plan with a runoff, however, is that under it, and under it alone, the winner of the presidency in popular votes would always be the winner of the presidency in the election.

Arguments for the Direct Vote Plan

The direct vote plan is the only electoral college reform that would deal with all of the problems of the present electoral college system, including: the faithless elector, the unit rule concerning a state's electoral votes, the constant two electoral votes per state, the contingent election procedure, and the uncertainty that the winner will win. It does so by totally abolishing the electoral college, electors, unit voting, the constant two, and the House contingent procedure. The direct vote plan with the runoff contingent procedure also ensures that the popular vote winner will always be the winner of the election. It is the only plan that will do this.

Under the direct plan, a vote for president wherever cast would count equally. Likewise, the advantages or disadvantages that any group or interest might have under the existing electoral college would be eliminated in favor of a system where every vote counts the same.

Two-party competition would be encouraged in each state—especially where a party is weak—since all votes cast for a candidate would count as part of the national vote totals. The direct vote plan would also encourage voter turnout generally, since a citizen would know that his vote would be counted as part of the national vote totals, no matter who carries the state.

Votes for minor-party candidates would be reflected in national vote totals in proportion to their actual vote strength. As a result regional minor parties and national minor parties would be placed on an equal footing.

The direct vote plan is the only electoral reform plan that would eliminate an intermediate counting system not based on current population, nor on census population, nor on the number of votes actually cast. The direct vote plan would be based solely on actual votes cast—votes which are totaled nationally. It meets, therefore, a basic test of equality.

The consequences of fraud and accidental circumstances would be lessened, in comparison with the present system, since small margins would not determine large blocs of electoral votes. Fraud could only affect the votes directly involved, which would be a minute fraction of national vote totals.

An extended period of catastrophic uncertainty as to who will be president as a result of what congressional deals would be avoided by the contingent runoff feature of most direct vote plans. The man finally chosen president by such a runoff would, of course, also be the popular vote leader.

Resort to a runoff election would be a relatively rare occurrence. In the thirty-seven elections for which popular votes are available, only one failed to produce a candidate with over 40 percent of the popular vote; and this single exception (1860) fell only .2 percent below 40 percent.

The separate and independent electoral base of president and Congress would be recognized and preserved by the direct vote plan.

It is appropriate that the only two national elective offices, the president and vice president, be determined in a national election with each citizen's vote counting equally.

The importance of each state in presidential elections would lie not in its population, but in the number of citizens who actually vote. In other words, the direct vote plan "penalizes efforts to restrict voting rights in any state by reducing that state's influence on the outcome."[37]

The direct vote plan would utilize the type of popular election now used for almost all governmental offices in this country, including state governors, United States senators, and members of the House of Representatives. It is not a revolutionary type of electoral system, but the one with which the American people are most familiar.

The direct vote plan is easily comprehended and, in fact, is the plan many citizens think now elects the president.

Arguments against the Direct Vote Plan

The direct vote plan would allow the election of a president with as little as 40 percent of the popular vote. Such a president would find it very difficult to govern.

The direct vote plan would have an undesirable impact upon the president elected, since it "would deflate his winning margin and along with it his decisive mandate to govern."[38]

Under the direct vote plan, minor parties would flourish and be rewarded for their efforts with national vote totals. This fragmentation of the popular vote would undermine the established two-party system.

The direct vote plan would eliminate whatever voting advantage may be conferred by the present electoral college on inhabitants of small states, large states, swing states, the South, metropolitan areas, minority groups—especially black voters, and/or urban, ethnic voters.

The direct vote plan specifically would deprive the small states of one of their most important political protections—the 2 extra electoral votes regardless of size. More generally, the elimination of the constant two would remove a major bulwark of federalism in the United States.[39]

Under the direct vote plan, fraud and accidental circumstances would no longer be localized but would affect and taint the entire national vote count.

In a popular election, a president could be elected through an overwhelming vote in a few sections of the country, yet have little support in many others. Such a possibility is unacceptable if the president is to represent all of the country.

The direct vote plan would be a blow to the role of states in the federal system and would hasten the trend toward elimination of other protections of states' rights, such as the equal representation of states in the United States Senate.

The importance of each state in presidential elections would lie not in its population, but in the number of citizens who happen to vote in a given presidential election.

The runoff feature would greatly encourage multiple candidates in the first election, followed by deals and bargaining for support in the second. Such a process is highly undesirable in our political system and, of course, very destructive of the existing two-party system.[40]

It would prove very difficult to hold the attention and secure the participation of the American public in an additional national run-off election. The expense of such an added election would also be prohibitive.

The direct vote plan would force candidates to campaign nationwide at considerably greater campaign expense and with much greater use of mass persuasion techniques such as television.

Hybrids and Other Plans

The four plans so far discussed are basic types of electoral college reform that have been repeatedly proposed and reproposed with minor variations over the years. Most "new" proposals that emerge to a temporary prominence and are subject to wide public discussion turn out, on analysis, to be one of the old classics clothed in new language, or, in the case of the most innovative plans, to be hybrids of elements of these plans.

This is not to suggest, however, that the ideas of electoral reformers have not, at times, been truly original. Early in the history of the electoral college, in 1808, Senator James Hillhouse of Connecticut proposed that senators serve a single, three-year term of office, with one-third of the senators retiring each year. Under the Hillhouse plan, the president would be chosen each year, by lottery, from among those retiring senators.

Another, even more ingenious plan, proposed by Senator Lazarus W. Powell of Kentucky in 1864, would provide for electors choosing a president by lot from among themselves in a very complex and multistage fashion.

Other innovative plans for selecting the president have also been advanced. Representative Thomas Montgomery of Kentucky introduced a constitutional amendment in 1822, which provided for election of the president by rotating geographic sections—once by the New England states, the next by the South, and so forth. Another similar plan along these lines, suggested in 1860 by Andrew Johnson, would have the North and South alternately elect the president. A proposal introduced by Representative Clement L. Vallandigham of Ohio in 1861 carried this sectional idea further by requiring that a president would have to be elected by a majority of electors in each of four regions.

Other plans that came out of the 1860s included an 1862 proposal of Senator Jerrett Davis to nominate candidates in any manner, with Congress selecting one of these nominees by a unanimous vote, and an 1869 amendment by Representative Charles R. Bucalew of Pennsylvania, which would simply give Congress the power to legislate the electoral process to be used. Finally, one of the most interesting hybrid proposals of recent years was advanced by Senator Hubert Humphrey in 1956, which would abolish electors while keeping the same number of electoral votes as at present. Each state would determine 2 electoral votes on a winner-take-all basis, while the remainder would be divided on a nationwide proportional plan basis.[41] Under this plan, in 1960 Nixon would have been elected president with 268.562 electoral votes to 260.159 for Kennedy.[42]

Three specific plans that were advocated during the 1969 and 1970 debates over the direct vote plan also deserve brief analysis here. The first of these, the Tydings-Griffin plan, became very important during 1970 Senate consideration of electoral reform. This plan would abolish the office of elector and provide that a candidate would be elected president if he received a plurality of popular votes of at least 40 percent *or* a plurality of popular votes less than 40 percent and a majority of electoral votes (apportioned and determined as present). If neither of these possibilities occurred, the decision would go to a joint session of Congress for choice between the top two candidates. Because it was favored by a number of key senators who were seen as potentially crucial to the prospects of the basic direct vote plan, the Tydings-Griffin plan was finally reluctantly accepted by Senate direct vote advocates in the closing months of 1970 electoral reform activity as part of a last ditch effort to save the direct vote plan.

The second major plan of the late 1960s was truly a hybrid. With the impressive title of the federal system plan, this proposal, introduced in March 1970 by Senators Thomas F. Eagleton of Missouri and Robert Dole of Kansas, provided three distinctly different ways that the president could be elected. On the election night a candidate would be elected president if he had received a national popular vote plurality and either pluralities in a majority of the states or pluralities in states containing a majority of the voters. If no candidate succeeded in meeting these requirements, then the election would be determined by the present electoral college, modified by the automatic casting of electoral votes. If no candidate received a majority of these votes, then the electoral votes of any third-party candiates would be proportionally reallocated to the two front runners in order to derive a majority electoral vote winner. This rather complex plan, explained at length by its sponsors, attracted little attention and support in the months following its introduction.[43]

The last plan, the Spong plan, emerged out of the October-November 1970 deadlock over electoral college reform and was frankly designed to be a possible compromise plan or, failing that, to be a proposal around which support could muster in the new 1972 Congress. This plan, developed by Senator William B. Spong, Jr., of Virginia, abolished the office of elector but provided that a candidate would have to receive both a majority of electoral votes (apportioned and determined as present) and a plurality of popular votes to be elected president on election night. If this did not occur, the election would go to a joint session of Congress for the final decision. In essence, this plan would eliminate the faithless elector and would also make it impossible for the electoral college's manner of apportioning and counting electoral votes to elect a popular vote loser. The winner in popular votes could, of course, still lose in the joint session of Congress contingent procedure.

In presenting arguments pro and con, we shall limit ourselves to the three contemporary hybrid plans: the Tydings-Griffin plan, the federal system plan, and the Spong plan. Since many of the same arguments are utilized for and against these proposals, these three plans will be treated together. It should also be noted that many of the arguments concerning these hybrid plans would also apply to future hybrid proposals. The ingenuity of scholars in creating new variations on electoral reform plans, has, after all, only been exceeded by the lack of originality of the hybrids created.

Arguments for the Hybrid Plans

The Tydings-Griffin, Spong, and federal system plans are essentially direct vote plans with variations and contingent features designed to avoid some of the possible problems of the direct vote plan. They all would eliminate the office of elector and substitute a more equitable contingent provision than the existing House procedure. The structure of the electoral college would also be maintained in all three plans as a check upon popular vote results.

Under the Tydings-Griffin plan, a resort to electoral vote results would be made only in the case that no candidate received 40 percent of the popular votes. Thus, deviation from the direct vote plan would occur only when the popular vote totals were insufficient to produce a 40 percent winner—a situation that would rarely occur.

Under the federal system plan and the Spong plan, recognition is given to the need for popular vote distributions throughout the various states. There is therefore a requirement for electoral college success in order to achieve election night victory.

All three of these plans avoid the necessity of a national popular vote runoff, with all of its attendant problems.

Arguments against the Hybrid Plans

All three electoral reform plans retain an electoral college somewhere in their complex proceedings, with all the inequitable distortions of the constant two and winner-take-all features. Electoral votes under each of these plans would still not be based equitably on current population, nor on census population, nor on the number of votes actually cast. An electoral reform plan that retains such electoral votes fails a basic test of equality.

All three electoral reform plans would allow the winner of the presidency in popular votes to lose the election either in electoral votes (the federal system plan) or through a joint session of Congress procedure (the Tydings-Griffin and Spong plans).

A joint session of Congress contingent procedure (as is used in the Tydings-Griffin and Spong plans) would mean that in case of an election deadlock, there could be an extended period of catastrophic uncertainty as to who will be president as a result of what congressional deals. The man finally chosen president by this procedure would not necessarily be the popular vote leader.

Each of these electoral reform plans introduces multiple ways by which a president might be selected. An electoral system should provide for one clear means of election of an officeholder, not contingent plan upon contingent plan.

All three of these electoral reform plans—but most of all the federal system plan—fail a basic requirement of clarity and easy comprehension. They are "undesirably complex"[44] —more so than either the direct vote plan or the existing electoral college system. The federal system plan, especially, defies simple explanation or easy understanding, so much as to dissolve the popular election mandate of a president resulting from this plan.[45]

4. Assessment: The Case for the Direct Vote Plan

The conception of political equality from the Declaration of Independence, to Lincoln's Gettysburg Address, to the Fifteenth, Seventeenth, and Nineteenth Amendments can mean only one thing—one person, one vote.

Gray v. Sanders

Yet time and again, the [House Judiciary] Committee members showed a profound reluctance to appreciate the importance and seriousness of the criticisms of direct Presidential election. They kept coming back to a single, abstract political dogma: one man, one vote, and each vote to be weighed in the same balance. The anticipated consequences of direct popular election seemed unable to affect their judgment; it was as if it had been divinely ordained that only one factor, one criterion was properly involved in deciding how we, as citizens of a democracy, should elect our President.

Irving Kristol and Paul Weaver,
"A Bad Idea Whose Time Has Come,"
New York Times Magazine

The summary of polemics presented in the preceding chapter purposely avoided any assessment of arguments; it is to this task that this chapter now turns. In order to make such assessments, obviously it is necessary for the authors to express value preferences and expose personal biases. This they do shamelessly—yet, it is also hoped, in a scholarly manner and according to systematic criteria.

Criteria for Evaluation

What are the goals of electoral college reform? What consequences should a desirable electoral reform plan have—and not have? These questions lie at the heart of the debate over the merits of specific plans. Occasionally an author identifies one or two goals in terms of which his preferred plan measures well, yet the literature of electoral college reform offers only an occasional attempt to systematically identify criteria for evaluation of reform proposals.[1]

We have sought to abstract and systematize such a minimal list of goals for electoral reform, which may be used as criteria for evaluating various plans.[2] To us, it seems that an electoral college reform should serve to further three broad goals:

1. It should contribute to democracy,[3] specifically—
   a. provide a basic equality of votes, and
   b. ensure that the winning candidate is the one who received the most votes.

2. It should ensure the effectiveness of the presidency, specifically—
   a. contribute to its legitimacy through providing a broad mandate,
   b. provide a clear, easily comprehended, and distinctive source for the president's mandate,
   c. ensure a quick and decisive verdict not subject to conflicting claims, and
   d. avoid a constitutional crisis that might arise either through an extended election deadlock or through questionable proceedings and deals in the course of a contingent procedure.

3. It should both preserve and invigorate the political system, specifically—
   a. maintain the existing two-party system and encourage effective two-party competition while recognizing the legitimate right of potential third and fourth parties to electoral influence,
   b. encourage popular political participation—especially voter turnout—while minimizing campaign expenditures,
   c. preserve federalism while securing an equitable electoral influence for all sections of the country in terms of campaign time and political attention,

    d. provide no systematic and inherent political biases favoring or hurting partisan, ideological, or categoric groups in American society, and

    e. avoid any incentive for electoral fraud and minimize the consequences of accidential electoral circumstances.

Having identified general criteria for evaluation, let us now turn to specific reform plans. We will look first at the electoral reform proposals that seem to have less current political support—the automatic, proportional, district, and hybrid plans.

Proposals with Less Support

The Automatic Plan

Proponents of the automatic plan usually start from the premise that the electoral college has served the American people well and that with the elimination of the possible problems that might be presented by a faithless elector and the House contingent procedure, it will perform even better.

This complacent satisfaction with the electoral college as a contemporary American political institution for "counting the votes,"[4] has been sharply criticized throughout this book. In chapter 1, which analyzed the electoral college today, it was concluded that the electoral college is a markedly imperfect institution that suffers from five noteworthy defects: the faithless elector, the constant two, the unit rule, the House contingent procedure, and the possibility that the winner of the popular vote will lose the election.[5] Of these five problems, the automatic plan would deal with only the first and fourth. In these terms, then, the automatic plan would appear to be a most inadequate reform.

The automatic plan also fails many of the criteria for evaluation of a reform plan. Like the present electoral college, the automatic plan would not aggregate votes equally nor ensure that the winning candidate would be the one with the most popular votes. In other words, the automatic plan—like the present system—does not correspond to democratic values nor further democratic procedures.

In terms of the criterion of "ensuring the effectiveness of the presidency," the automatic plan comes off slightly better. It probably would, to some degree, maintain presidential legitimacy through the exaggerated electoral vote strength that would still result from the multiplier effect. It should also be noted that under the automatic plan the source of the president's mandate is not made particularly comprehensible by the strange operations of the electoral college mechanism; the electoral procedure does not necessarily give rise to quick and decisive verdicts; and constitutional crises can quite possibly result from electoral college deadlock, subsequent political deals, and uncertain congressional activities.

It is in terms of the third criterion that the automatic plan shows what appeal it has. Indisputably, the automatic plan would not constitute a change from the present electoral college in this regard. The two-party system, political participation, federalism, electoral biases, and incentives or disincentives for fraud would remain unchanged. We should note, however, that as we argue later in this chapter, there is little evidence that the electoral college is, in fact, a vital support of the two-party system or a bulwark of federalism. It further seems doubtful that the present electoral college in any way encourages political participation or minimizes incentives for fraud. Finally, it will be shown that the electoral college does contain significant and systematic political biases—inherent advantages and disadvantages, which would, of course, be maintained by the automatic plan.

In those respects in which the automatic plan differs from the present electoral system, this reform appears reasonable. The office of elector does seem obsolete and should be abolished, and the House contingent procedure is thoroughly indefensible. In place of the last feature, however, the automatic plan would use a joint session of Congress procedure. While somewhat more equitable, this contingent arrangement still allows for massive problems and uncertainties—as well as inherent inequities—for the automatic plan, as well as for any electoral reform plan using it.

A last criticism of the automatic plan has to do with its very limited character. Even if the automatic plan is an improvement over the present electoral college system, its most important consequences might well be to head off permanently other much-needed broader electoral reforms.

The Proportional Plan

The proportional plan is clearly more inclusive than the automatic plan, and also, it might appear, more equitable. In the proportional division of electoral votes, in fact, lies much of the proportional plan's appeal. This reform, however, deals with just one more problem of the contemporary electoral college than the automatic plan—besides eliminating electors and the House contingent procedure, the proportional plan also does away with the unit vote. Two other serious problems—the constant two and the possibility of the winner losing—remain untouched by this reform.

In terms of the electoral reform criteria, the proportional plan, because of its inherent inequalities and possibilities for popular winner reversal, clearly fails to meet the criterion of contributing to democracy. It would further seem to be almost equally insufficient in terms of ensuring the effectiveness of the presidency. Any contribution the present electoral college makes to presidential legitimacy through the inflated majorities created by the multiplier effect, is, of course, eliminated by the proportional plan. The ability to obtain quick and decisive verdicts and to avoid constitutional crises would similarly be greatly weakened by the proportional plan because of the elimination of the unit vote. The only advantage that might be claimed for the proportional plan in terms of the second criterion is that of comprehensibility—and that only to the degree that the proportional division of inequitably determined blocs of electoral votes is an easily grasped concept.

Serious objections to the proportional plan arise in connection with the third criterion. While political participation might be encouraged, the consequences of fraud minimized, and federalism probably not affected, concern has been expressed that the proportional plan might have a serious effect on existing political parties. It is true that, as much as any plan, the proportional plan would weaken the two-party system through rewarding minor parties with fragments of electoral votes. We feel, however, as we will argue later in connection with the direct vote plan, that the relation of the presidential electoral system to the preservation of the two-party system is not substantial or significant, and, therefore, this concern is not well grounded.

It is in the remaining aspect of the third criterion—provision of no systematic and inherent political biases favoring or hurting partisan, ideological, or categoric groups—that the proportional plan is most glaringly deficient. In the last section of this chapter, data on the biases of each of the reform plans, as well as of the present electoral college, will be presented. Suffice it now to say that the proportional plan will be found to contain the greatest inequalities and biases of any of the plans. The reason for this is quite simple: under the electoral college, two features—the constant two and the unit rule—oppose each other in terms of their effects. The proportional plan completely eliminates one of these features, the unit rule, while retaining the other. As a result, the proportional plan transforms the presidential electoral system from one with countervailing biases to one with unidirectional biases.

The District Plan

The third reform plan contains many of the same features and problems as the proportional plan and introduces some distinctive ones of its own. As in the proportional plan, the unit rule is eliminated—but in the district plan only partially. The inequalities of an allocation of 2 electoral votes to each state and the possibility of the winner losing the election are maintained.

The district plan fails the first criterion of reform plans, as do both the proportional plan and the automatic plan before it. Under none of these plans would votes be counted equally, nor would the winning candidate necessarily be the one who received the most votes. In terms of presidential effectiveness the differences between the district plan and the proportional plan are ones of degree: the district plan probably would provide a somewhat larger electoral vote mandate than the proportional plan,[6] and thus might be thought more likely to provide a quick, decisive verdict and to avoid constitutional crises. In fact, however, this might well not be the case, since almost all district plans require a majority of electoral votes in order to avoid an electoral college deadlock, while almost all proportional plans require only a 40 percent electoral vote. As a result, it is impossible to say which plan makes election night deadlock most likely, but both plans share with the present electoral college system a very real possibility of such deadlock. It is in terms of comprehensiveness, however, that the district plan is most clearly inferior to the proportional plan. A complex system of district and state inequitably determined votes seems more complicated and obscure than the proportional plan—or the present system for that matter.

The district plan comes out slightly better than the proportional plan, however, under the third criterion. Minor parties, to the extent that they can carry electoral districts, would be encouraged, but only to a relatively minor degree. Political participation might, to a modest degree, be encouraged (probably less than under the proportional plan); federalism would probably remain unchanged; and fraud slightly discouraged. Finally, it should be noted that the district plan would also, as will be shown, introduce significant biases greater than under the present electoral college system but less than under the proportional plan.

It is in the unique features of the district plan that its most significant shortcomings arise. In most versions electors are retained (although effectively pledged) for unknown reasons or advantages. More important, however, is the district plan's utilization of local districts as the key to its new presidential politics. Such a district basis of the presidency, we feel, is neither necessary nor desirable. In addition to these objections, it should also be noted that politicians are unlikely to resist the opportunity to manipulate such district lines for partisan or ideological reasons—even while possibly respecting the necessity of numerical equality. We can, in fact, see no reason to introduce such presidential election districts as basic local elements of the only national political offices.

The Hybrid Plans

The three hybrid plans examined in the preceding chapter—the Tydings-Griffin plan, the federal system plan, and the Spong plan—all are based on the direct vote plan, but have an electoral college retained somewhere in the proceedings. As such, they immediately fail the first criterion of contributing to democracy, although it should be noted that the inequalities in these plans are less pervasive than in the previously discussed reforms. In addition, under each of the hybrid plans, the election of a candidate other than the popular vote leader would be possible—through a joint session of Congress contingent procedure, if not earlier.

In terms of the other two criteria, the hybrid plans would operate somewhat as the direct vote plan, to be discussed next, except that initial electoral deadlock and resort to contingent procedures would be made more likely, except in the case of the Tydings-Griffin plan, because of the addition of electoral vote to popular vote requirements. It is in terms of providing a clear, easily comprehended and distinct source for the president's mandate, however, that the hybrid plans most obviously fail. In each plan, the complexities of multiple roads to electoral victory would make the election of the president a confusing and unclear process and his mandate and source of legitimacy indistinct. Against whatever claim may be made for the perfection of such hybrid plans must be weighed their cost in terms of comprehension and, as a result, popular acceptance of the presidency.

The Direct Vote Plan

The direct vote plan has, as its basic attributes, simplicity and comprehensiveness. It is simple because it does not utilize electors or electoral votes, nor does it retain a constant two or a unit vote feature. All of these features, together with the House contingent procedure and the possibility of the winner losing, are swept away and replaced with a simple alternative: a nationwide popular vote for president, with all votes aggregated directly and equally. What complexity there is comes in the runoff feature: if no candidate receives 40 percent of the total initial popular vote, a second election would be held between the top two candidates to determine the winner.

The comprehensiveness of the direct vote plan lies in the fact that it is the only plan that deals with all five of the problems of the contemporary electoral college system. This it does through the simple expedient of totally abolishing the electoral college system in all respects, thus doing away with electors, constant twos, unit rules, House contingent procedures, and electoral reversal possibilities. Much of the appeal of this electoral reform, then, can then be seen to lie in this combination of simplicity and comprehensiveness.

In terms of the criteria for evaluation, the direct vote plan meets the criterion of contributing to democracy in that it—and it alone—treats all votes, wherever cast, equally, and it ensures that the winning candidate will always be the one who received the most votes. In fact, these two features of the direct vote plan are its real strength. If one holds to the principle that an electoral system must be compatible with these basic elements of democracy, then the direct vote plan is the only possible reform to support. On the other hand, if compatibility with these democratic principles is seen as a relative rather than absolute requirement for an electoral system, then the direct vote plan may be only a preferred alternative.[7]

We hold to the initial position, that compatability with democratic principles is an absolute requirement;[8] however, were we to rest on this view, we might fail to examine the direct vote plan in terms of its strengths and weaknesses in other aspects. Such a further examination is necessary, for to many an assertion that the direct vote plan is acceptable precisely and solely because of its compatability with democratic principles is insufficient. How, then, does the direct vote plan measure up in terms of the other criteria?

On the plus side, there seems to be little question that this reform provides an easily comprehended and distinctive source for the presidential mandate and would eliminate any systematic and inherent biases that might be contained in the present electoral arrangements. In addition, it seems reasonable to hold that the direct vote plan would encourage political participation—and especially voter turnout—because of the assurance it provides that all votes would have equal weight in determining the winner. In other regards, however, the consequences of the direct vote plan have been subject to widely varying interpretations and assessments.[9]

Among the criticisms of the direct vote plan which have been offered, the most notable are that this reform would damage federalism, encourage fraud, undermine the current two-party system, and introduce major problems because of the runoff contingent feature. In addition to these arguments, which we characterize as criticisms of a general nature, the direct vote plan has also been subject to criticisms of a parochial nature—that it eliminates various advantages that inhabitants of certain states, regions, or members of certain categoric groups enjoy under the present electoral college system.

Criticisms of a General Nature

FEDERALISM Critics of the direct vote plan have often attacked it on the grounds that abolition of the electoral college would seriously injure or even bring about the destruction of American federalism. The assumption here is that the present

apportionment of electoral votes according to a state's representation in Congress embodies the federal compromise, and, therefore, is an integral part of the federal system of government.

We doubt, however, that the electoral college is, in fact, a
central element of federalism in the contemporary United
States. Federalism is maintained by institutions and practices
other than that of the presidency, the only truly national office
in the United States. In the words of Herbert Wechsler, "the
existence of the states as governmental entities and as the services of the standing law is, in itself, the prime determinant of
our working federalism."[10] Together with the constitutional
guarantee of equal state representation in the Senate (probably
the only truly nonamendable constitutional provision), the very
fact of state and local levels of government engaged in crucial
decision-making activities is the essence of contemporary federalism—not a constant two allocation of electoral votes. We find
ourselves in agreement with Senator Bayh that "the Electoral
College system is not a fundamental ingredient in the Federal
system. It's more or less an accidental coincidental parallel."[11]
In fact, a linkage between the method of presidential selection
and federalism does not seem to exist even in popular conception, for, as Sayre and Parris point out, voters "perceive the
election as a national contest."[12] The direct vote plan, then,
would not entail a shift in popular acceptance of federalism;
rather it would ensure that the presidential selection process
would operate the way that the American people think it already does.

A particularly comprehensive view of the institutional balance
making up contemporary federalism has been provided by Senator Mike Mansfield (D., Mont.):

As I see the Federal system in contemporary practice, the
House of Representatives is the key to the protection of district interests as district interests, just as the Senate is the key
to the protection of State interests as State interests. These
instrumentalities, and particularly the Senate, are the principal
constitutional safeguards of the Federal system, but the Presi-

dency has evolved, out of necessity, into the principal legal bulwark beyond districts, beyond States, for safeguarding the interests of all the people in all the States. And since such is the case, in my opinion, the Presidency should be subject to the direct and equal control of all the people.[13]

We find ourselves in agreement with this assessment, made over a decade ago.

FRAUD Another charge frequently made against the direct vote plan is that it would do away with the defenses the electoral college provides against the effects of fraud and the consequences of localized accidental circumstances, such as inclement weather. As Alexander Bickel argues, "the electoral college system counts by states, focuses the closeness of the race on one or a few states ... and insulates recounts and other difficulties within these states." The implications of this in terms of fraud are made explicit by Theodore White: "Under the present electoral system ... crooks ... are limited to toying with the electoral vote of one state only, and then only when margins are exceptionally tight."[14]

This analysis, however, seems faulty when one considers the relative amount of fraud (or extent of accidental circumstance) necessary to accomplish an electoral reversal under the present electoral college system and the direct vote plan. In 1960 a shift of only 11,424 votes could have resulted in a different candidate winning; under the direct vote plan, an indeterminable, but certainly far greater shift of popular votes would have been necessary. In 1968, a shift of 53,034 votes could have given rise to an electoral college deadlock, but under the direct vote plan, a shift almost one hundred times as large, of a minimum of 4,491,395 votes, would have been necessary to force a runoff.[15]

The underlying reason for the greater possibilities of election reversals and deadlocks under the electoral college system is that it does not insulate the results of fraud and accidental circumstances within individual states, but rather magnifies their consequences enormously, to the extent that such fraud and accidents occur in marginal states. Certainly, the results of fraud and accidents in states already carried by a candidate are minimized, and even neutralized, but in those cases where fraud is most likely—in close, "swingable" states—the consequence of, and thus incentives for, fraud are enormous. A few thousand votes in a key state such as New York, under the electoral college, can deliver to a candidate an entire bloc of electoral votes representing as much as 16 percent of the popular vote.[16] Under the direct vote plan, on the other hand, fraud and accidental circumstances can affect only the relatively minimal number of votes directly involved.

We find no evidence, then, to support the notion that adoption of the direct vote plan would open any doors to electoral fraud. Rather, the observation of Neal Peirce seems pertinent: "Perhaps the best assurance of an honest vote count throughout the country lies in the expansion of a viable two-party system to every state and subdivision."[17] This raises the very important next question: What would be the likely effect of the direct vote plan on the two-party system?

POLITICAL PARTIES The most serious and substantial charge made against the direct vote plan has been that, if adopted, it would fundamentally undermine and change the existing two-party system. Alexander Bickel sums up the indictment against the direct vote plan in this regard:

> There is a strong possibility, if not probability, that under a system of popular election the run-off would be typical; the major party nomination would count for much less than it now does; there would be little inducement to unity in each party following the conventions; coalitions would be formed not at conventions but during the period between the general election and the run-off; and the dominant positions of the two major parties would not long be sustained. This sort of unstructured, volatile multi-party politics may look more open. So it would be—infinitely more open to demogogues, to quick-cure medicine men, and to fascists of left and right.[18]

Let us look at this set of arguments in terms of three interwoven but distinguishable possible effects: (1) the effects of direct election by itself (initially putting aside the runoff and related concerns) on third parties and two-party competition, (2) its effect on the underpinnings of the two-party system itself, and (3) its effects, due to the runoff feature, on party splintering and multiple candidacies.

One result of the direct vote plan would be to put all minor parties—whether they are regionally or nationally based—on an equal footing in trying to reach a somewhat difficult popular vote minimum of 20 percent. This figure—the least that a third party would have to have in order to deadlock an election if the two major parties split the remaining 80 percent—is a goal more demanding for the regionally based party and less demanding for the nationally based third party than the requirements of the present system.

Another consequence of the direct vote plan would be to remove the loopholes through which regional minor parties, capable of winning electoral votes in individual states, can exercise inordinate power in the presidential selection process. Under direct election, no third-party candidate could use a handful of electoral votes to dictate the choice of a president. As the *New York Times* editorialized:

Mr. Wallace can be a national threat with only 13 percent of the popular vote under the Electoral College; he cannot be a threat under popular election. Mr. Wallace is now able to resolve a deadlock on his own whim, bartering electoral votes for favors; the voters themseves would resolve any deadlock in the unlikely event one would occur under the direct election proposal through a run-off election.[19]

The direct vote plan would also have a beneficial effect upon two-party competition. Under it, a vote cast anywhere would be equally desirable. Parties would have to seek votes throughout the country, albeit it at possible greater cost and increased use of mass media.[20] As a consequence of this search for votes, political parties would have to be concerned with party structure and get-out-the-vote campaigns, especially in states and areas where they currently are a minority. Two-party competition would be strengthened—especially where it is weak now. Voters in one-party states would have special added incentive to vote. The members of the minority party in one-party states would no longer face the prospect of having their votes rendered meaningless by the effects of the unit rule; supporters of the majority party, on the other hand, would also have increased incentive to participate in the election because their votes, previously relatively unimportant in their own state, would now be counted in the national total for their party's candidate.

A second concern often expressed about the direct vote plan raises a fundamental question when it asks: If the electoral college is abolished, will an essential support for the two-party system also be eliminated? This question haunted the ABA Commission on Electoral College Reform during their 1966-67 study, leading to endorsement of the direct vote plan, and prompted them to review, in detail, the relevant political science literature on the basis of the two-party system. They found six generally cited reasons for the existence of two-party politics in the United States:

1. the persistence of initial form
2. the election of officials from single-member districts by plurality votes
3. the normal presence of a central consensus on national goals
4. a cultural homogeneity
5. a political maturity
6. a general tendency toward dualism

As the chairman of the ABA commission concluded:

> Some of the experts list the electoral college as a factor that may contribute; others ignore it; and some suggest that it is functionally opposed to two-partyism and that our party system may have survived despite the electoral college rather than because of it.[21]

A Brookings Institution conference of electoral reform experts in 1969 similarly downgraded the importance of the electoral college to the two-party system. At this conference,

> it was noted that many academic studies have identified the election of House members from single-member districts on a simple plurality basis as the major determinant of a two-party system. Most participants in the Brookings Conference, however, were unwilling to conclude that the presidential electoral system has no significant impact on party activity.

It should be recognized that this effect of the presidential electoral system lies in the individual, nondivisible nature of the office, rather than in the electoral college itself—it is the existence of a "single, national executive" that maintains a dualistic pattern of politics in the United States. While electoral votes are divisible, the presidency is not. As a result, in the words of political scientist Frank Sorauf, "the American election system offers no rewards of office for losing parties."[22]

A useful review of explanations for the maintenance of two-party politics has been provided by Sorauf. He has identified four broad types of theories explaining the two-party system: *institutional theories*, which include the prevalence of single-member, plurality elections and the single, national executive; *dualistic theories*, which stress an "underlying duality of interests in the American society" or a " 'natural dualism' within democratic institutions"; *cultural theories*, which base American party politics on political maturity and the development of a political culture that recognizes the necessity of compromise, the wisdom of pragmatism, and the need to avoid dogmatism; and *social consensus theories*, which trace two parties to an alleged prevailing acceptance of social, economic, and political institutions.[23] As Sorauf points out, the notable shortcoming with all of these theories is that they fail to explain *why* such consensus, cultural traits, duality of interests, or institutions themselves have developed. For our purposes, however, it is sufficient to note that nowhere in these theories of the causes of American party politics is there any significance given to the institution of the electoral college.[24]

Some years ago, historian James MacGregor Burns observed:

> The real protection of the two-party system is the existence
> of strong executive posts, such as President and Governor,
> around which parties polarize and which force third parties to
> amalgamate with major parties in order to achieve some of
> their desired ends.[25]

The real effect of the direct vote plan in terms of political parties is to explicitly recognize the presidency as based on a single-member national constituency—the very kind of electoral
system that has so often been cited as the institutional basis of
two-party politics.[26] We find, then, no body of literature
explicitly relating the electoral college to the preservation of
the two-party system and a significant body of literature suggesting, rather, that the single, indivisible office of the president
is one such element. Direct election would not disturb this
latter effect, but rather make this national office subject to
popular, direct determination.[27]

THE RUNOFF The third concern about the effect of direct
vote on political parties centers around the runoff contingent
feature of the direct vote plans debated in the late 1960s and
early 1970s. We consider this specific concern separately, for at
stake in the attack on the runoff contingent feature are charges
that it would considerably increase the cost, delay, and uncertainty of the presidential selection process and that it would
"encourage the proliferation of political parties in this country."[28]

   The first of these arguments—the cost, delay, and uncertainty
of direct vote—is based on the belief that a presidential election
runoff would entail added electoral burdens and expenses for
candidates and parties, would require a rapid ballot count (and
possible recount), would result in a considerable voting drop-off
for the second election, and would give rise to political deals
and maneuvering between the initial election and the runoff.[29]
Certainly, a second national election campaign would involve
some added burdens and expenses for both candidates and par-

ties, and the possibility of such a runoff would necessitate an efficient counting and certifying of the ballots (which is itself probably quite desirable). We are, however, less convinced that there would be a voting decline in the second election. Rather, it might well be that the suspense of a cliff-hanging decision, magnified, of course, by the mass media, would increase voter participation in the runoff.

Similarly, we do not feel that political deals or maneuverings would necessarily be the dominant feature of the period between elections. Such bargaining assumes that blocs made up of millions of American voters could be "delivered" by a candidate or party to another candidate or party without setting off incalculable but major countertrends and reactions. Rather, this interim period might be marked by millions of acts of choice between two clear alternatives by a voting public made attentive by the publicity and excitement generated by the initial election.

Two more basic questions that lurk behind the discussion of the runoff feature are: How likely, in fact, is such a runoff? And what are the alternatives to a contingent runoff—are they superior?

The likelihood question is speculative and necessarily difficult to answer, yet it should be noted that a runoff could occur only when a minor party, or parties, obtained a minimum vote exceeding 20 percent, while, at the same time, the two major parties were exactly evenly dividing the remaining vote of just under 80 percent. If a minor party or parties failed to exceed 20 percent, or even if they did, if the major parties were sufficiently uneven in strength that one of them exceeded 40 percent, there would be no runoff. As noted earlier in this chapter, for a runoff to have been necessary in the 1968 election, not only would George Wallace have had to have a shift *to him* of at least 4,491,395 votes, but this shift would have had to have been made up of a minimum of 2,500,855 Nixon voters and 1,990,540 Humphrey supporters in order for neither major party candidate to win in the initial election. The magnitude of these shifts—even in as close an election as 1968—is staggering, even more so when one realizes the likely countertrends that would be created by such shifts. In our view, then, the conditions that would give rise to a runoff are sufficiently demanding that resort to such a contingency would be relatively unlikely,[30] and if it were necessary, the consequences would not be particularly severe.

Putting aside for the moment the somewhat benevolent assessment of the runoff reached above, let us also ask what the alternatives to a runoff are. Essentially, they are the joint session of Congress contingent procedure and simple plurality election. The first alternative we have previously criticized on the grounds that it could entail delay and confusion as Congress considered the making of a president and that it could easily lead to a popular vote loser being elected president. Plurality election has considerable appeal from a simplicity standpoint,[31] and yet could lead to a candidate becoming president with only 25 or 30 percent of the popular vote. Such possible results, many feel, would be undesirable in terms of providing a sufficient mandate for the president to govern—a view we tend to share.

The "40 percent or runoff" feature was introduced into the direct vote plan as part of a compromise between the goals of providing a sufficient presidential mandate and avoiding runoffs as much as possible. As Republican William McCulloch of Ohio explained it:

> The 40-per cent figure is obviously a compromise. A higher figure would encourage third parties and thus increase the possibility of a run-off which no one really deserves. A lower figure would provide a very small mandate for the man elected President. . . .[32]

This compromise is, like all compromises, somewhat contrived, yet it looks appealing in comparison with the massive problems that would arise under the present House contingent arrangement, the somewhat similar pitfalls of a joint session of Congress procedure, and the undermining of the presidency that could result from a simple plurality election.

One last argument sometimes advanced for the belief that a direct vote for president with runoff would encourage multiple minor parties and candidates is drawn from the study of those southern state primaries with runoffs. Many scholars, most notably V. O. Key, Jr., have observed a relationship between multifactionalism and runoff systems, although often they hold that the use of a runoff is a result as much as a cause of such factionalism.[33] No matter what the cause and effect relationship, the experience with southern primaries is that a runoff procedure "rewards, maintains, and extends multi-factionalism."[34] The pattern that often emerges is that of multiple candidates running in the initial election and then politically selling their support to one of the top two contenders in the runoff.

We feel, however, that this analogy between presidential elections and state primaries is misleading and faulty. Southern primaries are elections within political parties, with only amorphous factions to limit candidates and guide voters. Presidential elections, on the other hand, occur within the context of two established national political parties with large reserves of traditional voters, multiple clues to rekindle party loyalties, and funds and organization sufficient to deter many potential minor candidates. One other major difference should also be noted—southern primaries with runoffs universally have a 50 percent rather than 40 percent requirement for initial election. Even with this higher figure, it has been found that 84.2 percent of such primary elections do produce a winner in the first election and do not need a runoff.[35]

In summary, we doubt that the runoff contingent procedure would have the effects on presidential selection politics and the national two-party system that are sometimes found in the case of southern primaries. Neither do we feel that the liabilities of the runoff feature are as significant as its critics hold—or for that matter, anywhere as great as the shortcomings of the present House contingent procedure, the joint session of Congress alternative, or a simple plurality election. In addition, we doubt that a direct vote plan with runoff would, in fact, frequently result in use of the runoff feature. When and if such a contingency did occur, however, the president of the United States would still be determined in an equitable manner that would assure that the candidate with the greatest popular support would become the president.

Four broad criticisms of a general nature have been examined and assessed. We have not felt these arguments against the direct vote plan to be persuasive and find ourselves supporting the direct vote plan as both the simplest and most comprehensive electoral reform.

Yet, we must also consider those criticisms of the direct vote plan that are of a parochial or self-serving nature. Opposition to electoral reform can arise not only out of concern about what such reform will do to democracy, the presidency, or the political system, but also out of concern about what it will do personally or to favored interests. What, then, will be the results of the direct vote plan for various groups who may be favored or hurt by the present electoral college? Who would be advantaged or disadvantaged by the direct vote plan? What are the biases of the electoral college that the direct vote plan would eliminate?

Criticisms of a Parochial Nature

A central conflict permeating the politics of electoral college reform in recent years has involved contradictory assessments of the biases of the electoral college.[36] Diverse groups and interests have been seen as advantaged or disadvantaged under the present mechanism for electing the president; often, however, these interpretations have sharply contradicted or differed from each other. Such opposing assessments can be seen in these sharply differing views of the electoral college held by two staunch opponents of the direct vote plan:

> The electoral college as it has evolved is so rigged that the big states count disproportionately. That is its critical attribute.

> My state of Nebraska has 92 100ths of 1 percent of the electoral vote. Based on the last election, we had 73 100ths of 1

percent of the popular vote. I'm not authorized to reduce the voting power of my state by 20 percent.[37]

Many arguments about electoral reform assume, as self-evident truths, various consequences of the electoral college system—that it favors some groups or disadvantages others—yet offer little solid evidence to support these assumptions. In this final section of chapter 4, we will be both synthesizing the available information on the biases of the electoral college and developing and utilizing new systematic data on this question as a means of assessing these parochial criticisms.

The electoral college system clearly does not operate as a neutral mechanism, but rather contains distinctive structural features that give rise to diverse and often conflicting biases. Among these sources of bias are:[38]

1. the constant two constitutional allocation of two electoral votes to every state, regardless of size. In the case of states with quite low populations, this can lead to startling results. During the elections of the 1960s, for example, Alaska, with one-half of the population of Delaware, enjoyed an equal number of electoral votes—the constitutional minimum of three.
2. the unit rule extraconstitutional provision. The result of this feature is that a candidate can win all of the electoral votes of states carried with even the slimmest of margins, while losing millions of popular votes in other states carried by the opposition. In 1924, for example, Democratic nominee John W. Davis received 136 electoral votes from states in which he had obtained 2 million popular votes, and no electoral votes from other states in which he had received 6 million popular votes.
3. the assignment of electoral votes (other than the constant two) to states on a population basis rather than on a voter turnout basis. In 1968 Connecticut and South Carolina each had 8 electoral votes based on their similar populations, yet the number of voters in Connecticut exceeded that in South Carolina by more than 590,000.[39]

4. the assignment of electoral votes on the basis of census population figures that do not reflect population shifts except every ten years. As a result, states that were growing quickly during the 1960s, such as Arizona, California, Colorado, Florida, and Texas, did not have their new population growth reflected in their electoral vote totals until the 1970 census, which established the electoral college vote for each state for the presidential elections of 1972, 1976, and 1980. Population changes in any state after 1970 will, therefore, not be reflected in the electoral college until 1984.

The result of these features is to ensure that the electoral college will always provide an imperfect and unreliable reflection of the popular vote for president. The contemporary electoral college is not just an archaic mechanism for counting the votes for president; rather, it is an institution that aggregates the popular vote in an inherently imperfect manner. To say that the electoral college introduces random distortions into the election of the president is only a half-truth, for the electoral college also contains a variety of systematic biases conferring advantages on some voters and imposing disadvantages on others.

There is an obvious need for a careful assessment of the biases of an institution whose abolition is so widely called for. In defending the electoral college or in supporting its elimination, one must, as Albert Rosenthal has argued,

consider the desirability of direct popular election of the president in terms of practical consequences as well as democratic theory. What forces in our society would be strengthened, and what weakened, if the change were made? Which needs would be likely to be served and which put aside?[40]

Electoral college reform is an issue in which political rhetoric has tended to create its own political realities. What, however, are the political realities concerning the biases of the electoral college?

CONVENTIONAL WISDOM Conventional wisdom about these

biases is both abundant and contradictory. Among the voters advantaged by the electoral college would appear to be inhabitants of small states, large states, swing states, the South, metropolitan areas, minority groups (especially black voters), and urban, ethnic voters.

There seems to be widespread agreement that the effective voting power for president of the 350,000 residents of Omaha, Nebraska, is not the same as that of the 350,000 residents of Oakland, California. What is not agreed, however, is whether the inhabitants of the small or the large state have the advantage. The case for the small-state advantage has often been based on the obvious fact that small states, with the added constant two electoral votes, have more electoral votes than their populations would otherwise entitle them to. As a result, it has been reasoned that small states enjoy a noteworthy advantage in the electoral college—an edge they would be loath to give up. In a 1936 article in *The American Political Science Review*, Joseph Kallenbach observed,

> The less populous states will object to any plan which reduces the advantages which they enjoy under the present electoral system growing out of representation of Senate as well as House seats in the apportionment of electoral votes.

Similarly, Herbert Wechsler concluded in 1955 that "whatever may be said in principle for simple popular election, it would so diminish the political importance of the states of small electorates that it has no hope of adoption." A similar belief was expressed by scholars as distinguished as Edward Corwin and Louis Koenig, who wrote in 1956:

> Above all, the ... [direct election] proposal runs afoul of the practical difficulty that no plan can make progress unless it is adapted to the federal arrangement. The less populous states will object, and with fatal effect, if their advantages under the present setup are put in jeopardy.[41]

This assessment of the electoral college as containing a small-state bias, however, gave rise to a notable paradox:

When the electoral vote of a State was divided by its population, a single voter in a small State was represented by a larger fraction of an elector than one in a large State; yet politicians and amateurs alike knew that somehow the influence of each large-State voter was greater than that of his counterpart in a small State.[42]

The result of this contradiction was to allow proponents of various points of view to cite different perceived consequences of the electoral college according to their own position at the moment. Senator Kefauver, chairman of the Senate Judiciary Committee's Subcommittee on Constitutional Amendments, once wryly recalled that

> there were instances in our [1961] hearings where a witness would dismiss the practical chances of direct national election proposals as depriving the small states of their electoral vote advantage and then attack the present system as favoring the large states over the smaller ones.[43]

Scholarly opinion during much of the 1960s differed on how to assess the big-state–small-state biases of the electoral college. As Robert Dixon sums up the ambivalent state of scholarship:

> Views do vary on what persons or groups are helped or hurt by the electoral college system. Arithmetically, the system obviously favors the smaller states. Practically, however, the system often has been said to favor the larger states, and more specifically the balance of power minorities within the larger states whose vote may determine the allocation of the entire electoral vote of the state. This large-state bias also has been said to extend to candidate selection and campaign emphasis.[44]

Two of the first works to demonstrate a clear understanding of the complex consequences of the electoral college and of various reform proposals, but which lacked mathematical substantiation of their conclusions, were 1964 and 1968 studies by political scientists Nelson W. Polsby and Aaron B. Wildavsky. In their analysis, they described the "constant two" and "unit rule" features as two different, countervailing forces having opposing consequences. Together, Polsby and Wildavsky argued, these two features result in a "current strategic advantage enjoyed by populous, two-party, urbanized states."[45]

The question of big-state–small-state advantage may be, some have suggested, an indeterminable or meaningless debate. Early in 1970 Senator Bayh threw up his hands at the endless controversy on the matter and suggested: "I just think that this is sort of an American roulette in which it's an happenstance as to whether the small states or the large states are advantaged."[46] Neal Peirce has further argued that the distinction itself between large and small states has not proven to be historically significant: "The arguments over the years, starting at the Constitutional Convention itself, on the subject of big- versus small-state interests and advantages might well be termed the Great Irrelevancy."[47]

Other states that are often cited as advantaged by the present electoral system are what are called "swing" states. Such states are decided by relatively small margins of popular votes and, if swung the other way, could deliver an entire bloc of electoral votes. As Allan Sindler argued in 1962,

> States safe for either party merit relatively less attention from both parties; attention must be concentrated on those states in which the election outcome is uncertain and, within that category, on those states in which large blocs of electoral votes are at stake.[48]

Thus, the swing-state hypothesis is, to a considerable degree, also caught up in the big-state hypothesis: the truly important states are those that are closely competitive and that have large blocs of electoral votes.

Additional states that are sometimes viewed as favored by the electoral college are the southern states. The traditional argument has been that the South, as a region, has been able to produce a solid bloc of electoral votes for Democratic candidates unblemished by any signs of Republican votes (which were eliminated by the unit rule). As a result, the South has been able to exercise inordinate influence over the Democratic party and national politics.[49] The case has also been made by Polsby and Wildavsky that under any alternative election system that recognizes the magnitude of the margin of popular votes, the South will gain additional strength over its present electoral college advantage. In other words, the South will "rise again" in political importance because of that region's large Democratic margins.[50]

The likelihood of the South gaining under a reform plan such as direct election, however, has been disputed in a later work by Harvey Zeidenstein entitled "The South Will Not Rise through Direct Election of the President, Polsby and Wildavsky Notwithstanding." Zeidenstein argued that in only one election since 1948 has the total winner's margin in the South exceeded that in the North, and that in no election during this period has the Democratic party proved to be politically indebted to the South for crucial support.[51] This analysis we find compelling, especially as the South has developed in recent years a two-party (and sometimes three-party) politics. Any characterization of the South as a Democratic bastion is dated both in terms of recent elections as well as likely long-term trends.

Another set of arguments about the biases of the electoral college revolve around the idea that the contemporary electoral college favors inhabitants of metropolitan areas, as well as minority groups, blacks, and urban, ethnic voters. Often these arguments are also asserted in the form of conclusions containing implicit or explicit defenses of the electoral college because of what is seen as a desirable bias:

> The system is in effect malapportioned in favor of cohesive interest, ethnic or racial groups within those big states, which often go very nearly en bloc for a candidate, and can swing the state's entire electoral vote.

> A reduction of the voting strength of the large states will mean a loss of political strength of urban and Negro voters.

> The interests favored by the present method of electing Presi-

dents are precisely those most urgently in need of favorable attention from the Federal government today.[52]

These conclusions, however, have been subject to criticism on a variety of grounds. Besides the fact that defense of the electoral college on the grounds that it benefits favored interests smacks of gross political cynicism, questions have been raised whether the identified "liberal" voting groups are also, in fact, *swing voters.* "Swing voters" have been defined as "those who can not be taken for granted,"[53] but the moorings of these liberal groups to one party seem more secure than for most voting groups.[54] In fact, the truly swing groups would seem likely to be those groups undergoing political transition, such as backlash and suburban groups, rather than the traditionally Democratic blocs of urban, blue collar, and black voters.[55] Being merely a part of the winning coalition does not necessarily mean that a group will be credited as being the decisive element—especially if that group's support had been taken for granted. At best, "the problem with a swing-vote theory . . . is that one of a number of voting groups can be identified as crucial,"[56] and those groups most likely to be so credited are those not traditionally part of the partisan coalition. As Senator Bayh has observed,

> The influence of minorities, as a result of the unit rule, is exaggerated by Professor Bickel simply because these groups are not composed of "swing" voters who can entice the major party candidates to bargain for their votes. It is a fact of political life, known alike to Democratic and Republican politicians, that these minorities traditionally vote Democratic.[57]

The difficulties of defending the electoral college on the grounds that it protects certain favored interests have been summarized by Neal Peirce in one effective sentence:

> To say that the electoral college should be retained to defend liberalism or big cities leads one down two odious roads: first, a political opportunism in which one would rather have a minority President he agrees with than a popularly chosen

one he disagrees with; and secondly, a possibly fatal mis-reading of the political tea leaves, in which one assumes that the political balances and realities of the past decades will hold true for the 1970's and time to come.[58]

The argument has also been made that urban minorities are advantaged by the electoral college not so much because of their swing character, but rather due to their being situated in the largest states, which are themselves, it is asserted, so advantaged that these urban minorities are likewise favored. Albert Rosenthal, for example, reasons:

Seven of the eight largest cities in the country are located in the seven largest states—New York, California, Pennsylvania, Illinois, Ohio, Texas, and Michigan. These states have a total of 210 electoral votes—only 60 less than the 270 needed to elect a President—and with the possible exception of Texas, they are closely balanced between the two parties (in the last five Presidential elections, [prior to 1967] each backed one party three times and the other twice). All seven have a greater proportionate urban population than the country as a whole, and the percentage of Negroes in their metropolitan areas already high is rising.[59]

These claims concerning the advantages enjoyed by urban and black voters under the electoral college have been, however, sharply qualified in a number of ways. First, it has been suggested that the central cities of urban areas are themselves not the key to populous states with large blocs of electoral votes. Along this line, William J. D. Boyd has pointed out:

No center city contains the necessary 50 percent of the people to dominate the state. . . . It now appears that no city will ever attain that dominance. The United States is an urban nation, but it is not a big-city nation. The suburbs own the future.[60]

The advantage that is asserted for urban areas may exist, but this advantage is likely to be one for suburban, not center city, interests.

Second, it has been pointed out that not all—probably not even a majority—of blacks live in big cities or in big states. Millions of blacks live in the medium to small population states of the South and other regions. As a result, Neal Peirce has argued,

If there were a direct vote system, blacks in Mississippi could combine their votes with those of blacks in Chicago, or Alabama blacks could see their votes counted equally with those of Negroes along the Eastern seaboard. Instead of being a big-city bloc, Negroes would become a national bloc.[61]

Paul Freund of the Harvard Law School has generalized the consequences of abolishing the electoral college for urban and minority interests with an interesting metaphor:

It may well be that direct popular vote will increase the weight of the minority and urban interests by enabling their votes, wherever cast, to coalesce with similar votes in other states. And attention will be paid to concentrations of voters in populous states, for where the nectar is thickest, the bees will naturally foregather.[62]

From our review of the existing literature on the biases of the electoral college, we conclude that there are gross inconsistencies and contradictions concerning who is really advantaged and disadvantaged, and, consequently, who would be favored or hurt by the direct vote plan. In order to assess these biases, then, it will be necessary to develop and utilize new systematic data on this question.

NEW APPROACHES AND ANSWERS Until recently there has been no sophisticated means of analyzing the actual influence of states and their citizens in the present electoral college system. In addition, there has been no reliable means of determining how the various reform alternatives would affect the influence of states and individual citizens in selecting the president.[63] Recent advances in game theory and the mathematical analysis of voting power, however, have made possible the development of techniques allowing for a reasonably sophisticated determination of the relative influence of the states and their citizens in the election of the president.

The inquiry into the electoral consequences of the present electoral college has been conducted on two levels. On the one hand, a determination of the relative power of the states in the present electoral college has been made by Irwin Mann and L. S. Shapley.[64] On the other hand, John F. Banzhaf III has calculated the relative power of individual citizen-voters within each state in the present electoral college and in various alternative systems.[65] The work of William Riker and Lloyd S. Shapley serves as a valuable transition between these works.[66]

The first of these works, the Mann and Shapley study, developed a "51-person, weighted majority game" to evaluate the electoral college. From it, they concluded that there is a slight systematic bias in favor of the large states in the present electoral college, as a result of the unit rule, but one not exceeding a 10 percent variation in power per electoral vote among the various states. This bias, in their opinion, is meaningful, though "not very important in the total consequences of the electoral college." However, in a footnote to their conclusions, Mann and Shapley suggested that in a multimillion-person game, taking the individual voters as the players, the voters in the large states actually might be favored with a bias that "quantitatively might be as much as double the one seen by treating the states as players."[67] The reason for this apparent contradiction is that Mann and Shapley (and later Riker and Shapley) felt that a citizen's voting power is inversely proportional to the square root of his constituency's population, not merely inversely proportional to the constituency's population.

The second study, by Riker and Shapley, dealt with weighted voting in legislatures[68] but pointed to an important conclusion concerning a delegate model with a weighted voting system, such as the electoral college:

A big district has distinctly more power than the power index of its delegate in the legislature would indicate. A new bias ... is therefore superimposed on the bias already discussed; both favor the larger districts at the expense of the smaller. The magnitude of this effect is surprisingly large. An estimate using techniques of probability theory, supported by numerical computations for some particular cases, indicates that the citizens' power indices are multiplied by a factor proportional to the square-root of their district population when we pass from the free-agent model to the delegate model.[69]

The crucial third study, that by John F. Banzhaf III, provided for the first time a systematic measure of the voting power of citizen-voters in each of the states under the electoral college, as well as for the proportional, district, and direct vote plans. These findings were published initially in the *Villanova Law Review* in 1968 and have been reprinted and cited since then in numerous publications.[70] Essentially, the "voting power" approach to the evaluation of the electoral college used by Banzhaf involves three distinct steps. First, a determination is made of the chance that each state has in a "51-person" game (actually fifty states plus the District of Columbia) of casting the pivotal vote in the electoral college. Next, an evaluation is made of the proportion of voting combinations to the number of all possible voting combinations in which a given citizen-voter can, by changing his vote, alter the way in which his state's electoral votes will be cast. Finally, the results of the first step are combined with the results of the second to determine "the chance that any voter has of affecting the election of the President through the medium of his state's electoral votes."[71] These calculations are normalized with the power index of the state whose citizens have the least voting power set at one and all other states having voting powers greater then one; the result is an index of *relative voting power* of each citizen vis-à-vis voters residing in other states.

Banzhaf, in his 1968 publication and various subsequent studies, used the voting power approach to devise data measuring the biases of the electoral college, as well as other major reform plans, for the electoral vote apportionment of the 1960s (presidential elections of 1964 and 1968). In two recent companion studies to this book, however, the voting power approach is utilized to measure the biases of the electoral college, and the reform proposals, for the electoral vote apportionment of the 1970s (presidential elections of 1972, 1976, and 1980).[72] Data drawn from these studies are presented in tables 7-10.

In each table, the first three columns give the electoral votes allotted each state in the 1972, 1976, and 1980 elections, the 1970 census population of each state, and the resulting relative voting power indices of a citizen-voter in each of the states. The fourth column provides additional statistical interpretations of the relative voting power column. This column lists the percent deviations from average voting power per citizen-voter for citizen-voters in each state.

The voting power per citizen-voter average is calculated by multiplying the number of citizen-voters in a state (which, for calculative purposes, Banzhaf assumes to be the state's population) times the relative voting power of the citizen-voters in that state. The sum of these fifty-one products (including that for the District of Columbia) is then divided by the total number of citizen-voters (i.e. population) in the nation to obtain the national average per citizen-voter.

Figures 2-5 graphically present the key data on the percent deviation from average voting power of citizen-voters under each plan. In each graph the populations of the various states are measured along the horizontal axis, and the percent deviations from average voting power (from column 4 of each table) of citizens residing in each state is represented on the vertical axis. A freehand line illustrates the general trend of the points.

The pattern of biases shown in figure 2 for the present electoral college and the automatic plan is quite revealing. With the exception of the twenty very small states at the extreme left-hand side of the graph, the plotting of states is almost linear, with the relative voting power of citizens increasing steadily with the size of the state population. This linearly increasing **advantage** of citizen-voters in the thirty-one most populous states is a result of the unit rule feature of the contemporary electoral college. The relative voting power of citizens in specific states departs from an exact linear relationship because electoral votes only approximate state populations. The citizens of the very small states at the extreme left-hand side of the graph also have a relative voting power that is disproportionately large in comparison with the population of these states. The increased relative voting power of the residents of these small states stems from the two electoral votes which are not based on population. The increased relative volting power of the citizens of the District of Columbia is disproportionately low, since the district has a population large enough to entitle it to four electoral votes but is limited to three electoral votes by the provisions of the Twenty-third Amendment.[73] The most disadvantaged citizens are those of the medium- to small-sized states, with from 4 to 14 electoral votes. The citizens of Massachusetts, the nation's tenth largest state, have a relative voting power approximately equal to that of the residents of Alaska, the smallest state. Therefore, the citizens of the forty states with a population size between that of Alaska and Massachusetts are at a disadvantage in comparison with the citizens of these two states and the nine largest states. The citizens of the nine largest states have a disproportionately large relative voting power, which increases in a direct relationship with the population. In terms of the percent deviations data, it can be observed that forty-five states have less than average voting power and only six states have more—the six most populous! The relative voting power data also show marked state size differences. Under the present electoral college in the 1970s, a citizen-voter in California has 2.546 times the relative voting power of a citizen-voter in the most disadvantaged "state"— the District of Columbia. To rephrase the title of Banzhaf's study, the present electoral college can be viewed as an institution providing a voter in California with "one man, 2.546 votes."

Figure 3, showing relative voting power under the proportional plan, reveals a significantly different bias. Disparities in the relative voting power of citizen-voters under the propor-

TABLE 7
Voting Power under the Present Electoral College in the 1970s
(Arranged by Size of State)

State Name[a]	Electoral Vote: 1972, 1976, 1980 (1)	Population 1970 Census (2)	Relative Voting Power[b] (3)	Percent Deviation From Per Citizen-Voter Average Voting Power[c] (4)
Alaska	3	300,382	1.587	-4.3
Wyo.	3	332,416	1.509	-9.0
Vt.	3	444,330	1.305	-21.3
Nev.	3	488,738	1.244	-25.0
Del.	3	548,104	1.175	-29.1
N. Dak.	3	617,761	1.107	-33.3
S. Dak.	4	665,507	1.366	-17.6
Mont.	4	694,409	1.337	-19.3
Idaho	4	712,567	1.320	-20.4
N.H.	4	737,681	1.297	-21.7
D.C.	3	756,510	1.000	-39.7
Hawaii	4	768,561	1.271	-23.3
R.I.	4	946,725	1.145	-30.9
Maine	4	992,048	1.119	-32.5
N. Mex.	4	1,016,000	1.106	-33.3
Utah	4	1,059,273	1.083	-34.7
Nebr.	5	1,483,493	1.035	-37.6
W. Va.	6	1,744,237	1.131	-31.8
Ariz.	6	1,770,900	1.123	-32.3
Ark.	6	1,923,295	1.077	-35.0
Oreg.	6	2,091,385	1.033	-37.7
Colo.	7	2,207,259	1.137	-31.4
Miss.	7	2,216,912	1.134	-31.6
Kans.	7	2,246,578	1.126	-32.0
Okla.	8	2,559,229	1.219	-26.5
S.C.	8	2,590,516	1.212	-26.9
Iowa	8	2,824,376	1.160	-30.0
Conn.	8	3,031,709	1.120	-32.4
Ky.	9	3,218,706	1.244	-25.0
Wash.	9	3,409,169	1.209	-27.1
Ala.	9	3,444,165	1.203	-27.5

TABLE 7 *(continued)*

State Name[a]	Electoral Vote: 1972, 1976, 1980 (1)	Population 1970 Census (2)	Relative Voting Power[b] (3)	Percent Deviation From Per Citizen-Voter Average Voting Power[c] (4)
La.	10	3,641,306	1.281	−22.7
Minn.	10	3,804,971	1.253	−24.4
Md.	10	3,922,399	1.234	−25.6
Tenn.	10	3,923,687	1.234	−25.6
Wis.	11	4,417,731	1.291	−22.2
Ga.	12	4,589,575	1.324	−20.1
Va.	12	4,648,494	1.316	−20.6
Mo.	12	4,676,501	1.312	−20.8
N.C.	13	5,082,059	1.462	−11.8
Ind.	13	5,193,669	1.446	−12.8
Mass.	14	5,689,170	1.459	−12.0
Fla.	17	6,789,443	1.611	−2.8
N.J.	17	7,168,164	1.568	−5.4
Mich.	21	8,875,083	1.648	−0.6
Ohio	25	10,652,017	1.815	9.5
Ill.	26	11,113,976	1.888	13.9
Tex.	26	11,196,730	1.881	13.5
Pa.	27	11,793,909	1.913	15.4
N.Y.	41	18,236,967	2.360	42.4
Calif.	45	19,953,134	2.546	53.6

Source: Longley and Yunker, "The Changing Biases of the Electoral College," p. 11.

[a] Includes the District of Columbia.
[b] Ratio of voting power of citizens of state compared with voters of the most deprived state.
[c] Percent by which voting power deviated from the average *per citizen-voter* of the figures in column 3. Minus signs indicate less than average voting power. Average voting power per citizen-voter = 1.658.

TABLE 8
Voting Power under the Proportional Plan in the 1970s
(Arranged by Size of State)

State Name[a]	Electoral Vote: 1972, 1976, 1980 (1)	Population 1970 Census (2)	Relative Voting Power[b] (3)	Percent Deviation From Per Citizen-Voter Average Voting Power[c] (4)
Alaska	3	300,382	4.442	277.2
Wyo.	3	332,416	4.014	240.9
Vt.	3	444,330	3.003	155.0
Nev.	3	488,738	2.730	131.9
Del.	3	548,104	2.435	106.7
N. Dak.	3	617,761	2.160	83.4
S. Dak.	4	665,507	2.673	127.0
Mont.	4	694,409	2.562	117.6
Idaho	4	712,567	2.497	112.0
N.H.	4	737,681	2.412	104.8
D.C.	3	756,510	1.764	49.8
Hawaii	4	768,561	2.315	96.6
R.I.	4	946,725	1.879	59.6
Maine	4	992,048	1.793	52.3
N. Mex.	4	1,016,000	1.751	48.7
Utah	4	1,059,273	1.680	42.6
Nebr.	5	1,483,493	1.499	27.3
W. Va.	6	1,744,237	1.530	29.9
Ariz.	6	1,770,900	1.507	28.0
Ark.	6	1,923,295	1.388	17.8
Oreg.	6	2,091,385	1.276	8.4
Colo.	7	2,207,259	1.411	19.8
Miss.	7	2,216,912	1.404	19.3
Kans.	7	2,246,578	1.386	17.7
Okla.	8	2,559,229	1.390	18.1
S.C.	8	2,590,516	1.374	16.6
Iowa	8	2,824,376	1.260	7.0
Conn.	8	3,031,709	1.174	-0.3
Ky.	9	3,218,706	1.244	5.6
Wash.	9	3,409,169	1.174	-0.3
Ala.	9	3,444,165	1.162	-1.3

TABLE 8 *(continued)*

State Name[a]	Electoral Vote: 1972, 1976, 1980 (1)	Population 1970 Census (2)	Relative Voting Power[b] (3)	Percent Deviation From Per Citizen-Voter Average Voting Power[c] (4)
La.	10	3,641,306	1.222	3.7
Minn.	10	3,804,971	1.169	-0.7
Md.	10	3,922,399	1.134	-3.7
Tenn.	10	3,923,687	1.134	-3.7
Wis.	11	4,417,731	1.108	-5.9
Ga.	12	4,589,575	1.163	-1.2
Va.	12	4,648,494	1.148	-2.5
Mo.	12	4,676,501	1.141	-3.1
N.C.	13	5,082,059	1.138	-3.4
Ind.	13	5,193,669	1.113	-5.5
Mass.	14	5,689,170	1.095	-7.1
Fla.	17	6,789,443	1.114	-5.4
N.J.	17	7,168,164	1.055	-10.4
Mich.	21	8,875,083	1.052	-10.6
Ohio	25	10,652,017	1.044	-11.4
Ill.	26	11,113,976	1.041	-11.6
Tex.	26	11,196,730	1.033	-12.3
Pa.	27	11,793,909	1.018	-13.5
N.Y.	41	18,236,967	1.000	-15.1
Calif.	45	19,953,134	1.003	-14.8

Source: Longley and Yunker, "The Changing Biases of the Electoral College," p. 23.

[a] Includes the District of Columbia.
[b] Ratio of voting power of citizens of state compared with voters of the most deprived state.
[c] Percent by which voting power deviated from the average *per citizen-voter* of the figures in column 3. Minus signs indicate less than average voting power. Average voting power per citizen-voter = 1.178.

TABLE 9
Voting Power under the District Plan in the 1970s
(Arranged by Size of State)

State Name[a]	Electoral Vote: 1972, 1976, 1980 (1)	Population 1970 Census (2)	Relative Voting Power[b] (3)	Percent Deviation From Per Citizen-Voter Average Voting Power[c] (4)
Alaska	3	300,382	2.857	132.8
Wyo.	3	332,416	2.716	121.3
Vt.	3	444,330	2.349	91.4
Nev.	3	488,738	2.240	82.5
Del.	3	548,104	2.115	72.4
N. Dak.	3	617,761	1.992	62.4
S. Dak.	4	665,507	2.185	78.0
Mont.	4	694,409	2.139	74.3
Idaho	4	712,567	2.111	72.1
N.H.	4	737,681	2.075	69.1
D.C.	3	756,510	1.800	46.7
Hawaii	4	768,561	2.033	65.7
R.I.	4	946,725	1.832	49.3
Maine	4	992,048	1.789	45.8
N. Mex.	4	1,016,000	1.768	44.1
Utah	4	1,059,273	1.732	41.1
Nebr.	5	1,483,493	1.599	30.3
W. Va.	6	1,744,237	1.581	28.8
Ariz.	6	1,770,900	1.569	27.9
Ark.	6	1,923,295	1.506	22.7
Oreg.	6	2,091,385	1.444	17.7
Colo.	7	2,207,259	1.488	21.3
Miss.	7	2,216,912	1.485	21.0
Kans.	7	2,246,578	1.475	20.2
Okla.	8	2,559,229	1.452	18.3
S.C.	8	2,590,516	1.443	17.6
Iowa	8	2,824,376	1.382	12.6
Conn.	8	3,031,709	1.334	8.7
Ky.	9	3,218,706	1.352	10.2
Wash.	9	3,409,169	1.313	7.0
Ala.	9	3,444,165	1.307	6.5

TABLE 9 *(continued)*

State Name[a]	Electoral Vote: 1972, 1976, 1980 (1)	Population 1970 Census (2)	Relative Voting Power[b] (3)	Percent Deviation From Per Citizen-Voter Average Voting Power[c] (4)
La.	10	3,641,306	1.321	7.6
Minn.	10	3,804,971	1.292	5.3
Md.	10	3,922,399	1.273	3.7
Tenn.	10	3,923,687	1.272	3.7
Wis.	11	4,417,731	1.242	1.2
Ga.	12	4,589,575	1.258	2.5
Va.	12	4,648,494	1.250	1.9
Mo.	12	4,676,501	1.246	1.5
N.C.	13	5,082,059	1.231	0.3
Ind.	13	5,193,669	1.218	-0.8
Mass.	14	5,689,170	1.196	-2.6
Fla.	17	6,789,443	1.177	-4.1
N.J.	17	7,168,164	1.145	-6.7
Mich.	21	8,875,083	1.114	-9.2
Ohio	25	10,652,017	1.087	-11.4
Ill.	26	11,113,976	1.080	-12.0
Tex.	26	11,196,730	1.076	-12.3
Pa.	27	11,793,909	1.064	-13.3
N.Y.	41	18,236,967	1.008	-17.9
Calif.	45	19,953,134	1.000	-18.5

Source: Longley and Yunker, "The Changing Biases of the Electoral College," p. 27.

[a] Includes the District of Columbia.
[b] Ratio of voting power of citizens of state compared with voters of the most deprived state.
[c] Percent by which voting power deviated from the average *per citizen-voter* of the figures in column 3. Minus signs indicate less than average voting power. Average voting power per citizen-voter = 1.227.

TABLE 10
Voting Power under the Direct Vote Plan in the 1970s
(Arranged by Size of State)

State Name[a]	Electoral Vote: 1972, 1976, 1980 (1)	Population 1970 Census (2)	Relative Voting Power[b] (3)	Percent Deviation From Per Citizen-Voter Average Voting Power[c] (4)
Alaska	3	300,382	1.000	0.0
Wyo.	3	332,416	1.000	0.0
Vt.	3	444,330	1.000	0.0
Nev.	3	488,738	1.000	0.0
Del.	3	548,104	1.000	0.0
N. Dak.	3	617,761	1.000	0.0
S. Dak.	4	665,507	1.000	0.0
Mont.	4	694,409	1.000	0.0
Idaho	4	712,567	1.000	0.0
N.H.	4	737,681	1.000	0.0
D.C.	3	756,510	1.000	0.0
Hawaii	4	768,561	1.000	0.0
R.I.	4	946,725	1.000	0.0
Maine	4	992,048	1.000	0.0
N. Mex.	4	1,016,000	1.000	0.0
Utah	4	1,059,273	1.000	0.0
Nebr.	5	1,483,493	1.000	0.0
W. Va.	6	1,744,237	1.000	0.0
Ariz.	6	1,770,900	1.000	0.0
Ark.	6	1,923,295	1.000	0.0
Oreg.	6	2,091,385	1.000	0.0
Colo.	7	2,207,259	1.000	0.0
Miss.	7	2,216,912	1.000	0.0
Kans.	7	2,246,578	1.000	0.0
Okla.	8	2,559,229	1.000	0.0
S.C.	8	2,590,516	1.000	0.0
Iowa	8	2,824,376	1.000	0.0
Conn.	8	3,031,709	1.000	0.0
Ky.	9	3,218,706	1.000	0.0
Wash.	9	3,409,169	1.000	0.0
Ala.	9	3,444,165	1.000	0.0

TABLE 10 *(continued)*

State Name[a]	Electoral Vote: 1972, 1976, 1980 (1)	Population 1970 Census (2)	Relative Voting Power[b] (3)	Percent Deviation From Per Citizen-Voter Average Voting Power[c] (4)
La.	10	3,641,306	1.000	0.0
Minn.	10	3,804,971	1.000	0.0
Md.	10	3,922,399	1.000	0.0
Tenn.	10	3,923,687	1.000	0.0
Wis.	11	4,417,731	1.000	0.0
Ga.	12	4,589,575	1.000	0.0
Va.	12	4,648,494	1.000	0.0
Mo.	12	4,676,501	1.000	0.0
N.C.	13	5,082,059	1.000	0.0
Ind.	13	5,193,669	1.000	0.0
Mass.	14	5,689,170	1.000	0.0
Fla.	17	6,789,443	1.000	0.0
N.J.	17	7,168,164	1.000	0.0
Mich.	21	8,875,083	1.000	0.0
Ohio	25	10,652,017	1.000	0.0
Ill.	26	11,113,976	1.000	0.0
Tex.	26	11,196,730	1.000	0.0
Pa.	27	11,793,909	1.000	0.0
N.Y.	41	18,236,967	1.000	0.0
Calif.	45	19,953,134	1.000	0.0

[a] Includes the District of Columbia.
[b] Ratio of voting power of citizens of state compared with voters of the most deprived state.
[c] Percent by which voting power deviated from the average *per citizen-voter* of the figures in column 3. Minus signs indicate less than average voting power. Average voting power per citizen-voter = 1.000.

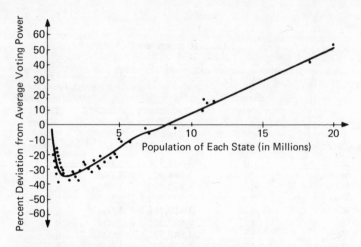

Figure 2 *Percent Deviations from Average Voting Power of States under the Present Electoral College in the 1970s*

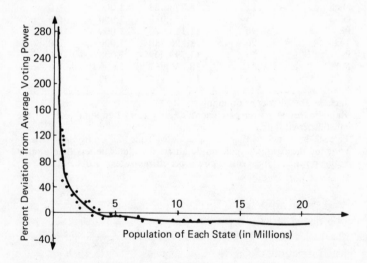

Figure 3 *Percent Deviations from Average Voting Power of States under the Proportional Plan in the 1970s*

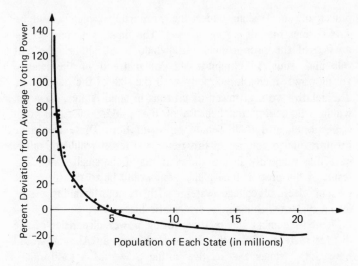

Figure 4 *Percent Deviations from Average Voting Power of States under the District Plan in the 1970s.*

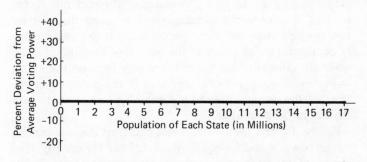

Figure 5 *Percent Deviations from Average Voting Power of States under the Direct Vote Plan*

tional plan arise from the fact that electoral votes are not apportioned strictly according to population (or to the number of actual voters) of the state. Small states have a considerably greater fraction of an electoral vote per capita than do large states. The result is a large, systematic bias in favor of the residents of small states. At the extremes, the relative voting power of an Alaskan under the proportional plan would be 4.442 times that of a New Yorker. The most important consequence of the proportional plan would be to abolish the unit rule and, thus, to eliminate the linear trend of the relative voting power increasing directly with the size of the population. The relative voting power of citizens in small states, however, would still be inflated because of the 2 added electoral votes corresponding to their Senate representation. There would be no unit rule to counteract this trend; the result would therefore be a bias markedly favoring inhabitants of the small states. The result of the proportional plan, then, would be to transform the present electoral college system, with its countervailing biases, into a system with a single, systematic bias.

Figure 4 depicts the relative voting power disparities of the district system. Under this electoral reform, an Alaskan would have 2.857 times the relative voting power of a Californian. The disparity between the citizens of the smallest and the largest states would not be as great as it would be under the proportional plan. However, by reducing the unit rule to the level of the congressional districts and retaining the constant two electoral votes per state, the net effect is to increase greatly the relative voting power of the citizens of the smallest states while the citizens of the larger states have their relative voting power significantly reduced. Again, as in the proportional system, relative voting power would generally vary inversely with the size of the population.

Finally, figure 5 demonstrates that under the direct vote plan, voting power would be equalized throughout the country. The disparities in relative voting power that are embedded in the present electoral college system, or inherent in the proportional or district plans, are the natural result of weighted voting systems. As Banzhaf concludes, "Of all systems, both present and proposed, the direct election is the only plan which guarantees to each citizen the chance to participate equally in the election of the President."[74]

Each of the preceding graphs shows the disparities inherent within each electoral system (except, of course, for the direct vote plan). Figure 6, using the percent deviation per citizen-voter data from the last column of tables 7-10, directly compares the four systems and shows a general tendency for the very smallest states to be most advantaged by the proportional plan, medium size states to be most advantaged by the district plan, some larger states to be most advantaged by the direct vote plan, and the largest states to be most advantaged by the existing electoral college system.

In summary, we note that the proportional and district plans have similar and extensive deviations from equality, with the proportional plan containing differences as great as 4.442 times between residents of different states. The present electoral college (and automatic plan) also contain strong, but less systematic biases, which are even then slightly less than those of the district plan. The direct vote plan, on the other hand, contains—by definition—no such voting power disparities.

The biases inherent in the present electoral college and various reform plans for inhabitants of different size states have thus far been shown. The data as presented up to now have not, however, dealt with the question whether various groups of voters may be similarly favored or disadvantaged because of their residency in various states. In order to examine this important question, the companion studies used the relative voting power data to determine the average voting power of various population categories under the electoral college and other plans as compared to the average voting power of the total population.[75]

The groups chosen were placed in two categories: regions and population groups. Regions chosen were East, South, Midwest, Mountain, and Far West groupings of states.[76] Population groups were blacks, and residents of urban areas, central cities, and rural areas (including both farm and nonfarm areas).[77] The average voting power of urban residents for the present electoral college, for example, was calculated by multiplying each state's relative voting power index (table 7, column 3) by the number of its urban residents. The sum of these products divided by the total number of urban residents in the nation equals the average voting power per urban resident. Finally, the percent deviation of this average from the per citizen-voter average was obtained.

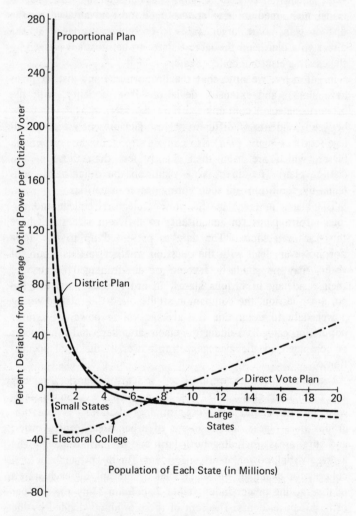

Figure 6 *Percent Deviations from Average Voting Power of States under the Present Electoral College, the Proportional Plan, the District Plan, and the Direct Vote Plan in the 1970s*

This percent deviation gives an indication of how this particular group in the electorate fares in comparison with other groups, as well as with all of the electorate. Since this analysis attempts to assess the argument that certain groups in the electorate exert inordinate voting power under the electoral college, national averages for various groups were calculated and are reported in figures 7 and 8. Similar data concerning the proportional plan are contained in figures 9 and 10, and for the district plan in figures 11 and 12.

Earlier it was found that the electoral college has countervailing biases which result in a net large state advantage and a disadvantage to states with four to fourteen electoral votes. Figures 7 and 8 now provide the additional information that the electoral college also favors inhabitants of the Far West and East, as well as central city and urban citizen-voters. In contrast, it discriminates against inhabitants of the Midwest, South, and Mountain states, as well as blacks and rural residents.

These data seem to confirm the urban, ethnic hypothesis in most respects. Urbanized areas and central cities are above the national average voting power for the electoral college. Rural voters, on the other hand, were found to be relatively disadvantaged.

The findings for one group, however, somewhat contradict the hypothesis as well as conventional wisdom concerning the biases of the electoral college. Black citizens have less than average voting power because of their high concentrations in small- and medium-sized states, such as Alabama, Georgia, Louisiana, and Mississippi, as well as the District of Columbia, in addition to the central cities of large states.

As suggested by conventional wisdom, the South appears to be disadvantaged by the electoral college and would stand to gain from the direct vote proposal. However, it should be noted that this bias has nothing to do with the small turnout in southern states or with the supposed bloc voting of southerners for the Democratic party. It merely measures the disadvantage stemming from the effect of the unit rule and the constant two.

Percent Deviations from National Average Voting Power for Various Population Categories under the Present Electoral College in the 1970s

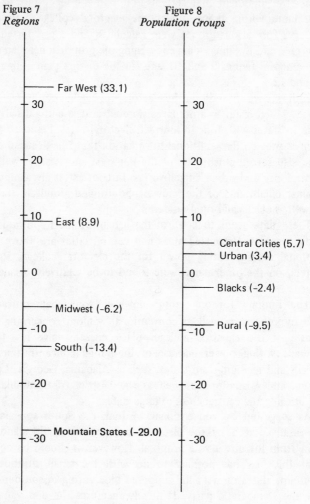

Figure 7
Regions

Figure 8
Population Groups

Far West (33.1)

30

20

10 — East (8.9)

0

Midwest (−6.2)

−10

South (−13.4)

−20

−30 Mountain States (−29.0)

30

20

10

Central Cities (5.7)
Urban (3.4)

0

Blacks (−2.4)

−10 Rural (−9.5)

−20

−30

Source: Longley and Yunker, "The Changing Biases of the Electoral College," pp. 30 and 33.

*Percent Deviations from National Average Voting Power for Various
Population Categories under the Proportional Plan in the 1970s*

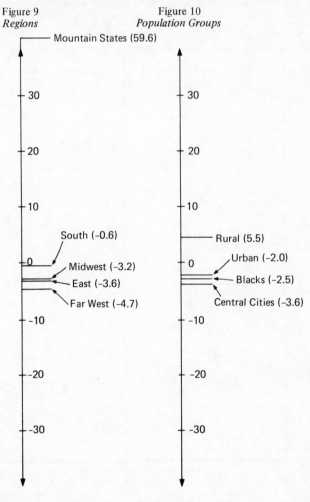

Figure 9
Regions

Mountain States (59.6)

30

20

10

South (-0.6)

0

Midwest (-3.2)

East (-3.6)

Far West (-4.7)

-10

-20

-30

Figure 10
Population Groups

30

20

10

Rural (5.5)

Urban (-2.0)

0

Blacks (-2.5)

Central Cities (-3.6)

-10

-20

-30

Source: Longley and Yunker, "The Changing Biases of the Electoral
College," p. 33.

*Percent Deviations from National Average Voting Power for Various
Population Categories under the District Plan in the 1970s*

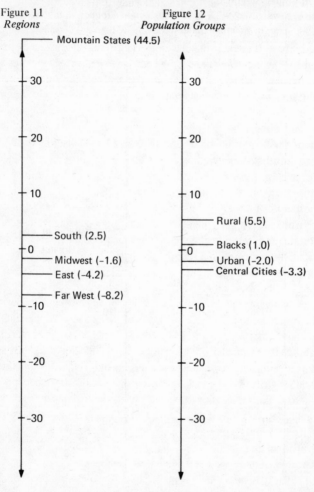

Figure 11
Regions

— Mountain States (44.5)

- 30
- 20
- 10
— South (2.5)
- 0
— Midwest (−1.6)
— East (−4.2)
— Far West (−8.2)
- −10
- −20
- −30

Figure 12
Population Groups

- 30
- 20
- 10
— Rural (5.5)
— Blacks (1.0)
- 0
— Urban (−2.0)
— Central Cities (−3.3)
- −10
- −20
- −30

Source: Longley and Yunker, "The Changing Biases of the Electoral College," p. 34.

We have also examined the effect of the three most frequently proposed reform plans on the a priori voting power of these groups. The direct vote plan, of course, introduces no deviations from average voting power; hence, all groups, as well as all citizen-voters, would have average voting power.

The proportional and district plans, however, both produce marked deviations. For the population categories previously discussed, these biases are in the opposite direction of those introduced by the electoral college. We earlier found the proportional plan to have a large and unidirectional bias sharply favoring inhabitants of the smallest states. In terms of the population groups, this reform plan also confers marked advantages upon some and disadvantages upon others. It greatly advantages inhabitants of the Mountain states and rural citizen-voters. Inhabitants of the South, Midwest, East, and Far West, as well as urban, black, and central city citizen-voters are discriminated against by the proportional plan.

The district plan has a similar yet somewhat lesser set of biases. It sharply advantages inhabitants of the smallest states, the Mountain and Southern states, and rural citizen-voters. Inhabitants of the states of the Midwest, East, and Far West, and black, urban, and central city citizen-voters are, on the other hand, disadvantaged by the district plan.

Since conventional wisdom has little to say about the particular biases imposed on these diverse groups by the proportional and district plans, these new data can serve as a staring point for the formulation of new wisdom. We find rural voters to be advantaged, while citizens in metropolitan areas are, in general, slightly disadvantaged. These conclusions are the opposite of our findings with respect to the electoral college. Finally, the regional data reveal only slight biases in both plans, except that the Mountain states are greatly advantaged by both the proportional and district plans.

In terms of percent deviations from average voting power for the 1970s, it is interesting to note that the following groups are most advantaged by the electoral college: residents of the Far West, East, urban areas, and central cities. The Mountain states are most favored by the proportional plan, whereas the South is most advantaged under the district plan. Rural citizen-voters are equally well-off under the proportional and district plans. Finally, the direct vote plan with its equal treatment of all votes is the best presidential selection method for Midwest residents and blacks.

In spite of some modest questions that might be raised about the basic voting power approach,[78] we have reached, by using systematic data derived through this approach, some very useful conclusions. Specifically, residents of large states, urban areas and central cities, and the residents of the Far West and the East have been found to be advantaged by the electoral college. More generally, we have also found that the electoral college is an institution that operates with noteworthy inequity. While the biases of the electoral college are not cumulative and unidirectional, they are significant and introduce a complex element of citizen inequality into the American political system.

The basic question of whether members of those population groups that are favored by the existing electoral college system should thereby seek to retain that electoral system and thus their favored position we cannot answer, except to note our uneasiness with a position that seeks a politically favored position for any interest or group in a democracy. This dilemma has been particularly well expressed by one writer in the following words, with which we close:

> In ethical terms, it may be difficult for those who are dedicated to the advancement of the democratic process and to its "one man, one vote" corollary to support the perpetuation of a patently shrewd system because it may be deemed to be good for certain elements, and to attempt to rationalize that therefore it is also good for America. On the other hand, to endorse a change which from a purist point of view would be more "democratic," but which might entail the sacrifice of a significant and perhaps justifiable measure of urban minority leverage is not an easily tenable position either.[79]

5. Direct Vote: A Goal Nearly Reached

*I believe that if this joint resolution passes, it will be a
crowning achievement in my own life. I am approaching
my 82nd birthday. Fate has been kind to me in giving
me many birthdays. The abyss awaits me. I have not too
many years to live, and I am happy to know that the
passage of this joint resolution, which I am hopeful
will occur, is a real event in my life.*

> Representative Emanuel Celler,
> in the closing minutes of 1969
> House debate on House Joint
> Resolution 681, the direct vote plan.

Electoral reform? Don't chuckle, chum.
You're knocking 'an idea whose time has come.'
It passed the House though 70 demurred;
It's possible the Senate has concurred.
Now watch the pressure build upon each state
Until three-quarters of them (38)
Abolish the electors from the scene.
Then, rid of that archaic in-between
The people will be grateful for the chance
To vote exactly as they do in France.

> W. H. von Dreele, from the
> October 7, 1969, issue of *National Review.*

Obstacles to Constitutional Change

The obstacles to constitutional change that have hindered
electoral reform have proved to be formidable. In this chapter,
we shall consider these obstacles in terms of two broad categories: four obstacles of an institutional or structural type and
four obstacles of a belief (both myth and reality) type.

The first obstacle of an institutional or structural type is the previously mentioned multiplicity of proposals, which were described and analyzed in chapters 3 and 4. The willingness of proponents of electoral college reform to scatter among automatic, proportional, district, direct vote, and other plans has been historically one of the greatest hindrances to successful reform of the electoral college. A constitutional amendment, if it is to be enacted, requires a broad consensus sufficient to overcome multiple hurdles; with support for reform dissipated among various alternatives, the formation of such a broad consensus is made impossible. The history of electoral college reform efforts has been more one of a permutation of plans than one of an aggregation of support for one plan, and in this lies much of the failure of reform efforts.

There exists a strategy, however, that offers the possibility of uniting the proponents of various plans in support for one. In terms of a legislative decision-making situation, this strategy goes as follows: If there is a strong consensus that *some* reform is very much needed, and if the proponents of one plan, such as the direct vote plan, can control the voting process so that other reform proposals are acted on first, then the possibility exists that as other proposals are voted down (probably with the help of the proponents of the direct vote plan), the supporters of other plans will move over to support the direct vote plan "rather than have no reform at all." This scenario depends on several critical elements: the existence of a strong consensus for some change, the control of the voting process by direct vote plan advocates, and a willingness on the part of those who have their preferred plan defeated to join with those who had helped defeat them. Without anticipating too many surprises later in this chapter, it can be noted here that this strategy, in fact, worked almost perfectly for the direct vote proponents in several stages of House and Senate decision-making, such as in the House Judiciary Committee, on the House floor, and in the full Senate Judiciary Committee. It failed in the final stage of the legislative process—on the Senate floor—only because of an inability of direct vote advocates to control the voting process—or, more precisely, to get any vote at all. Save for this problem (which was, however, decisive), the above discussed strategy was utilized and found to be effective during the 1969 and 1970 congressional activities and showed how, to some extent, the problem of a multiplicity of proposals could be overcome.

The second institutional obstacle to electoral reform involves the very mechanism of the constitutional amending process itself. The procedure is relatively simple: Constitutional amendments are proposed by a two-thirds vote of both House and Senate or, although never used, by a national constitutional convention called by Congress at the request of three-fourths of the states. They are ratified by action of three-fourths of the state legislatures or, used only for the repeal of prohibition, by three-fourths of special state conventions. Congress specifies which of the latter two options will be used for a given constitutional amendment it proposes.

Inherent in this procedure are multiple veto points. A majority opposed to a possible amendment may effectively kill it in the appropriate committee of either the House or Senate. One-third plus one of the House members (146, or less if not all representatives vote) or one-third plus one of the Senate members (34, or less if not all senators vote) may kill an amendment in one of the chambers.[1] Finally, nonaction by *either* house of the state legislature in but thirteen states (one-quarter plus one of the fifty states) will doom a measure. The road to electoral reform, then, is rocky and long and can be traversed only in a vehicle propelled by strong, persistent, and well-distributed support.

A third obstacle to electoral reform is, like the previous one, an obstacle relevant to any attempted constitutional change, but has to do more with the symbolic character of change. In its most general sense, this involves a general reluctance to "tamper with a Constitution that has served us well." This conservatism toward constitutional change puts a heavy burden of proof upon the reformer who must substantiate the necessity of change. This obstacle, then, is closely related to a fourth obstacle of a symbolic character—a reluctance to really believe in the possibility of a breakdown of the electoral college system and a contemporary constitutional crisis until we actually have one. Although the electoral college has teetered on the brink of deadlock in three of the last six presidential elections, the fact remains that there has not been any overt manifestation of electoral college breakdown in contemporary times—such as the election of a clear popular vote loser, a deadlock in the electoral college, or a deadlock in the House of Representatives. It may well be that it will take a major malfunctioning of the electoral college system in order to achieve a reform to avoid such malfunctioning. In its absence, the tendency to put off until tomorrow worrying about what has not happened today may well prevail.

Four further obstacles to reform can be identified in terms of beliefs—both mythical and real. These beliefs have been examined in considerable detail in the preceding chapter, so they will be only briefly summarized here.

The first of these is the belief that the electoral college is an essential prop to federalism and that without a presidential electoral counting mechanism based on states, the character of the United States federal system will undergo a fundamental change.

The second belief is somewhat similar and complementary. This is that the electoral college is a vital support for the American two-party system. Presumably, this support comes about through the electoral college's suppression of minor or third parties, a feature of the electoral college, we have argued, that operates most unevenly. The electoral college does make things quite difficult for nationally based third parties because of the winner-take-all system in each state; however, at the same time the electoral college provides incentives for regionally based third parties to seek inordinate power through carrying blocs of electoral votes by thin margins and by deadlocking the electoral college in the case of a near two-party standoff.

The third belief about the electoral college is one of the most common recurring beliefs expressed about that institution and one that is clearly incorrect. This is that the present electoral college preserves the power of the small states. As discussed in the preceding chapter, this simply is not the case and probably can be most clearly labeled as myth. It is also, however, a salient political reality as an argument and proved to be perhaps the most potent element in the direct vote plan's defeat in the Senate in 1970.

The last obstacle to electoral college reform is a belief directly contradictory to the preceding one and is perhaps both the most substantial argument and the most bothersome problem for many direct vote advocates today. This is the belief that the present electoral college benefits large states, urban interests, ethnic minorities, and/or black voters. As analyzed in chapter 4, there is much to this belief, at least as far as the large-state advantage goes, and seemingly persuasive arguments can also be made concerning urban interests and various ethnic minorities. It is intriguing, however, to find, in the last two obstacles, directly opposing arguments being advanced in defense of the present electoral college system.

Late in 1960 historian James MacGregor Burns summed up very well the conventional assessment of the prospects of electoral college reform in the following words:

> There is little hope for a major overhaul of the electoral college. The opposing groups are simply too strong. Each of them gets enough out of the present system to be willing to settle for it when the chips are down.[2]

The truly fascinating question of electoral college reform activity during the 1960s, which came so extraordinarily close to success, is how were these many and varied obstacles to constitutional change so very nearly overcome?

Activities during the 1960s

The period from 1960 through 1968 served as a building period for the electoral college reform movement, which was to emerge in vigorous form during 1969 and 1970. During these eight years a series of events occurred, which were to transform electoral reform, and specifically the direct vote plan, from an idea with little hope of success into a proposal whose time seemingly had come.[3] Among these events were two extremely close and uncertain presidential elections, which demonstrated many of the perils and pitfalls of the existing electoral college system;[4] the reapportionment of almost all states, decreasing the rural bias of state legislatures and the House of Representatives; a series of congressional hearings of considerable educational value; the publication of several influential studies of the electoral college; and a fortuitous sequence of association and individual endorsements for the direct vote plan over a two-year period.

The 1960 election, the first close election in twelve years, revived concerns about the possibility of electoral college deadlock, especially in light of the selection by the voters of Alabama and Mississippi of fourteen unpledged electors devoted to that goal and the efforts of Henry D. Irwin, an Oklahoma elector, to add to that number.[5] Immediately resulting from this concern were the 1961 hearings of the Constitutional Amendments Subcommittee of the Senate Judiciary Committee,[6] conducted by Senator Estes Kefauver of Tennessee. These hearings, which undoubtedly told all (or more) about Henry D. Irwin than the senators had really wanted to know,[7] produced, however, no major new push for electoral reform. The 1963 supplemental hearings of the committee[8] were a one-day affair focusing on the effects of the 1962 reapportionment decision, *Baker* v. *Carr*,[9] on the electoral college and likewise had little immediate impact on reform efforts.

In January of 1963, however, a sequence of association activities commenced, which were to have great importance to electoral reform. The United States Chamber of Commerce in that month initiated an internal information campaign, which was to lead to a 1965 advisory referendum of its membership[10] and, in 1966, to that association being the first to commit itself to electoral college reform along the lines of a direct vote plan (although it was also to find the district plan acceptable). This developing endorsement by the United States Chamber of Commerce between 1963 and 1966, quickly seconded by the ABA in 1967, proved to be one of the decisive developments moving electoral college reform and the direct vote plan out of the realm of abstract advocacy and into the world of possible congressional enactment.

Several events from 1963 on concerned the leadership and activities of the Constitutional Amendments Subcommittee of the Senate Judiciary Committee. Late in 1963, following the death of Senator Kefauver, freshman Senator Birch Bayh was offered the chairmanship of this seeemingly unimportant subcommittee by Senate Judiciary Committee Chairman James Eastland. Senator Bayh accepted the post and within two years had achieved the unheard of accomplishment, for a freshman senator, of successfully piloting a constitutional amendment—the Presidential Disability Amendment—through the congressional shoals. During this time, Senator Bayh was vigorously assisted by the ABA, whose support he was later to enjoy concerning electoral reform. After the successful enactment of the Presidential Disability Amendment in 1968, both Senator Bayh and the ABA were receptive to new campaigns for constitutional change.

The call to such a campaign was provided by the congressional messages of President Lyndon Johnson in January 1966 and January 1967.[11] Although these messages supported an automatic type of electoral plan, they also served to focus public attention on the electoral college, and, more specifically, to galvanize the interest of the ABA and Senator Bayh in the issue of electoral reform.

A few days after President Johnson's 1966 message, electoral reform was given additional support by the release, by the United States Chamber of Commerce, of the results of the advisory referendum of its membership: 91.5 percent for abolishment of the electoral college and replacement of it by either the direct vote or district plans and only 8.5 percent opposed. As a result of this referendum, the direct vote and district plans jointly became the official dual policy of the chamber—the first important endorsement for direct vote of the 1960s.

The response of the ABA to these events was to establish, in February of 1966, a blue-ribbon Commission on Electoral College Reform to study the electoral college and various proposed reforms.[12] The response of Senator Bayh was likewise to prove significant: he scheduled hearings of the Constitutional Amendments Subcommittee for February and March of 1966.

It should be recognized that at the opening of these 1966 hearings, Senator Bayh was by no means a direct vote advocate. In fact, in his opening statement on February 28, 1966, Senator Bayh listed several reasons why he considered direct popular election to be out of the question as a possible reform alternative.[13] In place of a direct vote, he suggested the administration-proposed automatic plan—a quite reasonable position for a freshman senator.

On May 18, 1966—only 2½ months later—Senator Bayh reversed this position and came out in favor of the direct vote for president, with a joint session of Congress contingent procedure. This was, of course, a startling change for the senator, one which could be to some great degree attributed to the educational effect of the hearings over which he had presided in the preceding months. It was, of course, not easy for Senator Bayh to shift from the administration-backed automatic plan, of which he was the Senate sponsor, to the direct vote plan; as he admitted, the administration is "not at all happy with us."[14] This move was, however, an important one, for it gave the direct vote plan something it had never had previously—the support of the chairman of one of the congressional committees concerned with constitutional amendments—in addition to a skilled, persistent, and devoted advocate.

During 1966 support for electoral reform continued to grow. On the same day that Senator Bayh announced his conversion to direct vote, the first Gallup poll on the direct vote plan was published. It showed 63 percent of respondents favoring the direct vote concept, 20 percent opposed, and 17 percent with no opinion. Another poll, this one of legislators in all fifty states, was taken during the summer of 1966 by Senator Quentin N. Burdick (D., N.Dak.), with the results being released in

December. The Burdick poll showed that of all the state legislators, 58.8 percent favored the direct vote idea, 9.7 percent
preferred the present system, 21.2 percent supported the proportional plan, and 10.2 percent chose the district plan. Even
more important than this aggregate data, however, was the
finding that direct vote was favored by 50 percent or more of
those legislators responding in forty-four of the fifty states, support which gave rise to hope that ratification of a direct vote
plan by thirty-eight states might well be accomplished.[15]

One other event of 1966, also to set the stage for following
activities, was the suit, by the State of Delaware, against the
use by the various states of the unit rule, winner-take-all procedure for determining electoral votes. Although the Supreme
Court, later in the year, refused to hear the suit, this legal
action did at least partially achieve its goal of illuminating the
inequities of the unit rule aspect of the electoral college system.[16]

Early in 1967 the movement for electoral college reform received a major push with the release of the report of the ABA's
Commission on Electoral College Reform,[17] which condemned
the existing electoral college system and called for a direct vote
for president with a runoff if no candidate received 40 percent
of the popular vote. This widely reported and discussed advocacy came only days before the official ratification of the Presidential Disability Amendment—likewise sponsored by the ABA
after a study commission's recommendations—as the Twenty-
fifth Amendment to the Constitution. It was assumed by many
that this new ABA commission's support for a direct vote constitutional amendment would likely result in change. This
expectation was quickly underscored by the ABA's House of
Delegates' approval of the commission's report, on February 13,
1967, by a vote of 171 to 57, thus officially committing the
ABA to this new constitutional amending campaign.

The direct vote plan that Senator Bayh had advanced in May
of 1966 differed from that proposed by the ABA in 1967 in
one very significant aspect—the procedure to be followed in the
contingency that no candidate received 40 percent of the popu-

lar vote. The Bayh proposal had provided for a joint session of Congress selection process in this case; however, the ABA recommended a runoff between the top two candidates. Soon after the commission made public its recommendations, Senator Bayh—in what was to prove to be a momentous decision— deferred to the ABA and modified his plan to include a runoff. It was this feature of the direct vote plan, proposed by the ABA commission and subsequently adopted by Senator Bayh, which, in spite of its desirability in terms of ensuring that the popular vote winner would always win the election, later proved to be one key element of the plan's downfall.

During May, July, and August of 1967, the Constitutional Amendments Subcommittee of the Senate Judiciary Committee, chaired by Senator Bayh, held extensive hearings on electoral college reform, especially in light of the developments of the past year. The resulting 703 pages of testimony and exhibits[18] were highlighted by endorsements of the direct election of the president by three earlier leading advocates of alternate plans:[19] Lucius Wilmerding, author of a 1958 study entitled *The Electoral College,* Professor Paul David of the University of Virginia and formerly associated with the Brookings Institution, and Professor Joseph F. Kallenbach of the University of Michigan, author of an important 1960 article, "Our Electoral College Gerrymander."[20] What proved to be of even more importance, however, was the testimony of a young New York lawyer, John F. Banzhaf III, on July 14, 1967, who discussed his soon-to-be-published computer study of the electoral college and supplied the subcommittee with tables drawn from this study.[21]

Mr. Banzhaf's subsequent article, published early in 1968 in the *Villanova Law Review* under the intriguing title "One Man, 3.312 Votes: A Mathematical Analysis of the Electoral College," proved to have a major impact upon subsequent congressional and scholarly discussion about the biases of the electoral college.[22] Its first presentation in the 1967 hearings opened up an area of systematic analysis of the electoral college which heretofore had been marked by speculation and hunch.[23]

Another publishing landmark of this period was the appearance, in April of 1968, of a major analysis of the electoral college in terms of its functioning, its historical roots, and the case for its abolishment: Neal R. Peirce, *The People's President.* This monumental work, marked both by the care of its scholarship and the force of its arguments against retention of the electoral college, served—and continues to serve—as a standard reference work for electoral college critics and defenders. With this publication, analysis and debate about the electoral college system underwent a qualitative improvement—and the direct vote plan received a significant boost.

The two last events of the 1960-68 period both directly concerned the 1968 presidential election and were discussed in detail in chapter 1. The closeness of the election, together with widespread concern about the possibility of an electoral college deadlock and George Wallace playing a significant role in the selection of a president, led to intensified interest in electoral reform. When Nixon elector Dr. Lloyd W. Bailey of North Carolina cast his vote on December 16 for Wallace instead, the stage was set for legislative action on electoral college reform in 1969 and 1970.

1969 and House Action

The first event of 1969 concerning electoral reform grew out of the last event of the preceding year: the decision of Nixon elector Bailey to cast his electoral vote for Wallace.[24] As Dr. Bailey, a John Birch Society member, later explained it, he decided on this action because the United States was "dangerously close" to becoming a democracy and because he disapproved of some of the early appointments of prospective-president Nixon. He also pointed out that he had taken no pledge to support Nixon, although he had agreed to be part of a "Nixon slate" of electors in a state not listing the names of individual electors on the ballot.[25]

Unlike in the case of faithless electors of earlier years, Dr. Bailey's action did not go without congressional challenge.

When the House and Senate met in joint session on January 6, 1969, to count the electoral votes cast in the respective states, objection was made to Dr. Bailey's vote by Senator Edmund Muskie (D., Maine) and Representative James G. O'Hara (D., Mich.) along with six other senators and thirty-seven other representatives. Under the terms of an 1887 statute the two bodies then moved to separate deliberations on the disputed electoral vote, with a rejection of the vote by both House and Senate necessary to invalidate it.

The House debate was marked by a feeling of many members that elector Bailey had violated his trust, but Congress lacked any power to remedy the matter without a constitutional amendment. In contrast, the Senate debate explored some of the issues in fuller fashion. Senator Muskie, ironically fighting to preserve an electoral vote for the Nixon-Agnew ticket, argued that (1) electors, in effect, bind themselves when they agree to be part of a slate of electors in a state using the short ballot not listing individual electors, (2) the Supreme Court, in placing Wallace on the ballot in Ohio in 1968 had spoken of the need to ensure citizens an effective voice in the selection of the president—a concept violated by Bailey's action, and (3) to allow his act to stand unchallenged would be to establish a precedent encouraging future electors to unpredictable actions. To this, Senator Bayh added the observation that he hoped this debate would "galvanize this Congress to find an equitable way of electing the President."

The dangers in congressional challenges to properly certified electoral votes, however, were stressed by Senator Howard H. Baker, Jr. (R., Tenn.), who also pointed out that this challenge, if successful, might "diminish pressures" for more basic electoral reform. Senator Sam J. Ervin, Jr. (D., N.C.) asserted that Congress has no control or review over electors. Senator Karl E. Mundt (R., S.Dak.), long a district plan supporter, observed that the congressional district in which Dr. Bailey lived had favored Wallace. Senator James B. Allen (D., Ala.) stressed the need for the "free elector system" and declared "the Senator from Maine would expect to make of the electors robots."

Throughout the debate in both houses, there was general dismay about the possibility of electors casting unexpected votes; however, there was also a feeling that after-the-fact congressional challenges were not the appropriate mechanism for eliminating this evil. The challenge to Dr. Bailey's vote was rejected by both the House (229 to 169) and the Senate (58 to 33); the result of the debates in both houses on January 6 was to give considerable new impetus to congressional attempts to abolish or modify the electoral college through the constitution amending process.[26]

The other major event of the early months of 1969 was the initiation of lengthy hearings on electoral reform by both the Constitutional Amendments Subcommittee of the Senate Judiciary Committee on January 23 and the full House Judiciary Committee on February 5. These exhaustive investigations of electoral college reform—together running in printed form to over two thousand pages of testimony, statements, and exhibits in volumes weighing over two pounds each—will be discussed in detail subsequently. An immediate effect of these hearings, however, was further to stimulate an already gushing outpouring of articles, essays, and pamphlets on the electoral college and its reform.

Much of this literature had, of course, been directly provided by the uncertainties and fears of the 1968 presidential election.[27] Together with other materials arising from the electoral reform activities of 1966-68, this literature emerged in late 1968 and early 1969 in a veritable wave of writings ranging from the *New Republic* to the *New Yorker* and from the *Journal of the American Bar Association* to *Playboy*.[28] Perhaps most noteworthy among this flood of material were the series of articles written by members of the ABA's Commission on Electoral College Reform outlining their case for the direct election of the president[29] and a widely discussed series of essays by Alexander M. Bickel of the Yale University Law School arguing against the direct vote plan and for—at most—the automatic plan of electoral reform.[30]

One of the few occasions of presidential involvement in electoral reform activities occurred at this point, with President Richard Nixon sending a long-awaited message on electoral reform to Congress. He asked for prompt congressional action and proposed that the office of elector be abolished (as in the automatic plan), that each state's electoral votes be divided in some manner (as in the district or proportional plans), and that a popular vote runoff (as in the direct vote plan) be held in case no candidate received 40 percent of the electoral votes.

This presidential statement, which suggested that Congress was not giving serious attention to electoral reform, was ill-received by congressmen deeply engaged in such efforts. In addition, his statement was subject to widespread criticism on the grounds that such a "conglomerate plan" made up of bits and pieces of various proposals confused and complicated reform activities.[31]

Another significant event of this period occurred on March 25 when the state of Maine enacted a new law providing for two of its four electoral votes to be determined by the voters of each of its two congressional districts, and the other two on a statewide, winner-take-two basis. Democratic Governor Kenneth M. Curtis opposed this district plan, but allowed the bill, once passed, to become law without his signature. This district plan, to become effective with the 1972 election, will be the first use of this method of determining electoral votes since an isolated instance—for partisan purposes—by Michigan in 1892.[32]

It was, however, in the hearings of the Constitutional Amendments Subcommittee of the Senate Judiciary Committee and of the full House Judiciary Committee that the major events of early 1969 were occurring. The House hearings were held over a period of five weeks, and unlike many such hearings, involved the full committee rather than a smaller subcommittee.[33] This was of considerable importance, for as opinion within the committee swung toward the direct vote plan—partly through the effect of the hearings and partly because of the emerging views of the leadership of the Judiciary Committee—the entire membership of the committee was affected.

Initially, both Chairman Emanuel Celler (D., N.Y.) and ranking minority member William M. McCulloch (R., Ohio) were uncommitted and possibly even undecided about various electoral reform plans. Celler, the most senior member of the House of Representatives, having served in the House since March 4, 1923, pointed out in his opening statement:

> I, myself, have introduced two ... measures. One, House Joint Resolution 179, would abolish the present electoral college system and establish in its place a national, direct election. This proposal incorporates recommendations of the American Bar Association. ...
>
> I have also introduced H. J. Res. 181 which would reform but not abolish the electoral college. It would retain the present electoral vote distribution among the states, but would eliminate the office of electors. ... This proposal represents the recommendations of former President Johnson.[34]

The ambivalence on the part of the House Judiciary Committee leadership made it possible for the committee hearings to fulfill a somewhat rare function—that of educating the committee members and leaders. During the five weeks of the hearings, Chairman Celler, Representative McCulloch, and most of the committee members involved themselves to a considerable degree in the question of electoral reform. One analysis of the activities of the committee members during the hearings, for example, found their activity roles falling into three broad types, with several subcategories (table 11). What is most intriguing in this analysis is the high degree of participation—either active or passive—by most committee members. Only three of thirty-five members generally failed to attend committee hearings, which for most provided opportunities for clarification, knowledge-seeking, advocacy, and resolution of problems.

Over one hundred witnesses or statements came before the House Judiciary Committee in the course of the hearings, ranging from William T. Gossett, president of the ABA, to Chaim H. Zimbalist, a former member of the Missouri General Assem-

TABLE 11
Representative Role Types in 1969 House Judiciary
Committee Hearings on Electoral College Reform

I. *The Active Participant*
   A. The Opinionated Moderator
      Emanuel Celler   (D., N.Y.)
   B. The Issue Expert-Opportunist
      Clark MacGregor   (R., Minn.)
   C. The Knowledge-Seeker
      Richard Poff   (R., Va.)

II. *The Passive Participant*
   A. The Delegate-Clarifier
      Robert Kastenmeier (D., Wis.)
      Don Edwards   (D., Calif.)
      John Conyers   (D., Mich.)
      Andrew Jacobs, Jr. (D., Ind.)
      Charles Wiggins   (R., Calif.)
   B. The Knowledge-Seeker
      Joshua Eilbert   (D., Pa.)
      William McCulloch (R., Ohio)
      Henry Smith III   (R., N.Y.)
      Thomas Meskill   (R., Conn.)
      Charles Sandman, Jr.(R., N.J.)

III. *The Nonparticipant Follower*
      Jack Brooks   (D., Tex.)
      William St. Onge   (D., Conn.)
      Edwin W. Edwards (D., La.)

D. The Tradition Advocate
   Edward Hutchinson (R., Mich.)
   David Dennis   (R., Ind.)
E. The Delegate-Clarifier
   William Ryan   (D., N.Y.)
   Abner Mikva   (D., Ill.)
F. The Problem-Solver
   Robert McClory   (R., Ill.)

C. The Tradition Advocate
   John Dowdy   (D., Tex.)
   Walter Flowers   (D., Ala.)
   James Mann   (D., S.C.)
D. The Problem-Solver
   Michael Feighan   (D., Ohio)
   Peter Rodino, Jr.   (D., N.J.)
   Byron Rogers   (D., Colo.)
   Harold Donohue   (D., Mass.)
   William Hungate   (D., Mo.)
   Jerome Waldie   (D., Calif.)
   William Cahill   (R., N.J.)
   Thomas Railsback   (R., Ill.)
   Edward Biester   (R., Pa.)
   Hamilton Fish, Jr.   (R., N.Y.)
   R. Lawrence Coughlin(R., Pa.)

Source: Chris A. Bowers, "A Role Analysis for the House Judiciary Committee *Hearings on Electoral College Reform: 1969*" (Unpub-
lished paper, Lawrence University, June 1970), pp. 3-4.

bly. Of the major testimony, about seventeen people favored
the direct vote plan, including William Gossett, Robert Storey,
James C. Kirby, Jr., and John D. Feerick, all of the ABA's
Commission on Electoral College Reform; John F. Banzhaf III,
of computer analysis fame; George Meany, the president of the
AFL-CIO; Clarence Mitchell, Jr., the director of the Washington
Office of the NAACP; and Neal Peirce, by now associate editor
of the Center for Political Research. Testimony favoring retention of the present electoral college system in some form came
from Alexander Bickel, of Yale Law School, and Harvie Williams, executive secretary of the American Good Government

Society, Inc. The district plan was supported by Michael D. Jaffe, general counsel of the Liberty Lobby, John C. Lynn, legislature director of the American Farm Bureau Federation, and J. Banks Young, Washington representative of the National Cotton Council of America. Finally, the proportional plan was supported by Mr. Young (in addition to the district plan), I. Martin Wekselman of the American Jewish Council, Richard M. Scammon, director of the Elections Research Center (who, however, preferred the direct vote plan), and John N. Mitchell, attorney general of the United States.

The last testimony was to prove especially important, for the immovable insistence of the attorney general that direct vote lacked strong support in Congress[35] and in the states, while the proportional plan had much, considerably irritated Chairman Celler and led to a heated exchange, including:

The Chairman: What concrete evidence is there in support of the proportional plan? What other evidence? We already have the evidence indicated favoring direct election. Now what evidence of support do you have in support of the proportional plan?

The Attorney General: Mr. Chairman, as far as legal evidence or polls, they do not exist. But based on the input that we have ... the proportional plan will have a much greater chance of ratification.

The Chairman: Of course, I don't like to pry into your research too much, but do you care to give us more detail than the generalization that you have just expounded? Specifically which were the specific methods, who were the people that you spoke to in support of the proportional representation method throughout the country which led you to believe that the direct election system will not be ratified?

The Attorney General: Primarily, Mr. Chairman, the people in the State organization, both Republican and Democrat. . . .

The Chairman: Would you care to give us the names of those with whom you came in contact and who gave you those conclusions? We could call them to testify before the committee.

The Attorney General: This would be a long list. . . .

The Chairman: Who were these people? Were they officials of the Government and/or legislators?

The Attorney General: They run the entire spectrum. . . .

The Chairman: These men that you speak of have not communicated their views to this committee. Is there any reason why they should not have done so on an important issue of this sort?

The Attorney General: I cannot answer to that, Mr. Chairman, because I have no idea what their intentions were.[36]

Despite the futility of this exchange, Chairman Celler was able to elicit from the attorney general a promise that the administration would support a direct vote plan should Congress happen to approve one. More important, however, was that the chairman of the House Judiciary Committee had felt personally challenged by the Mitchell testimony about the lack of congressional interest in the direct vote plan, and at least partially due to this, now took upon himself the task of selling the direct vote for president.[37]

Another individual's House testimony also proved to be of considerable—although quite different—importance. This was a repeat performance, for the House committee, of the 1967 Senate testimony of John F. Banzhaf III, now a George Washington Law School professor. His findings about the inequities of the present electoral college, as well as the proportional and district plans, had enormous impact on the committee members, especially as it tended to "dispel [the] small state weighted power myth."[38]

One last feature of the committee hearing stage of the legislative process should be stressed. This was the strong, unified, and complementary activities of the several high status associations now working for the direct vote plan. From the opening day of the hearings when Representative Celler noted that one of the measures under consideration "incorporates recommendations of the American Bar Association,"[39] to the final committee report 3½ months later when it was observed that "the Committee finds the statement of William T. Gossett, . . . president of the American Bar Association, persuasive"[40] to the floor debate when Representative Celler stated:

> The U.S. Chamber of Commerce was most active in conjunction with the A.B.A. in endeavoring to secure wavering votes directed toward the approval of this popular method. I have been in conference with the representatives of the U.S. Chamber of Commerce, and they have indicated very strong approval,[41]

the support of the ABA, United States Chamber of Commerce, and other groups for the direct vote plan was never far from the surface. These groups had considerable impact on the legislative process because of what political scientist David Truman once identified as "the deference accorded a high-status group . . . [which] not only facilitates the acceptance of its propaganda but also eases its approach to the government."[42] In addition, these groups—especially the ABA—also have influence as providers of technical and expert knowledge which backstops allies and impresses the undecided. A final resource of the associations supporting direct vote lay in the very fact of their common cause. As Representative Celler later noted:

> The hearings before the Judiciary Committee indicated that such diverse organizations as the AFL-CIO, the U.S. Chamber of Commerce and the American Bar Association have all united in support of the direct popular election method. I have been in Congress for a great many years. I know of no case or no bill where you had the unified support of such diverse groups as the American Bar Association, AFL-CIO, or the U.S. Chamber of Commerce representing business, large and small, and the labor organizations that I have mentioned. Yet they have all agreed not only to support this bill but to go out into the highways and byways after it is passed by the

Congress and urge the voters in the various states to ratify this constitutional amendment.[43]

In April of 1969 the House Judiciary Committee, having completed its extensive hearings, started to work in executive session on preparing its final bill. On April 17 the committee adopted a key section of the direct vote plan as a basic element of its "clean" bill. The next day, President Nixon spoke again on electoral reform, indicating his preference for a proportional plan, while also agreeing to work for a direct vote plan if one were to pass Congress. The impact on the committee members of the president's latest statement, however, seemed to be negligible.

In crucial committee votes on April 29 and 30, the House Judiciary Committee first approved and then ordered reported a rewritten clean bill, House Joint Resolution 681, providing for a direct vote for president, essentially identical to that proposed by the ABA. The vote in each case was 28 or 29 for (one member was absent for the first vote) and 6 opposed.[44] This action was the first time since 1956 that any electoral reform amendment had been reported out of a congressional committee, and the first time ever for a direct vote plan. Although there was some question whether it could be enacted in time for the 1972 election, this point seemed minor in comparison with the strong committee endorsement—as Chairman Celler put it, "I'm so happy about getting this [committee vote] that I don't give a damn when it becomes effective."[45] On May 16 the committee issued its report on House Joint Resolution 681,[46] and the stage seemed set for floor action—after the House Rules Committee approved an appropriate rule.

In the thirty-seven days between June 17 and July 27, the Rules Committee managed to shoehorn in four days of hearings on the issue of whether a rule should be issued concerning House Joint Resolution 681.[47] These hearings were marked by some notable friction between Representative Celler, testifying on behalf of a favorable rule, and Rules Committee Chairman William M. Colmer (D., Miss.), who apparently thought little either of direct election of the president or of Representative Celler. Besides posing a series of rather unfriendly questions suggesting that Representative Celler's committee had not fully considered some important questions, Chairman Colmer also engaged in the rather rude practice of talking to committee members near him, ignoring Celler, while committee members friendly to Celler's position were questioning him. At one point, Representative Ray Madden (D., Ind.), engaged in a dialogue with Celler, stopped to ask, "Could I get the Chairman's attention, please?," and continued:

This is the greatest piece of legislation, and it should have been passed 60 years ago, that this Congress has had an opportunity to consider.

There is Harding. There was a shining example of why a bill like this would have prevented all those scandals and probably—nobody was interrupting when the Chairman was asking several questions.

The Chairman: The Chairman apologizes.[48]

In spite of this personal factor, the House Rules Committee finally did, on July 24, issue a favorable rule for the direct vote measure, limiting debate to a total of six hours, three for each side, and allowing amendments. Why Representative Celler requested—as he in fact did—an "open" rule such as this is an interesting question. One line of speculation is that allowing amendments to be proposed and then voted down would be a convenient way of activating the strategy outlined earlier in this chapter, of turning proponents of other plans into "last chance for electoral reform" supporters of direct vote.

Meanwhile, in the Senate, things were not going at all well for direct vote advocates. The similarly exhaustive hearings by the Constitutional Amendments Subcommittee of the Senate Judiciary Committee had not resulted in the near unanimity of opinion of the House Judiciary Committee. Rather, the Senate subcommittee proceeded to junk the direct vote bill of subcommittee chairman Birch Bayh, replacing it, by a 6-to-5 vote, with a district plan having few prospects. In effect, the result was greatly to increase the difficulties of direct vote supporters, since they would now have to convince the parent committee, chaired by direct vote opponent Senator James O. Eastland (D., Miss.) to override its "expert-matter" subcommittee and reinstate the direct vote plan. Senator Bayh expressed optimistic hope that his subcommittee could be so reversed; others, however, were far more pessimistic. The *New York Times* editorially expressed these doubts, declaring: "It is painfully apparent that the memory of what Senator Bayh called a 'brush with catastrophe' in last November's Presidential election has begun to recede; apathy is upon us."[49]

At this point, it was becoming evident that favorable House action on electoral reform might be the desperately needed catalyst to get direct election moving again in the Senate. If the House approved the direct vote plan, and especially if it favored it by a healthy margin, possibly this would influence the Senate committee. Without it, there could be no prospects for electoral reform.

On September 10, 1969, the House of Representatives commenced consideration of House Joint Resolution 681 in what was the first full-scale floor debate over electoral reform in the House since 1826. Representative Celler, as chairman of the House Judiciary Committee and author of the resolution, led off with a speech outlining five, by now familiar faults of the present electoral college system: the constant two allocation of electoral votes to the states, the unit rule, winner-take-all procedure, the House contingent election of the president, the possibility of an election's winner losing the electoral college, and the occurrence of faithless electors.[50] The present electoral college system, Representative Celler concluded in his colorful manner, is "barbarous, unsporting, dangerous, and downright uncivilized."[51]

Many amendments were offered on a variety of aspects of electoral reform—including one by Representative Joe D. Waggonner (D., La.) that would have raised the runoff percentage from 40 to 50 percent. This amendment was initially passed on a 43 to 33 standing vote, but was then defeated on a subsequent 71 to 91 teller vote demanded by Representative Celler.

Another amendment was an innocuous proposal by Representative Richard H. Poff (R., Va.) to add the word "inability" to the conditions of death or withdrawal of presidential candidates and proved to be the only amendment to be adopted. Sixteen other proposals, including automatic, proportional, and district plans were rejected by the House in a series of votes on September 17.

With most amendments out of the way, the House of Representatives prepared, on September 18, 1969, to move to a final vote on House Joint Resolution 681. On the eve of the crucial final vote, Representative Celler and other direct vote supporters were reported to be concerned about their ability to muster the necessary two-thirds vote of the House. Defeating hostile amendments required only a majority, but final passage would necessitate a much more difficult two-thirds; and as many as 159 House members—well over one-third—had earlier expressed their preference for the district plan. The key to the two-thirds vote, then, would lie with the supporters of alternative plans that had been voted down. One such congressman was Representative Poff, who had joined with Representative Dennis and Representative Dowdy to introduce a substitute district plan. On September 12 Representative Poff stated that if his preferred electoral reform plan lost, he would support direct vote—a plan he had strongly opposed in the House Judiciary Committee—rather than have no reform. This action by a man who had been personally outspoken in opposition to the direct vote plan was thought by some observers to be important in "showing the way by which supporters of other plans could become supporters of direct vote."[52]

On September 18 one final attempt was made by direct vote opponents to block final action. Representative Dennis, to the end a staunch opponent of direct vote, moved to recommit House Joint Resolution 681 to the House Judiciary Committee with instructions to substitute and rereport a district plan. This last-minute action was rejected by the representatives in a 162 to 246 roll call vote, and the House then proceeded to pass House Joint Resolution 681 by a resounding vote of 338 to 70, 66 more votes than needed—or, in other words, a margin of votes almost as large as the total opposition. Eighty-three percent of the House members voted for the direct vote plan— amazingly the exact percentage of support that direct vote had received in the House Judiciary Committee five months earlier.[53]

The two House roll call votes of September 18 allow for some rather interesting analyses of patterns of support and opposition. On the first vote, to recommit House Joint Resolution 681 and substitute the district plan, the vote was 162 in favor, and 246 opposed.[54] Breaking these figures down by party shows that Democrats opposed recommittal by 62 to 166, while Republicans supported it 100 to 80. More interesting, however, is the finding that when northern Democrats and southern Democrats are separated, almost all northern Democrats opposed the recommittal motion (6 to 140), while most southern Democrats supported it (56 to 26). In other words, 156 of the 162 votes for recommittal and substituting of the district plan came from Republicans and southern Democrats.

The vote on final passage of House Joint Resolution 681 shows a similar pattern. The overall final vote was 338 to 70, with Democrats supporting it by 184 to 44, and Republicans by 154 to 26. Among the Democrats, practically all northern Democrats favored final passage (142 to 3), while southern Democrats were divided (42 to 41). Of the 70 votes against final passage, 26 came from Republicans and 41 from southern Democrats.

A very interesting observation about these two votes concerns the shift of representatives for recommittal to a vote for final passage of direct vote. There were no significant numbers of shifters among northern Democrats—almost all had originally opposed recommittal and only well under one-third of the fifty-six southern Democrats supporting recommittal shifted to final support for direct vote. In the case of the Republicans,

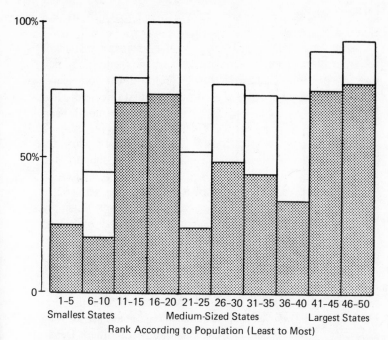

Figure 13 *House Voting on Recommittal and Final Passage of House Joint Resolution 681 (By Size of States)*
Shaded areas represent percentage voting against recommittal of House Joint Resolution 681. Shaded areas plus additional unshaded areas represent percentage voting for final passage of House Joint Resolution 681.

however, a considerable shift occurred; almost three-fourths of the one hundred Republicans favoring recommittal followed the lead of congressmen like Representative Poff in supporting direct vote on final passage, giving House Joint Resolution 681 its needed two-thirds vote.

Other variables were also investigated in order to see to what extent they might be related to House voting on electoral reform. Figure 13 shows the percentage of congressmen voting against recommittal and for passage, according to groups of similarly sized states. From this table one can observe some variations among congressmen from different size states, but no consistent pattern corresponding to state size. Generally, there

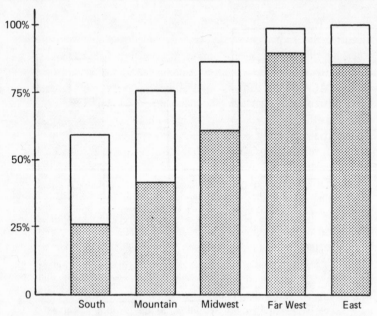

Figure 14 *House Voting on Recommittal and Final Passage of House Joint Resolution 681 (By Region)*
Shaded areas represent percentage voting against recommittal of House Joint Resolution 681. Shaded areas plus additional unshaded areas represent percentage voting for final passage of House Joint Resolution 681.

would appear not to have been a tendency for support or opposition to direct vote to come predominantly from either the large or small states.

Figure 14 similarly shows congressional voting by regions. Here one can see a slight pattern of less support for direct vote by congressmen from southern and Mountain states than from other areas. Overall, region appears to have had some importance in the recommittal and final votes, although this relationship is likely as much due to the next factor as to regional interests alone.

This final factor, which also has a considerable regional cast to it, is the liberalism or conservatism of the House members. It is in regard to this factor that the strongest and clearest patterns of House voting on electoral reform are found. For this measure, the scores given to each congressman on his 1969 votes by the Americans for Democratic Action (ADA) and its conservative counterpart, the Americans for Constitutional Action (ACA), were utilized.[55] The mean (average) ADA score of those representatives supporting recommittal was a very low 8.7, and the ACA score was a high 72.4. In other words, recommittal of House Joint Resolution 681 was supported by a group of very conservative representatives. It was opposed, on the other hand, by a mixed group of moderate and liberal representatives with a mean ADA score of 53.8 and a mean ACA rating of 26.9. The supporters of recommittal, then, had a distinctive ideological cast, while the opponents were more bi-ideological or mixed in their character.[56]

This pattern was similarly present in the vote on final passage. Those voting for passage were a mixed group with a mean ADA score of 40.5 and an ACA rating of 39.1. Those voting against the direct vote plan on final passage, however, were on the average very conservative—their average ADA score being 11.5 and their ACA rating, 73.3.[57]

From this voting analysis of the two crucial House roll calls, we conclude that neither size of state nor, to any great degree, region were important in House voting, but rather that the recommittal vote was supported, and the final passage of direct vote opposed, by very conservative southern Democratic and Republican representatives, and that House Joint Resolution 681 obtained its overwhelming final margin because of the last-minute shift of some southern Democratic and many Republican, less conservative representatives to the direct vote plan.

The approval by the House of Representatives of the direct vote plan had considerable widespread impact. The *New York Times*, after reviewing some of the gloom surrounding Senate prospects for electoral reform, noted:

After Thursday's House vote, this pessimism lifted like a sun-struck marsh cloud. In the face of such a demonstration of popular support from wary and politically hard-nosed Congressmen, how could the Senate stand in the way? Or, at least, that was the warm flush of early reasoning.[58]

Anthony Lewis of the *New York Times* viewed the House action as demonstrating "a historical truth—that in choosing a President, at least, we are no longer a collection of states but a Nation."[59] Columnist Max Lerner, on the other hand, took the opportunity to decry the fact that now "each of us will become a statistical item in a single, vast national count."[60]

The assumption about the inevitability of final approval of the direct vote amendment was given additional support on September 24 with the timely release of the results of a Gallup poll on electoral reform taken in November 1968. At that time, the Gallup organization asked 1,530 respondents: "Would you approve or disapprove of an amendment to the Constitution which would do away with the Electoral College and base the election of a President on the total vote cast throughout the nation?" and found that 81 percent approved, 12 percent disapproved, and 7 percent had no opinion. With commentators making much of the similarity of this 81 percent popular support to the 83 percent approval the direct vote plan had received both in the House Judiciary Committee and in the full House, the direct vote plan seemed unstoppable.

Another event occurring in September ended an eventful month on a triumphant note for electoral reform advocates. President Nixon, who had been soundly criticized for his lack of leadership on electoral reform,[61] announced, on September 30, that he now supported the direct vote plan, and "unless the Senate follows the lead of the House, all opportunity for reform will be lost this year and possibly for years to come."[62] Representative Carl Albert, Democratic floor leader in the House, acidly complimented the president for his belated support and added, "You can't criticize his flexibility."[63] As it turned out, however, the lack of timeliness of President Nixon's support for direct vote would be matched, in the Senate, by its lack of substance.

Another event of 1969 boosting the spirits of many electoral reform advocates was the publication by the *New York Times*, on October 7, of the results of a survey of state legislature leaders and governors concerning the prospects of state ratification of a direct vote constitutional amendment.[64] The *New York Times* found that, overall, nine states could be said to strongly favor a direct vote amendment, twenty-one somewhat, six undecided, six somewhat opposed, and eight strongly opposed. Most of the opposition was found to be in southern, midwestern, and Mountain states, yet even in those areas, nearly one-half of the states favored direct vote or were undecided. While these findings encouraged many direct vote proponents, others noted that the survey sought to assess state legislative opinion prior to the matter becoming an actual legislative issue, and that it did not take into account the fact that either chamber of a two-house state legislature can block a state from ratifying a constitutional amendment. Even disregarding for a minute these uncertainties, the data as given also showed that, at best, a direct vote amendment would have to prevail in at least two of these states now considered opposed, while losing in none of those favoring it or undecided, in order to obtain the thirty-eight states needed for ratification.

One final item brought 1969 to a somewhat somber end. In spite of the House action of September and subsequent events, Senator Eastland, chairman of the Senate Judiciary Committee, announced on November 3 that full committee action on electoral reform—which direct vote supporters had been counting on to reinstate the direct vote plan in place of the subcommittee approved district plan—was being "indefinitely" postponed, at least until after the committee had disposed of the Haynsworth nomination to the United States Supreme Court. This delay in committee action—which was to stretch deep into 1970 as controversy developed first over Haynsworth and then over the succeeding Carswell nomination—caused electoral reform to lose the heady impetus developed from the events of September and October of 1969. By the time direct vote would be reported by the Senate Judiciary Committee late in April of 1970 and would come up for floor consideration in September of 1970, the resounding House vote, the Gallup poll, President Nixon's support, and the *New York Times* survey of state legislatures would all seem distant and far removed. In 1969 direct vote for president achieved its peak of support; in the coming year, it would be subject to frustrating delay, massive debate, and—ultimately—ignoble defeat.

1970 and Senate Action

The immediate and urgent problem for Senate direct vote supporters in the early months of 1970 was to find some way of getting the direct vote plan out of the Senate Judiciary Committee.[65] Senate Joint Resolution 1 had been killed in the Subcommittee on Constitutional Amendments, and the full committee chairman, Senator Eastland, seemed disinclined to allow his committee to resurrect it. Through the ample powers available to him as chairman, Senator Eastland might be able to delay committee action on electoral reform indefinitely—unless Senator Bayh, the Senate chief sponsor of Senate Joint Resolution 1, could outmaneuver him.

Much to the surprise of Senator Eastland (and perhaps also of Senator Bayh), such a successful outflanking did in fact occur on February 3. In an adroit parliamentary move on that day, Senator Bayh moved that the Senate Judiciary Committee vote on the pending nomination of G. Harold Carswell to the United States Supreme Court on February 9 *and* vote on Senate Joint Resolution 1 and other electoral reform plans by April 24. By so linking the Carswell nomination, strongly supported by Chairman Eastland, to the direct vote plan, Senator Bayh succeeded in making agreement on a voting date for electoral reform a condition for agreement on voting on the Carswell nomination. Senator Eastland, it was reported, noted the success of this maneuver "with some admiration."[66]

On April 13 Senator Eastland announced a suitable surprise in return: supplemental hearings by the full Senate Judiciary Committee on electoral college reform, to be held starting in two days with himself presiding and featuring various witnesses hostile to the direct vote plan.[67] Bayh angrily responded to this insult to himself and his subcommittee's earlier hearings by terming Senator Eastland's move "the most blatant disregard for senatorial courtesy in my eight years in the Senate."[68] The only consolation offered him was the opportunity to add several witnesses favoring direct election on the last day, following testimony critical of the direct vote plan by initial witnesses such as Theodore H. White, Professor Alexander Bickel of Yale Law School, and Richard N. Goodwin, former assistant to Presidents Kennedy and Johnson.[69] In retrospect, it is unclear what real function these last-minute hearings served, except perhaps to provide a foretaste of the possibilities for obstruction by southern parliamentarians when aroused.

As the time for Senate Judiciary Committee voting on electoral reform drew near, it was reported that direct vote was having serious trouble in getting even the bare majority of 9 out of 17 committee votes. One key figure appeared to be Senator Joseph Tydings, a direct vote supporter, who might nevertheless vote against Senate Joint Resolution 1 as long as it contained a runoff feature.[70] Eventually, Senator Tydings was persuaded to advance his preferred alternative on the Senate Floor rather than allow electoral reform to die in committee by voting against it. It was through decisions such as his that electoral reform hung in the balance.

On April 23 the moment of voting finally arrived for the direct vote plan as the Senate Judiciary Committee rejected an automatic plan by a vote of 7 to 9, a district plan by 6 to 10, and—in a crucial and close vote—a proportional plan by 8 to 9.[71] The committee then, by a vote of 11 to 6, ordered Senate Joint Resolution 1 reported. As Warren Weaver of the *New York Times* noted, the strategy of the direct vote supporters worked perfectly: they invited other reform plans to be brought out first and then voted them down, leaving a simple choice—direct vote or nothing.[72] The result of the use of this strategy—which had earlier worked so well in the House—was again to give direct vote a strong mandate consisting of first-, second-, and even third-choice supporters. By the committee vote on April 23, the revived constitutional amendment emerged from the committee phase of the legislative process—somewhat like the Phoenix from the ashes—with renewed hope and expectations for final enactment.[73]

The electoral reform proposal was not, however, to move rapidly to the next stage of floor consideration buoyed by recent committee success. Rather, another long period of delay was to ensue before the final committee report was issued. The majority had agreed to write its majority report in a week; however, it found itself taking five weeks to do so. The minority of the committee had agreed to write its minority report in two weeks, but instead took eleven—starting after the majority completed its work.[74] Whether the Senate would have passed the direct vote plan if it had come to a floor vote soon after House approval will never be known; what is clear, however, is that—in the words of one legislative observer—"that year [between House and Senate action] really cooled things off."[75]

Finally, on August 14, 1970,[76] nearly four months after the favorable committee vote, the Senate Judiciary Committee formally reported Senate Joint Resolution 1 to the Senate floor. In the committee report on the measure the majority argued, in a familiar manner, for direct election of the president with a runoff if no candidate received 40 percent of the popular vote. In separate views accompanying the majority statement, Senators Griffin and Tydings stated their position that although they supported the direct election plan, an alternate to the runoff procedure was necessary.[77] Specifically, they proposed a plan where a president could be elected by either a 40 percent popular vote or, failing that, by a majority of electoral votes. Only if neither mechanism determined a president would there be a resort to a joint session of Congress procedure. This plan—the Tydings-Griffin plan—had been advanced earlier in the Senate Judiciary Committee, but rejected. In the coming months, however, it would emerge as a key element of a possible "compromise direct election plan," but one which would be embraced by direct vote supporters too late to help electoral reform prospects to any great degree.

The committee minority, consisting of Senators Eastland,

McClellan, Ervin, Hruska, Fong, and Thurmond, was also not likely to remain silent in its views. In a dissent over twice as long as the majority statement, they outlined their convictions that the direct vote plan would destroy the two-party system, undermine federalism, damage the separation of powers, radicalize public opinion, encourage electoral fraud, and necessitate national control of the electoral process. They concluded their dissent with the ringing declaration:

> It will not do to say that the electoral college is antiquated or outmoded; no more viable institution, nor a more salutary one, will be found today. Let us, if need be, repair it; but let us not abandon it for the sake of a mathematical abstraction, or because we are angry that the world is not perfect.[78]

By late August and early September, Washington activity on electoral reform had begun to pick up. By this time there had emerged an astonishing alliance among five major national interest groups in support of the direct vote plan: the League of Women Voters of the United States, the ABA, the UAW, the AFL-CIO, and the Chamber of Commerce of the United States.[79] This unity among groups more often found on opposing sides was unprecedented—especially the agreement between labor and the Chamber of Commerce. The series of group endorsements for direct vote stretching over the past four years had been an important factor in building and maintaining interest in electoral reform; now the very unity of their coordinated efforts would further enhance the attractiveness of the direct vote plan. As one involved lobbyist put it, "The effect is beyond the mathematics of 5 ones equal 5. There is a geometric effect far beyond that. ... The march to Capitol Hill together is very significant. ... The effect is magnified enormously."[80]

In addition to coordinated contacting of individual senators,[81] the five major groups also cooperated in a formal request for a meeting of President Nixon with their respective presidents: George Meany of the AFL-CIO, Edward L. Wright of the ABA, Arch Booth of the Chamber of Commerce, Leonard Woodcock of the UAW, and Mrs. Bruce Benson of the League of Women Voters, hopefully on or about September 11.

This request took the form of a letter from Mr. Booth of the Chamber of Commerce, which was sent to the White House on August 24. Three weeks went by without any answer, while the presidents of the different associations fretted about whether they should plan a Washington trip or not. Finally, on September 10—the day before the requested meeting date—a telegram was received from a rather low-level White House functionary stating that the president was unavailable for the hoped for meeting with the organization presidents. No alternative time for such a meeting was mentioned, and it was indicated that the president's position on electoral reform was already quite clear.[82]

But was it? The most recent statement of the president on electoral reform had been nearly one year earlier, on September 30, 1969, when, in the flush of overwhelming House passage of House Joint Resolution 681 (and possibly also as a result of badgering by Senator Bayh), President Nixon had finally expressed support for the direct vote plan. In the year since then, there had been persistent reports of a change of mind concerning the 1969 endorsement[83] —sufficient in fact to lead a White House aide, on April 8, to deny them. As far as affirmative statements or actions on behalf of direct vote, however, there had been absolutely none—a situation which left Senate Joint Resolution 1 floor manager Senator Bayh rather plaintively remarking, "a half-dozen well-timed phone calls from the President or visits by his personal staff could be tremendously helpful."[84]

On September 11, probably not by coincidence the day for which the association presidents had sought their meeting, President Nixon broke his silence by including electoral reform in a catch-all message to Congress on unfinished business. After restating his support for the House-passed plan, he chided the Senate, noting: "Unfortunately, the Senate has not completed action. Time is running out. But it is still possible to pass the measure and to amend the Constitution in time for the 1972 elections."[85]

This presidential expression of support for direct election was generally dismissed as weak, untimely, and responding to events rather than showing leadership. One Senate aide characterized the president's position on electoral reform as one of "benign neglect;" another noted that Nixon was getting exactly what he wanted out of it: making liberals happy by being in favor of it, and yet not pushing hard enough to pass it.[86] That the president could exercise considerable leadership on the issue was evident: of the twelve or so undecided senators, eight were Republican and presumably subject to influence by administration pressure.[87] As one lobbyist put it, "if he issued strong marching orders, it could pass."[88] Yet, an aide to one of the key Republican opponents to direct vote acknowledged that there was no Nixon pressure on them as to their position nor had he seen any signs of administration pressure on Republican moderates. The reason, he felt, was simply that the Nixon administration had a number of legislative concerns and this one was relatively low. In short, there were many matters of greater importance to the administration than electoral reform.[89]

In a column in the *New York Times* appearing at about this time, Tom Wicker attempted to answer the question why, as he quoted one direct vote supporter, "the President hasn't delivered a vote." Wicker suggested that the president's actions (or nonactions) might be explained by three reasons: (1) he was a reluctant and unenthusiastic convert to the direct vote cause and might just be unwilling to commit any significant effort to it; (2) he might have considerable reluctance to act in a way to add luster and prestige to Senator Bayh, the man who had led the successful fights against the confirmation first of Clement Haynsworth, then of G. Harold Carswell, and who now was being discussed as a dark horse presidential candidate; and (3) he might have concluded that direct vote would hurt his reelection prospects in 1972.[90] No definitive assessment of these three theories can be made here, although it might be noted that there was widespread Washington opinion in support of all three. Whatever the reason or reasons, the fact remains that the Nixon administration made little, if any, sincere effort to secure electoral reform in 1970. The consequences of this inaction in terms of the 1972 and subsequent elections will be his—and the nation's—to bear.

Senate debate on Senate Joint Resolution 1 formally opened the day after Labor Day, September 8, 1970, ten days short of one year after House passage of the direct vote plan. Senator Bayh, as the floor manager of the bill, led off by calling direct vote "the only system that is truly democratic, truly equitable and truly responsive to the will of the people."[91] Major supportive efforts in the opening days were provided by Senators Howard H. Baker, Sr. (R., Tenn.) and Henry Bellmon (R., Okla.), both of whom stressed the small-state interest in the direct vote plan. Senator Bellmon, for example, illustrated one consequence of the present electoral college system by introducing into the *Congressional Record*, on September 9, a table showing that in the 1968 election, sixteen states had no visits from either major party candidate—all relatively small states with from three to ten electoral votes.[92]

Rhetorical counterattacks against the direct vote plan were launched and maintained by three leaders of the opposition—Senator Carl T. Curtis (R., Nebr.), Roman L. Hruska (R., Nebr.) and Strom Thurmond (R., S.C.). Senator Curtis, for example, stressed the runoff provision as "the fatal defect" which could only cause "doubt and confusion." Senator Hruska expressed his opinion that direct election of the president was "the most mischievous and dangerous constitutional amendment that has ever received serious consideration by the Congress" and "to adopt it would be to set out on a vast uncharted sea, with no guarantee that the slightest political breeze might not capsize and destroy our ship of state."[93]

Most of the debate, however, was not up even to these rhetorical standards, but was, as one senator described it, "boilerplate"[94] designed to fill time and the *Congressional Record*. This was in spite of the fact that, starting on September 8, the Senate had been operating on an unusual double-shift schedule, debating electoral reform until 3 P.M., and then turning to other business late into the evening. This was necessary because of a push by the Senate leadership for adjournment by October 15, formalized in a bipartisan agreement of September 10,[95] which quickly broke down. The relation between the pressure of time and the desultory debate on Senate Joint Resolution 1 was simple: electoral reform was being killed by talk and inaction—in other words, by a filibuster. If direct vote opponents could delay long enough, Senate Joint Resolution 1 would likely be lost in the closing frenzy of the session without the possible awkwardness of an actual vote.

What made possible this type of cavalier treatment of a reform backed by 81 percent of the American people and voted for by 83 percent of the House was its peculiar character. Electoral reform is not a "gut issue" clearly determining gains and losses for affected interests. "For the lobbyists, this issue is not important to them. They will not hate you for how you vote."[96] Nor is the issue one on which there is clear constituency pressures generating clues or demands for action. Instead, it is one in which narrow advantage is neither clearly defined nor the deciding issue; one which calls for evaluations of a difficult type. For many senators, such an issue is somewhat a "pain in the neck" since they can in no way benefit or hurt themselves, yet a large amount of time is required in order to really understand it. The result of these aspects of the issue is a tendency to grasp at political symbols as a means of justifying political decisions and to build elaborate cases for dubious propositions. In short, electoral reform turned out to be an issue in which political rhetoric tended to create political realities.[97]

A political reality that Senator Bayh and direct vote supporters found themselves facing in mid-September was a simple one—they did not have the votes. For over a year, the story had been the same: if direct vote could get to the Senate floor, it could count on 51, or 55, or 58 votes—always at least 7 to 10 short of the needed two-thirds vote of 66 or 67. After concluding yet another count, one senior Senate staff aide was reported, on September 10, to have flatly told a direct vote supporter, "You haven't got the votes now and you're not going to get them."[98] On September 14 the *New York Times* reported in one front-page article, dishearteningly entitled "Electoral Reform Is in Deep Trouble," that Senator Bayh and allies were debating in an empty Senate chamber, there was no evidence of President Nixon pushing in any way for direct vote, five major interest group presidents had been unsuccessful in contacting or meeting with the president, Senate Joint Resolution 1 seemed stuck at the 58-vote level, and possibly the ghosts of Haynsworth and Carswell—along with a faint dream of the presidency—were indirectly killing electoral reform.[99]

The sources of the difficulties for the direct vote plan lay in several different directions. First, there was clear and outspoken opposition by southerners to the idea of abolishing the electoral college on the grounds that an important bulwark of states' rights would thus be breached. The president, they reasoned, is now elected by state voters; under a national popular election this "state element" of the presidency would be lost. In addition, concern was also expressed that abolishment of the electoral college's recognition of the role of individual states might lead to attacks on other institutions recognizing individual states—in particular, the United States Senate and its basis in equally weighted states.

Other darker thoughts may have also occurred to southerners—that direct vote might increase voting turnout in their states, especially among the blacks, or that electoral reform was an attempt to block George Wallace and other traditional opportunities of the South in the electoral college system. For whatever motives, the fact remains that the South was the source of much of the opposition to direct vote, and—as will be shown—of the successful filibuster against electoral reform.

Opposition also came from nonsouthern sources: from staunch conservatives opposed to changing the Constitution, from some small-state senators convinced that direct vote would leave their states helpless in the hands of large populous states, and even from one liberal Democratic senator who found himself agreeing that direct vote might be "the most deeply radical amendment which has ever entered the Constitution of the United States."[100]

One issue, however, tended to cut across size, sectional, and ideological lines—a concern about the possible consequences of the runoff procedure incorporated in Senate Joint Resolution 1. As the legislative assistant to one direct vote supporter put it, "Everyone is much scared of the runoff feature."[101] Some compromise on this point seemed needed, but how would it be implemented, and along what lines?

The problem for direct vote advocates was that if they prematurely accepted some alternative to runoff, they would, by doing so, give up their trump card. As a consequence, during September, key aides and participants fidgeted and fudged concerning whether the direct vote plan might be, was about to be, or perhaps already had been, changed in this respect. By late September, however, it was apparent to all that the direct vote plan would be modified by some sort of contingent procedure containing a remnant of an electoral college, together with an ultimate joint session of Congress decision, perhaps along the lines of the earlier presented Tydings-Griffin plan. Yet, the specifics of such a modification of the direct vote plan were not the crucial concern of the moment. Perhaps direct vote supporters could patch up the direct vote plan and pick up a few vitally needed votes by adopting the Tydings-Griffin plan or some other modification; however, the truly crucial question facing electoral reform was not that. It was, how would *any* vote on electoral reform be obtained?

As debate droned on into a second week, the fate of the direct vote plan became increasingly bound up in the pressure for adjournment. This took the form of lengthy negotiations between allies—partners, however, with different objectives. The goal of Senator Bayh, together with his chief aides Jason Berman and P. J. Mode,[102] was simple: to keep pressure up for Senate Joint Resolution 1 as long as necessary to bring it to a final vote. On the other hand, Senate Majority Leader Mike Mansfield, with his key aides Dan Leach and Charles Ferris,

wished to see the Senate move as quickly as possible through
its business on the way to the scheduled October 15 adjournment. Both senators shared a common desire to see the direct
vote plan passed; however, at times, they sharply differed concerning the possibility of moving on to other Senate business.[103]

On Monday, September 14, Senators Mansfield and Bayh and
their aides spent more than six hours from mid morning to late
afternoon trying to work out, with direct vote opponents, a
schedule for voting on electoral reform.[104] The alternative to
some agreement with the opposition allowing for an eventual
vote would be, all knew, a cloture motion. Such a parliamentary move would involve introduction of a petition, signed by
sixteen senators, calling for a vote on whether debate should be
terminated. Under Rule 22 of the Senate Rules, a cloture vote
would then be held two legislative days after introduction of
the petition, and, if approved by two-thirds of those present
and voting, would cut off discussion and require a vote after
only one hundred hours of additional debate. The Senate has
always been reticent about imposing such a gag upon itself,
and, consequently, resort to cloture proceedings in order to
terminate lengthy debate is always a drastic move.

Such a cloture petition was now prepared and ready for Senator Mansfield to introduce. Senator Bayh, however, tended to
oppose its introduction—at least as long as any shred of hope
remained that some compromise allowing for a vote would be
worked out by other means. The reason for Senator Bayh's
opposition to use of a cloture petition at this time was a simple
one—he did not have the votes to pass it. As he noted on September 14, two or three direct vote supporters would not vote
for cloture of debate, thus making the necessary two-thirds vote
almost impossible to obtain.[105] To Mansfield men, however, a
cloture vote was really the last chance for getting a vote on
electoral reform[106] —unless the opposition would agree to a
voting timetable.

On Thursday, September 15, two important meetings of
direct vote opponents were held: the southern Democrats in the

morning, presided over by Senator Richard Russell (D., Ga.)[107] , and the Republicans at midday. It was at the first caucus that the key decision dooming electoral reform was made: the southern Democrats would under no circumstances agree to any kind of vote on electoral reform. The decision to utilize (or, more exactly, to continue to utilize) a filibuster to defeat electoral reform was not necessarily a reflection of concern that they lacked votes to defeat the direct vote plan on an outright vote, but rather a coolly calculated strategy. The reliance upon extended debate was seen as the best tactic to be used to prevent any possibility of Senate Joint Resolution 1 passing, especially since their ability to block direct vote with a Tydings-Griffin plan removing the runoff feature was more in question. Consequently, as one key southern Senate aide put it, a filibuster was the safest way of assuring failure for electoral reform.[108]

In order for the southern filibuster to be effective, tacit acquiescence would be necessary from Republican opponents of Senate Joint Resolution 1. This, in fact, was obtained at midday on September 15, when the Republican opposition caucused. In that meeting, there was considerable sentiment for agreeing to a timetable allowing the direct vote plan to come to a final vote, since it was thought the votes to defeat it were available. The views of the southern Democrats were reported, however, with the result that the decision was made not to go along with a voting agreement nor to try to force a vote on the southern Democrats through voting for cloture. As one key Republican aide explained it, there would be little advantage in treating an ally like that.[109]

Direct vote supporters had been aware of these crucial meetings occurring in the morning and midday of September 15[110] and were curious to find out what had been decided. Therefore, early in the afternoon of September 15, Senator Bayh rose on the floor of the Senate and announced that he was about to pose a series of unanimous consent requests pertaining to voting on electoral reform and wished senators to be notified and called to the floor. Senator Bayh then moved through a series of 7 different unanimous consent requests on various pending electoral reform proposals. Senator Ervin objected to each, including one objection to voting on four of his own amendments. To this manifestation of the southern decision not to allow any vote on any electoral reform proposal, Senator Bayh responded with the biting observation: "I think it is unconscionable to suggest that the Senate does not have the courage to stand up and vote on the merits of an issue as vital as this."[111] Senator Bayh then yielded the floor to Senator Mansfield who, at 2:56 P.M., introduced the long awaited cloture petition.[112] The Senate was now committed to a vote, but a vote on the very difficult matter of cloture of debate, to be held one hour after the 10 A.M. opening of the Senate session on Thursday, September 17.[113]

Between September 15 and 17, as counts of the senators were made and remade, it became clear that cloture was not likely to be voted—at least on this first attempt. The major purpose this first vote would serve, then, would be a test of strength—a test that would be avidly examined by all key parties: Senator Bayh and other proponents of a "let's wait them out" strategy, Senate Majority Leader Mansfield concerned about keeping the Senate moving toward adjournment, Senator Hruska and other Republicans who thought they had the votes to defeat direct vote on an outright vote, and Senator Ervin and other southerners who just did not want to take any chances. This initial test of strength, however, would be played out against a backdrop of Senator Bayh's public confession that he did not have sufficient votes for cloture—maybe 62, but not 66 or 67, together with the knowledge that since introduction of Rule 22 allowing cloture in 1917, only eight of the fifty-one cloture petitions introduced in the United States Senate have been approved.[114]

Supporters of direct vote at this time began to develop an important new issue in their favor—the propriety of unlimited debate or a filibuster being used against a constitutional amendment that would itself require a two-thirds vote of the Senate together with a subsequent three-fourths approval by the states in order to be enacted. As the *New York Times* editorially observed on September 18, "The excuse offered in defense of unlimited debate is that it can forestall precipitous action by a bare majority." Yet, direct vote could not be enacted by any such bare majority, but would rather require an "extraordinary majority" of two-thirds. As Senate Majority Leader Mansfield argued on September 18, the use of unlimited debate against such a measure "abuses the clear purpose and interests of the Senate rules." Similarly, Tom Wicker of the *New York Times* wrote on September 17, "There may be reason to vote against direct election of Presidents, but there is no reason for voting against consideration of the issue."[115]

It was the question whether the Senate would be allowed to vote on electoral reform that was before the Senate as it prepared to vote on cloture shortly after 11 A.M. on September 17. On a roll call vote of 54 to 36, the Senate then failed to invoke cloture on Senate Joint Resolution 1. With ninety senators present and voting, sixty were necessary for cloture to pass; consequently, the attempt fell 6 votes short. Even more disheartening was the realization that even if all ten additional senators were present and voting unanimously for cloture, the vote still would be insufficient. The minority of thirty-six voting against cloture was, and would continue to be, sufficient to block voting on electoral reform until and unless significant defections occurred.[116]

The reaction to the vote by direct vote supporters was guarded. Senator Mansfield observed that Senate Joint Resolution 1 was "still breathing," but he would have to examine the cloture vote closely to see where to go next. In words with an ominous ring, he added "I don't want to go through an exercise in futility."[117] Senator Bayh's aides, however, felt they had correctly predicted almost every vote, and with ninety-seven instead of ninety senators present, cloture would have had 62 rather than 54 votes—still, however, 3 crucial votes short. In an interview only a few hours after the vote, the view was repeatedly stressed: Senator Mansfield could not deny them a second cloture vote when they were this close.[118]

Late in the following week, while consideration of Senate

Joint Resolution 1 dragged on inconclusively, Senator Bayh moved to force Senator Mansfield's hand. Starting on Thursday, September 24, he began to object to all unanimous consent requests for the Senate to act on business other than the pending matter—electoral reform. In addition, he also objected to committees meeting while the Senate was in session, which was still for extraordinarily long hours. The Senate operates on the unanimous consent request;[119] with Senator Bayh making objection to any request other than an agreement for voting on Senate Joint Resolution 1, the Senate's business came to an effective halt. Senate Majority Leader Mansfield, by now despairing of any hope of an October 15 adjournment,[120] responded in the only possible way—he introduced a second cloture petition, to be voted on September 29.

The second vote was viewed by all as a crucial final vote. Senator Bayh termed it a test of the Senate's ability to function as a responsible instrument of government. The *New York Times* editorialized on the day of the vote: "A vote against cloture today is a vote against any reform of the Presidential electoral system within the foreseeable future." Senator Mansfield observed, not too subtly, "This is an extremely important vote. It could very well be the tell-tale vote."[121]

The second cloture vote was held shortly after 1 P.M. on Tuesday, September 29. In the closing minutes of debate on that day prior to the vote, direct vote opponent Senator Ervin urged the Senate not to invoke cloture, since there were many different ideas about the election of the president, and we "should not attempt to solve this problem in the last days of a harried and hurried session."[122] Following this summary of four years of congressional hearings and two years of congressional actions, the Senate proceeded to reject cloture on Senate Joint Resolution 1 a second time, by 53 to 34. With eighty-seven senators present and voting, 58 votes were needed for cloture; consequently the second cloture attempt fell 5 votes short—an insignificant gain of 1 vote in return for ten days of effort. The minority of 34 was itself still sufficient to block cloture, even if all thirteen missing senators supported cloture.

Perhaps most discouraging was the absence of any signs of movement or change in voting patterns. Senator Gordon Allott (R., Colo.) shifted from a vote for cloture on the first vote to a vote against; Senators Long (D., La.) and Byrd (D., W.Va.) shifted from against cloture to for it. There were also some minor differences concerning who was absent for the vote.

Following the vote, Senator Bayh ceased objecting to unanimous consent requests for the Senate to consider other business. Senator Ervin pledged a major effort in the next Congress for "genuine reform." The *New York Times* editorially concluded that "Yesterday's vote in the Senate . . . all but dooms the nation to another round of electoral roulette in 1972." [123] One last act in the politics of electoral college reform, however, remained still to be played out—namely a third cloture effort.

On October 2, perhaps out of despair of ever seeing the Senate resolve the issue, Senator Mansfield introduced a third cloture petition, to be voted on in the following week, on October 6. The purpose of this last gasp was somewhat unclear, unless it was to try one more time to persuade the reticent opponents of Senate Joint Resolution 1 to agree to a voting timetable that would give direct vote at least a decent burial. No matter what the motive for the cloture motion, a result was a meeting, on Monday afternoon, October 5, of the most unlikely people. Starting at about 3:30 in United States Capitol room number S220, the back portion of Senator Mansfield's Capitol office, the confrontation involved Senators Bayh, Baker, Griffin, Byrd, Spong, Dole, Ervin, and Hruska, as well as Bayh aides P. J. Mode and Jason Berman, and Mansfield aide Charles Ferris. No one person presided; however, the purpose of the meeting was clear to all: Could electoral reform—in any compromise form—be brought to a vote? Accounts somewhat differ as to the details of what happened—mention is made both of Senator Hruska's ominous silence and of his negative reaction to proposed compromises; some reports indicate that Senator Ervin objected on behalf of the southern caucus; and apparently the meeting became somewhat emotional, especially when

Senator Bayh realized that the opposition had no intention of agreeing to any compromise plan for electoral reform. After about one hour, the meeting in S220 adjourned and compromise efforts collapsed.[124]

With the failure of the October 5 meeting to lift the filibuster, electoral reform died in 1970. Within hours of the meeting, the third cloture petition was withdrawn and Senate Joint Resolution 1 was indefinitely postponed—at least until after the congressional recess to November 16. Although sporadic attempts were made later in November and December to revive a compromise electoral reform plan along the lines of the Spong plan,[125] these efforts were ineffective and only resulted in reports "that several Senators are extremely tired of Senator Bayh's political moves."[126] The opposition to the direct vote plan was thus able to block in the Senate a plan that had exhibited so many signs of strength and support. Who were these successful opponents in the Senate?

An analysis of the roll call cloture votes helps in answering this question. As indicated earlier, the Senate division on the first cloture vote, on September 17, was 54 to 36.[127] Breaking these figures down by party shows that Democrats supported cloture 33 to 18, while Republicans were more evenly divided, 21 to 18. More interesting, however, is the finding that when we separate northern Democrats from southern Democrats, we find the division to be northern Democrats 30 to 2, and southern Democrats 3 to 16, a startling regional difference within the Democratic party. Of the 36 votes against cloture on the vote, 34 came from either Republicans or southern Democrats.

The second cloture vote, of September 29, shows a similar pattern.[128] The Senate vote was 53 to 34, with the party breakdown being Democrats 34 to 15 and Republicans 19 to 19. The regional division on this issue within the Democratic party was also quite evident: northern Democrats voted 32 to 2 in favor of cloture, southern Democrats voted 2 to 13 against it. Of the 34 votes against cloture on the second vote, 32 came from either Republicans or southern Democrats.

In addition to analysis of party and regionalism within

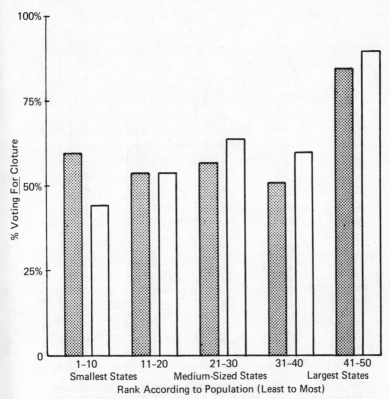

Figure 15 *Senate Voting on Cloture of Debate on Senate Joint Resolution 1 (By Size of States)*
Vote no. 1 is shaded; vote no. 2 is not shaded.

party—which was found to be quite important—the votes were also examined to see if there were marked small-state–large-state differences (see figure 15). Those senators from the twenty-six states with 8 or less electoral votes (six or less congressional districts) were found to have divided on the first roll call 25 to 21, and to have evenly split on the second 23 to 23. [129] Figure 15 additionally illustrates the lack of importance of state size in the cloture votes. Although there are differences, there

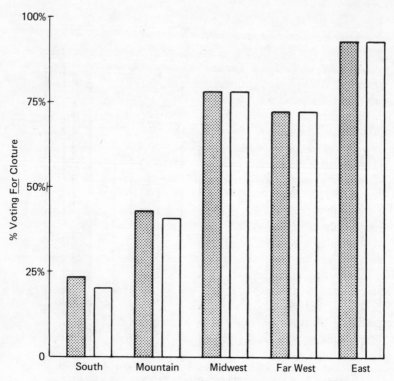

Figure 16 *Senate Voting on Cloture of Debate on Senate Joint Resolution 1 (By Region)*
Vote no. 1 is shaded; vote no. 2 is not shaded.

does not appear to have been any systematic voting pattern according to size of state. In spite of the political rhetoric about the small-state protections being threatened by the direct vote plan, the voting in the Senate does not seem to indicate political strength of these concerns.

Region, a factor earlier mentioned as important in party voting patterns, was itself explicitly evaluated. Figure 16 presents the votes on the two cloture motions by regions; in it the opposition to direct vote is clearly localized to a high degree in the South and, to a lesser degree, in the Mountain states.

The last factor examined, which also has a considerable

regional cast to it, is the liberalism and conservatism of the senators. For this measure, the scores given each senator on his 1970 votes by the ADA and its conservative counterpart, the ACA, were utilized.[130] On the first cloture vote, the mean (average) ADA score of those senators supporting cloture was 65.1 and the mean ACA score was 25.2. Cloture was opposed by a somewhat more ideologically distinct group with a mean ADA score of 14.2 and an ACA score of 73.3.[131] The pattern was almost identical on the second cloture vote: supporters of cloture had a mean ADA score of 65.9 and ACA score of 25.1. Cloture opponents had mean ADA scores of 14.1 and ACA scores of 71.5.[132]

On both cloture votes, then, the supporters of cloture were a moderately liberal group of senators, while the opponents of cloture were somewhat more clearly conservative. More generally, we can say that size of state was not important in the Senate defeat of the direct vote plan, but rather that Senate Joint Resolution 1 was defeated by a filibuster strongly supported by southern senators and, to a lesser degree, by Mountain state senators together with allied support by Republicans, these senators together compromising a clearer conservative opposition to electoral college reform. Electoral reform, which had started off the decade of the 1960s as an idea dismissed as without hope, ended in 1970 as a concept widely supported, but defeated.

Prospects

The defeat of Senate Joint Resolution 1 in the Ninety-first Congress meant that electoral reform, if it is to be again advanced, must travel the same route as before—of committee hearings, struggles for committee votes, floor consideration, and agonies in getting a final affirmative vote—and this in both Houses.[133] Certainly, discouragement over facing this prospect again is sufficient to shake even the most committed direct vote advocate. Another fact, however, must also be kept in mind: the 1976 and possibly subsequent elections will be held under the traditional electoral college system, modified only by Maine's use of the district plan. As a result, a presidential election may yet provide the American people and their political leaders with tragic evidence of the potentially disastrous shortcomings of the present system. At that point, the politics of electoral college reform will become lively again.

Appendix A

1970 State Populations and 1972-80 Electoral College Apportionments

	Population 1970	Population Change from 1960 to 1970		Electoral College Vote 1972-80	Change in Electoral College Vote
		Number	Percent		
Ala.	3,444,165	+ 177,425	+ 5.4	9	−1
Alaska	302,173	+ 76,006	+33.6	3	
Ariz.	1,772,482	+ 470,321	+36.1	6	+1
Ark.	1,923,295	+ 137,023	+ 7.7	6	
Calif.	19,953,134	+ 4,235,930	+27.0	45	+5
Colo.	2,207,259	+ 453,312	+25.8	7	
Conn.	3,032,217	+ 496,983	+19.6	8	
Dela.	548,104	+ 101,812	+22.8	3	
D. C.	756,510	− 7,446	− 1.0	3	
Fla.	6,789,443	+ 1,837,883	+37.1	17	+3
Ga.	4,589,575	+ 646,459	+16.4	12	
Hawaii	769,913	+ 137,141	+21.7	4	
Idaho	713,008	+ 45,817	+ 6.9	4	
Ill.	11,113,976	+ 1,032,818	+10.2	26	
Ind.	5,193,669	+ 531,171	+11.4	13	
Iowa	2,825,041	+ 67,504	+ 2.4	8	−1
Kans.	2,249,071	+ 70,460	+ 3.2	7	
Ky.	3,219,311	+ 181,155	+ 6.0	9	
La.	3,643,180	+ 386,158	+11.9	10	
Maine	993,663	+ 24,398	+ 2.5	4	
Md.	3,922,399	+ 821,710	+26.5	10	
Mass.	5,689,170	+ 540,592	+10.5	14	
Mich.	8,875,083	+ 1,051,889	+13.4	21	
Minn.	3,805,069	+ 391,205	+11.5	10	
Miss.	2,216,912	+ 38,771	+ 1.8	7	
Mo.	4,677,399	+ 357,586	+ 8.3	12	
Mont.	694,409	+ 19,642	+ 2.9	4	
Nebr.	1,483,791	+ 72,461	+ 5.1	5	
Nev.	488,738	+ 203,460	+71.3	3	
N. H.	737,681	+ 130,760	+21.5	4	
N. J.	7,168,164	+ 1,101,382	+18.2	17	
N. Mex.	1,016,000	+ 64,977	+ 6.8	4	
N.Y.	18,190,740	+ 1,408,436	+ 8.4	41	−2
N. C.	5,082,059	+ 525,904	+11.5	13	
N. Dak.	617,761	− 14,685	− 2.3	3	−1
Ohio	10,652,017	+ 945,620	+ 9.7	25	−1
Okla.	2,559,253	+ 230,969	+ 9.9	8	

	Population 1970	Population Change from 1960 to 1970 Number	Percent	Electoral College Vote 1972-80	Change in Electoral College Vote
Oreg.	2,091,385	+ 322,698	+18.2	6	
Pa.	11,793,909	+ 474,453	+ 4.2	27	−2
R. I.	949,723	+ 90,235	+10.5	4	
S. C.	2,590,516	+ 207,922	+ 8.7	8	
S. Dak.	666,257	− 14,257	− 2.1	4	
Tenn.	3,924,164	+ 357,075	+10.0	10	−1
Tex.	11,196,730	+ 1,617,053	+16.9	26	+1
Utah	1,059,273	+ 168,646	+18.9	4	
Vt.	444,732	+ 54,851	+14.1	3	
Va.	4,648,494	+ 681,545	+17.2	12	
Wash.	3,409,169	+ 555,955	+19.5	9	
W. Va.	1,744,237	− 116,184	− 6.2	6	−1
Wis.	4,417,933	+ 466,156	+11.8	11	−1
Wyo.	332,416	+ 2,350	+ 0.7	3	
U.S.	203,184,772	+23,861,597	+13.3	538	

Appendix B

Recent Empirical Research on the Electoral College

Brams, Steven J. and Morton D. Davis. "The 3/2 Rule in Presidential Campaigning." *American Political Science Review* 68 (March 1974): 113–34.

Colantoni, Claude S., Terrance J. Levesque, and Peter C. Ordeshook. "Campaign Resource Allocations Under the Electoral College." Forthcoming in *American Political Science Review*.

Davis. See Brams and Davis.

Dickens. See Spilerman and Dickens.

Goetz, Charles J. "An Equilibrium-Displacement Measurement of Voting Power in the Electoral College." Paper delivered at the Annual Meeting of the American Political Science Association, New Orleans, 4–8 September 1973.

———. "Further Thoughts on the Measurement of Power in the Electoral College." Paper presented at the annual meeting of the Public Choice Society, 4 May, 1972.

Hinich, Melvin J. and Peter C. Ordeshook. "The Electoral College: A Spatial Analysis." Paper delivered at the Annual Meeting of the Midwest Political Science Association, May 1973. Also in *Political Methodology*, vol. 1.

Hinich, Melvin J., Richard Michelson, and Peter Ordeshook. "The Electoral College vs. a Direct Vote: Public Bias, Reversal, and Indeterminate Outcomes. *Journal on Mathematical Sociology*, forthcoming.

Levesque. See Colantoni, Levesque and Ordeshook.

Longley, Lawrence D. "The Electoral College." *Current History* 67 (August 1974): 64–69 ff.

Longley, Lawrence D. and John H. Yunker. "Who is Really Advantaged by the Electoral College—and Who Just Thinks He Is? Paper delivered at the Annual Meeting of the American Political Science Association, Chicago, 7–11 September 1971.

———. "The Changing Biases of the Electoral College." Paper delivered at the Annual Meeting of the American Political Science Association, New Orleans, 4–8 September 1973. Also in Senate Judiciary Committee, Subcommittee on Constitutional Amendments, *Hearings on Electoral Reform*, 93rd cong., 1st sess., 26 and 27 September 1973, pp. 187–217.

Longley. See also Yunker and Longley (1973 and 1975).

Nelson, Michael C. "Partisan Bias in the Electoral College." *The Journal of Politics* 37 (November 1974): 1033–48.

Ordeshook. See Colantoni, Levesque and Ordeshook; and Hinich, Michelson and Ordeshook.

Paris. See Sayre and Paris.

Power, Max S. "A Theoretical Analysis of the Electoral College and Proposed Reforms." Ph.D. dissertation, Yale University, 1971.

———. "The Logic and Illogic of the Case for Direct Popular Election of the President." Paper delivered at the Western Political Science Association Meeting, Albuquerque, 8–10 April 1971.

———. "Logic and Legitimacy: On Understanding the Electoral College Controversy." In *Perspectives on Presidential Selection,* edited by Donald R. Matthews. Washington, D.C.: The Brookings Institution, 1973.

Sayre, Wallace S. and Judith H. Paris. *Voting for President: The Electoral College and the American Political System.* Washington, D.C.: The Brookings Institution, 1970.

Sindler, Allan. "Basic Change Aborted: The Failure to Secure Direct Popular Election of the President, 1969–70." In *Policy and Politics in America,* edited by Allan Sindler. Boston: Little, Brown and Company, 1973.

Spilerman, Seymour and David Dickens. "Who Will Gain and Who Will Lose Influence Under Different Electoral Rules." Discussion paper, Institute for Research on Poverty, University of Wisconsin-Madison, December 1972. Also forthcoming in *American Journal of Sociology.*

Sterling, Carleton W. "The Political Implications of Alternative Systems of Electing the President of the United States." Ph.D. dissertation, University of Chicago, 1970.

———. "The Failure of Bloc Voting in the Electoral College to Benefit Urban Liberal and Ethnic Groups." Paper delivered at the Annual Meeting of the American Political Science Association, Los Angeles, September 1970.

———. "The Electoral College: The Representation of Non-Voters." Manuscript.

———. "The Electoral College and The Impact of Popular Vote Distribution." *American Politics Quarterly* 11 (April 1974): 179–204.

Uslaner, Eric M. "Pivotal States in the Electoral College: An Empirical Investigation." In *Annals of New York Academy of Science,* edited by Lee F. Papayanopovlos, *Proceedings of the Conference on Quantitative Methods, Measures and Criteria.* vol. 219. New York: New York Academy of Science, 1973.

Uslaner, Eric M., "Spatial Models of the Electoral College: Distribution Assumptions and Biases of the System." Paper delivered at the Annual Meeting of the American Political Science Association, Chicago, August 29-September 2, 1974.

Yunker, John H. and Lawrence D. Longley. "The Biases of the Electoral College: Who Is Really Advantaged?" In *Perspectives on Presidential Selection,* edited by Donald R. Matthews. Washington, D.C.: The Brookings Institution, 1973.

———. "The Electoral College: Its Biases Newly Measured for the 1960's and 1970's." *Sage Professional Papers in American Politics* 3 (August 1975).

Yunker. See also Longley and Yunker (1971 and 1973).

Zeidenstein, Harvey. *Direct Election of the President.* Lexington, Mass.: Heath-Lexington Books, 1973.

Notes

Chapter 1

1 Neal R. Peirce, *The People's President: The Electoral College in American History and the Direct-Vote Alternative* (New York: Simon & Schuster, 1968), p. 108. The election of 1964 is omitted from this discussion, since while some rather bizarre election systems could have reversed the results, no reasonably democratic system could have. This is also true for the election of 1972.

2 U.S., *Constitution*, Art. 2, sec. 1. The congressional apportionment in effect in 1960—and consequently the electoral vote apportionment—was based upon the 1950 census. As a result, the president chosen in 1960 to serve from 1961 to 1965 was selected by an electoral college apportioned according to population distributions of 1950.

3 This latter feature gives a considerable advantage to states with low voter turnout, since no matter what level the turnout, the electoral vote—based on population—remains constant. In 1960 Mississippi and Kansas both had 8 electoral votes, but Mississippi had a voter turnout of 25.5 percent, while Kansas had a turnout of 70.3 percent. The resulting difference is quite startling: Mississippi had an average of 1 electoral vote per 37,271 voters, while Kansas had 1 electoral vote per 116,003 voters. Peirce, *The People's President*, p. 139. On a regional level, the effect of this feature is evidently to the advantage of the South: in the 1960 election, the South had 17.8 percent of the national vote, but controlled, with that, 27.2 percent of the nation's electoral votes. It seems to be a curious feature of the electoral college that low levels of voter participation are rewarded.

4 There are, at present, seven different modes of choosing the nominees for presidential elector, ranging from election by state party conventions (thirty-five states) to selection by the governor on recommendation of the state party committee (one state). Thirty-five states use what is called the short ballot. On such ballots, the names of the electors are omitted entirely. For a state-by-state analysis, see Peirce, *The People's President*, pp. 338-39.

5 This difficulty in determining which candidate—Nixon or Kennedy—received the most votes in the 1960 election is discussed in detail later in this section.

6 See note 27.

7 An example from a single state can best illustrate this. In the 1960 election, Nixon received 50.1 percent of the two-party vote in California and, thanks to the winner-take-all provision, consequently received 100 percent of that state's electoral votes—32, or 15 percent of Nixon's total. This phenomenon was not sufficient to help him decisively, however, for of the twelve largest states in 1960,

Kennedy was to carry nine—for an electoral vote total of 207, while Nixon was to win only three—for an electoral vote count of 70. None of these states were carried by votes of over 55 percent except for Massachusetts, whose voters supported their home state candidate by over 60 percent.

For a statistical examination of the relationship between state population size and degree of competitiveness for each of the postwar presidential elections, 1948-68, see John H. Yunker and Lawrence D. Longley, "The Biases of the Electoral College: Who Is Really Advantaged?", in *Perspectives on Presidential Selection* ed. Donald R. Matthews (Washington, D.C.: The Brookings Institution, 1973), pp. 172–203.

8 Actually the multiplier effect was comparatively weak in 1960. This can be shown by determining the disparity between the winning candidate's popular vote percentage and his electoral vote percentage. In the elections of the twentieth century, this difference has ranged from a low of 3 percent (1916) to a high of 40 percent (1912). The 1960 election magnification of 12 percent is the second lowest of the twentieth century and is considerably below the average of 22 percent. The comparable 1968 magnification was 13 percent, also considerably below the average for the elections of this century. Data adapted from Peirce, *The People's President*, pp. 315-16. The 1972 magnification was a very high 36 percent.

9 This research by Professor Bischoff was commissioned by Neal Peirce for his study of the electoral college and is summarized on pages 141-45 of ibid., especially p. 142.

10 4,480 in Illinois and 4,491 in Missouri.

11 The same vote shift in Illinois and Missouri, plus 1,148 in New Mexico, 58 in Hawaii, and 1,247 in Nevada. The popular vote in Hawaii was so close that its electoral vote was still in question on the day the electoral college met.

12 Peirce, *The People's President*, p. 108. An important qualification to keep in mind concerning this type of analysis about how many voters in which states could have deadlocked or reversed an election is that shifts in voting patterns are not isolated in individual states, but are part of national trends. The shifts that would have accomplished the electoral changes outlined here would have most likely been part of national or regional shifts not limited to just two or five states. Or, conversely, to swing these key states, there would have to be vote switching of considerably greater magnitude than just 9 or 12 thousand.

13 Richard M. Nixon, *Six Crises* (Garden City, N.Y.: Doubleday, 1962), pp. 395, 412, and 413. Some recent accounts have questioned who initiated the discussion about checking out the Illinois and Texas returns—Eisenhower or Nixon.

14 This gave rise to one of the truly priceless moments of American politics on January 6, 1961. Presiding over the new Congress in his capacity as outgoing vice president—and, therefore, being addressed as "Mr. President" (of the Senate)—Nixon announced the electoral

vote results from the first state: Alabama–6 votes for Senator Byrd of Virginia and 5 votes for Senator Kennedy of Massachusetts, then added with some irony "the gentleman from Virginia is now in the lead." A full account of this scene can be found in Peirce, *The People's President*, pp. 17-19.

15 The material in the preceding paragraphs is drawn from ibid., pp. 102–04. Nixon never chose to claim that he had actually won in 1960, probably because of the complexities of showing this to be so, as well as the likely poor loser image this would generate. It is interesting that the Democratic National Committee used this exact calculation of Alabama's 1960 vote in determining convention representation in 1964, thus seemingly accepting a count in which Kennedy ran second in popular votes. Ibid., p. 104.

16 Tom Wicker, from his preface to ibid., p. 9. It is also evident that it is impossible to say who would have won in 1960 given a direct vote for president, since it is unknown where the vote for unpledged electors would have gone if the only choice were between Nixon and Kennedy—assuming, of course, that this was the only choice.

17 Ibid., p. 107.

18 One result of the action of Henry Irwin was that Oklahoma, in 1961, passed the nation's most stringent law binding electors to oaths to support their party's nominees or face penalties up to a fine of one thousand dollars. Such laws, however, are probably unconstitutional on the grounds that the Constitution provides for electors *voting*, which implies a freedom of action. See James C. Kirby, Jr., "Limitations on the Power of State Legislatures over Presidential Elections," *Law and Contemporary Problems* 27 (Spring 1962): 495-509.

19 Material adapted from Peirce, *The People's President*, p. 168.

20 League of Women Voters of the United States, *Who Should Elect the President?* (Washington, D.C.: League of Women Voters, 1969), p. 29.

21 The type of third party that one might or might not favor is, of course, an individual choice; however, traditionally, regional third parties have been most often associated with the southern region and have gained their impetus from questions of particular concern to them, usually the race issue. See V. O. Key, Jr., *Public Opinion and American Democracy* (New York: Knopf, 1963), pp. 100-10.

22 Alabama, Arkansas, Florida, Georgia, Louisiana, Mississippi, North Carolina, South Carolina, Tennessee, Texas, and Virginia.

23 Alabama, Georgia, Louisiana, Mississippi, and South Carolina. Wallace actually carried the first four of these states, plus Arkansas, but not South Carolina. His electoral vote total on election day was 45; however, a North Carolina Nixon elector later added his vote to these, resulting in 46 electoral votes for Wallace—almost precisely the figure used here.

24 "Wallace Candidacy Raises Fears of Electoral Stalemate," *Congressional Quarterly Weekly Report*, July 19, 1968, pp. 1816-17.

25 As we note elsewhere, Wallace's electoral vote total was later increased by 1 and Nixon's decreased by a like amount, by the actions of an individual Nixon elector.

26 This national percent difference should not be confused with the previously discussed percent difference in states other than those carried by a third-party candidate.

27 An electoral college majority in 1968 was 270 votes out of a total of 538, while in 1960 it was 269 votes out of a total of 537. The reason for this change was that the total electoral college vote rose temporarily to 537 for the 1960 election to accommodate the new states of Alaska and Hawaii, while in 1968 the total electoral college vote had increased permanently to 538 electoral votes due to the Twenty-third Amendment, giving the District of Columbia 3 electoral votes.

28 But see note 12.

29 30,631 votes in New Jersey, 10,245 in Missouri and 12,158 in New Hampshire. Based on "Final 1968 Presidential Election Results as reported to Congressional Quarterly by the Governmental Affairs Institution," in *Politics in America*, 3rd ed. (Washington, D.C.: Congressional Quarterly, 1969), p. 127. This analysis is, of course, based solely on the actual November election results. If one takes into account the later action of Nixon elector Dr. Lloyd W. Bailey in voting for Wallace, different results are found since only 32 rather than 33 electoral votes would have to shift. In this case, a shift of 41,971 votes from Nixon to Humphrey in New Jersey (30,631), Missouri (10,245), and Alaska (1,095) could have deadlocked the election. This latter measure is the one used by Senator Bayh in the Foreword to this book.

30 Bailey's action gave rise to debate by both houses of Congress on January 6, 1969, over a challenge to his vote by Senator Edmund Muskie (D., Maine) and Representative James G. O'Hara (D., Mich.), which was finally defeated. For a more detailed discussion, see chapter 5.

31 Judson L. James, *American Political Parties: Potential and Performance* (New York: Pegasus, 1969), p. 52.

32 James A. Michener, *Presidential Lottery: The Reckless Gamble in Our Electoral System* (New York: Random House, 1969), pp. 16 and 56. Another plan, widely reported during the months of the election, had been advanced by Gary Orfield, an assistant professor of government at the University of Virginia, in an article in the *Washington Post* of July 7, 1968. The Orfield proposal, quickly adopted by then Representative, later Senator, Charles E. Goodell (R., N.Y.) and Representative Morris K. Udall (D., Arizona), would have the leaders of both parties pledge that if the 1968 election resulted in an electoral college deadlock, they would provide sufficient House votes to elect whomever had been the popular vote winner. This plan, of course, could have been as easily implemented in the electoral college as in the House of Representatives. "Wallace Candidacy Raises Fears of Electoral Stalemate," p. 1820.

33 This potential tension actually appeared in a rather subtle form in the campaign statements of the two candidates about the possibility of electoral college deadlock. Humphrey stressed the need to follow the prescribed constitutional contingent procedure, while Nixon stated his belief that "whoever wins the popular vote should be the next President of the United States." Quoted in "The Electoral College," *Congressional Quarterly Guide to Current American Government* (Spring 1970), p. 144.

34 A Wallace position paper of late 1967 stressed this possibility: "If the election is that close, it is entirely possible that it might be settled by negotiation in the Electoral College before it reaches the House of Representatives. Before you go into the House, you go into the Electoral College. If we hold the balance of power, we may decide the question in the Electoral College because one party may have a major concession to make to the people of our country, a solemn covenant to them." "Wallace Candidacy Raises Fears of Electoral Stalemate," p. 1812.

35 Senator Birch Bayh, quoted in "The Electoral College," *Congressional Quarterly Guide to Current American Government* (Spring 1970), p. 144.

36 "Wallace Candidacy Raises Fears of Electoral Stalemate," p. 1818.

37 Wallace, it has been alleged, collected affidavits from each of his pledged electors affirming that they would follow his directions about how to vote. Such affidavits, of course, would have no legal standing, but would serve, presumably, as reminders to the Wallace electors when and if the time came to switch to a major-party candidate.

38 Among the nastiest rumors of the 1968 election was that if electoral college deadlock appeared immanent and if the new House appeared likely to elect Nixon, outgoing President Johnson might reconvene the old Congress for the purpose of moving the meeting time of the new Congress back beyond January 6 so that the old, Democratic Congress could choose the new president. This rumor never had any substance, but illustrates both the suspicions generated by threatened deadlock and the frightening possibilities under the contingent proceedings.

39 The parallel process of Senate election of a deadlocked vice president has been used only once, in 1837.

40 Presumably the House would adopt many of the House rules used in 1825, but the precise manner by which the House would proceed would itself be subject to considerable controversy. See "Wallace Candidacy Raises Fears of Electoral Stalemate," p. 1819.

41 Peirce, *The People's President*, p. 133.

42 "House Membership in the 91st Congress, 1st Session," *Congressional Quarterly Weekly Report*, January 3, 1969, pp. 38-39.

43 Much of this material is adapted from the analysis presented in "Wallace Candidacy Raises Fears of Electoral Stalemate," pp. 1821-22.

44 "House Candidate Pledges," *Congressional Quarterly Weekly Report*,

October 25, 1968, p. 2956. The pledges were made as a result of widespread speculation that the election might go to the House and that in that case representatives would vote for the nominee of their party. For Democrats in districts that were expected to go to Nixon or Wallace, this was potentially a detrimental campaign issue. In order to protect themselves, candidates pledged to follow the mandate of their districts and to vote in the House for the winner of their districts, regardless of party affiliation.

45 Compiled from *Apportionment in the Nineteen Sixties* (New York: National Municipal League, 1967), pages unnumbered, and Luman H. Long, ed., *World Almanac, 1969* (New York: Newspaper Enterprise Association, 1968), pp. 907-08.

46 Ibid.

47 This incomplete analysis of possible voting alignments in the House highlights another aspect of the inequality of the contingent election scheme. One man, representing the 285,278 citizens of Nevada, would cast one-fiftieth of the vote for president. At the same time, had the Illinois, Maryland, Montana, and Oregon delegations voted along party lines, they would have been divided and would have lost their vote; over 15 million people would, therefore, have been disenfranchised. This is in addition to the total and automatic disenfranchisement of the 700,000 residents of the District of Columbia.

48 The possibilities inherent in this period of uncertainty as the House moves through successive ballots was fascinatingly described in a fantasy written in early 1968 by Russell Baker of the *New York Times*, entitled *Our Next President: The Incredible Story of What Happened in the 1968 Elections* (New York: Dell, 1968). Two less realistic fictional accounts of possible events surrounding electoral college deadlock in 1968 and subsequent House contingent activities are Theodore G. Venetoulis, "1968: The Year No President Was Elected," in *The House Shall Choose* (Margate, N.J.: Elias, 1968), pp. 154-77; and Sherwin Markman, *The Election* (New York: Random House, 1970). The latter novel includes a black insurrection in California complicating House activities.

One can carry this type of analysis on and on—for example, to show how a Democratic Senate might have had to choose a vice president between Spiro Agnew and Curtis Le May, if, as some September predictions suggested, the Wallace-Le May ticket ran ahead, in electoral votes, of the Humphrey-Muskie ticket and thus became the second ticket, thus excluding Senator Muskie from Senate consideration.

49 Peirce, *The People's President*, pp. 189-90. This relationship, however, may be becoming indistinct through consensus. The latest Gallup poll results (Fall 1968) show the abolition of the electoral college and its replacement by direct vote favored by 81 percent of the American people.

50 The unit rule became common as early as 1832, although South Carolina continued to use a district division of presidential electoral votes as late as 1860, and Michigan used such a system for one elec-

tion in 1892. Maine adopted the district plan effective for the 1972 election. "Electoral College Reform," *Congressional Quarterly Weekly Report,* March 28, 1969, p. 440.

51 Thomas Hart Benton, quoted in Peirce, *The People's President*, p. 152.

52 Lucius Wilmerding, Jr., *The Electoral College* (Boston: Beacon Press, 1958), pp. 93-94.

53 Ibid., p. 87.

54 For the sake of simplicity, we are here assuming a Kennedy plurality in 1960.

55 This, of course, is different from the number of times a candidate who has failed to receive a majority—over one-half of all the votes cast—has become the president. This has occurred fifteen times—in the elections of 1824, 1844, 1848, 1856, 1860, 1876, 1880, 1884, 1888, 1892, 1912, 1916, 1948, 1960, and 1968. This comprises 39 percent of the elections for which popular totals are available.

56 U.S., Congress, Senate, Subcommittee on Constitutional Amendments, Senate Judiciary Committee, *Hearings on Election of the President*, 89th Cong., 2nd sess., and 90th Cong., 1st sess., February and March 1966, May, July, and August, 1967, p. 369.

57 Alexander Hamilton, *The Federalist* (New York: Modern Library, n.d.), p. 441.

Chapter 2

1 John Dickinson, quoted in John P. Roche, "The Founding Fathers: A Reform Caucus in Action," *American Political Science Review* 55 (December 1961): 799. John P. Roche describes the convention delegates as "first and foremost superb democratic politicians" who "*made* history and did it within the limits of consensus," and the convention itself as "a *nationalist* reform caucus which had to operate with great delicacy and skill in a political cosmos full of enemies to achieve the one definitive goal—popular approbation." Ibid.

2 Richard C. Welty, "Who *Really* Elects Our Presidents?", *Midwest Quarterly* 2 (Autumn 1960): 23.

3 This first assessment of the probable consequences of a direct vote for the president seems reasonably accurate for this historical period. What was not anticipated, of course, was the later development of political parties able to popularize national contenders, inform the nation's electorate about them, and actively engage in aggregating support for candidates across state lines.

4 Charles A. O'Neil, *The American Electoral System* (New York: Putnam, 1887), pp. 3-4, and J. Hampden Dougherty, *The Electoral System of the United States* (New York: Putnam, 1906), p. 1.

5 Peirce, *The People's President*, p. 43.

6 The practical effect of this provision would be to retain the same state proportions as if the selection had been by a joint session of Congress, as had been proposed in the earlier congressional selection plan.

7 This change in the contingent procedure from the Senate to the House was due to the fears that the Senate, which had already been given treaty ratification powers, and advice and consent responsibilities, was accumulating too much authority in comparison with the House of Representatives.

8 William T. Gossett, "Electing the President: New Hope for an Old Ideal," *American Bar Association Journal* 53 (December 1967): 1103.

9 Peirce, *The People's President*, p. 52.

10 Roche, "The Founding Fathers," p. 811.

11 Felix Morley, "Democracy and the Electoral College," *Modern Age* 5 (Fall 1961): 377.

12 Roche, "The Founding Fathers," p. 811.

13 James Madison, quoted in Peirce, *The People's President*, p. 37.

14 John P. Feerick, "Electoral College: Why It Was Created," *American Bar Association Journal* 54 (March 1968): 254, and Peirce, *The People's President*, p. 262.

15 Feerick, "Electoral College," p. 255.

16 "The Electoral College," *Congressional Quarterly Guide to Current American Government* (Spring 1970), p. 141.

17 Michener, *Presidential Lottery*, p. 9.

18 These thirty-two states and the District of Columbia use what is called the *short ballot* for president, where the ballot lists only the presidential contenders, but not the electors. Three other states also use the short ballot in those areas with voting machines. Fourteen states retain the long ballot, listing both presidential candidates and electors. Alabama, uniquely, lists the names of electors, but leaves it up to the voter to know to whom they are pledged—if at all. In 1960 five Alabama Democratic electors were pledged—to Kennedy, while six were unpledged. In 1964, all Alabama electors under the Democratic column were unpledged; no electors were pledged to the incumbent Democratic president, Lyndon Johnson. League of Women Voters, *Who Should Elect the President?*, p. 4.

19 Quoted in Peirce, *The People's President*, p. 64. An interesting and more eloquent echo of these sentiments was expressed by James Russell Lowell, a Republican elector in Massachusetts in 1876, who was urged to switch his vote from Hayes to Tilden in order to resolve the political uncertainties of that year. He responded: "In my own judgment I have no choice, and am bound in honor to vote for Hayes, as the people who chose me expected me to do. They did not choose me because they have confidence in my judgment but because they thought they knew what the judgment would be. If I had told them that I should vote for Tilden, they would never have nominated me. It is a plain question of trust." Quoted in ibid., p. 124.

20 Adapted from Peirce, *The People's President*, p. 124. The faithless elector of 1956 was a particularly interesting case. When asked why he voted for Walter Jones, a local judge, instead of Adlai Stevenson

as pledged, this individual, W. F. Turner of Alabama, tersely replied, "I have fulfilled my obligations to the people of Alabama. I'm talking about the white people." Harry L. Selden, "The Electoral College: Does It Choose the Best Man?", *American Heritage* 13 (October 1962): 142. In 1972, Roger MacBride, a Va. Nixon elector, cast an unexpected vote—for Libertarian Party candidate John Hospers.

21 See James C. Kirby, Jr., "Limitations on the Power of State Legislatures over Presidential Elections," *Law and Contemporary Problems* 27 (Spring 1962): 495-509.

22 See chapter 1, pp. 7, 12-17.

23 Peirce, *The People's President*, pp. 74 and 76. The legislature chose presidential electors also, for a brief period, in the reconstructed state of Florida in 1868 and in the newly admitted state of Colorado in 1876. "The Electoral College," *Congressional Quarterly Guide to Current American Government* (Spring 1970), p. 141.

24 See Peirce, *The People's President*, pp. 74-78. The district division of electoral votes had been common early in the nineteenth century but completely disappeared by 1836. It momentarily reappeared in Michigan in one election late in the nineteenth century for particular partisan reasons. In 1969 Maine resurrected the district division of electoral votes through adoption of a plan, to go in effect with the presidential election of 1972, allowing for determination of two of its four votes on the basis of its two congressional districts.

25 See ibid., pp. 71-74. The Twelfth Amendment, however, also provided that if a subsequent election were thrown into the House, the choice would be from the top three candidates rather than from the top five as previously; that if by inauguration day no president had been selected, the new vice president would become president; that a vice president would need a majority of electoral votes (previously he only needed the second highest number), and that the age, citizenship, and residency requirements would be the same for the vice president as for the president.

26 Ibid., p. 88.

27 Historian Eugene H. Roseboom writes that "fortune seemed to reserve her smiles for the Republicans during these years, but in this case asinine blundering by the Illinois Democrats would seem to be a more logical explanation," Eugene H. Roseboom, *A History of Presidential Elections* (New York: Macmillan, 1959), p. 247; quoted in Peirce, *The People's President*, p. 90.

28 See Michener, *Presidential Lottery*, pp. 78-91, and Paul L. Haworth, *The Hayes-Tilden Disputed Presidential Election of 1876* (New York: Russell and Russell, 1966).

29 What the House action might have been in 1825 had its widely revered and very powerful Speaker been among the candidates that could be considered is unknown but subject to interesting speculation. Clay had but 13 percent of the popular vote, but institutional loyalty would have been very potent.

30 Thomas Jefferson, quoted in Peirce, *The People's President*, p. 132.

Chapter 3

1 Robert L. Tienken, *Proposals to Reform Our Electoral System* (Washington, D.C.: Library of Congress Legislative Reference Service, January 1966; revised and updated, July 1, 1968), p. 17.

2 Peirce, *The People's President*, p. 151. In addition to this incredible diversity, the opening days of the first session of the Ninetieth Congress in 1967 resulted in thirteen different constitutional amendments in the Senate alone, and the comparable senatorial total in the first days of the Ninety-first Congress in 1969 was an additional eleven. The House of Representatives, always prone to outdo the Senate at least numerically, managed to produce over fifty proposals within thirty days of its convening in January 1969.

3 This is the subject of chapter 5, "Direct Vote: A Goal Nearly Reached."

4 In fact, it could be argued that to a degree the automatic plan enhances this possibility, since it would eliminate the possibility of one or two electors switching to a popular vote leader in order to give him a clear electoral college majority. On the other hand, the absence of such elector behavior also cuts the other way—the automatic plan eliminates the possibility of one or two electors switching so as to deny a popular vote leader a clear electoral college majority.

5 Peirce, *The People's President*, p. 177-81.

6 While many joint session procedures provide for choice from among the top two contenders, some provide for the choice to be from among the top three. All establish a majority vote requirement in the joint session. Inherent in any plan incorporating a choice from among the top three candidates is the possibility of a deadlock in the joint session just a dozen or so days away from inauguration day.

7 Wallace S. Sayre and Judith H. Parris, *Voting for President: The Electoral College and the American Political System* (Washington, D.C.: The Brookings Institution, 1970), p. 150.

   Another student of electoral reform, but by no means a defender of the present system, observes: "The indirect electoral college system ... is a remarkable instrument. It produces majorities even when the voters cannot; it amplifies the majorities that the voters do produce; and it provides rather sharp disincentives to those who would, by becoming candidates, decrease the possibilities of a majority popular decision." Max S. Power, "A Theoretical Analysis of the Electoral College and Proposed Reforms" (Ph.D. Dissertation, Yale University, 1971), p. 116.

8 Quoted in Tom Wicker column, *New York Times*, September 17, 1970.

9 Alexander M. Bickel, "Direct Election of the President," *New Republic*, September 26, 1970, p. 9.

10 Sayre and Parris, *Voting for President*, p. 62.

11 John D. Feerick, "The Electoral College: Why It Ought to Be Abolished," *Fordham Law Review* 37 (October 1968): 43.

12 Viscount John Morley, quoted in Michener, *Presidential Lottery*, p. 138.
13 The story of the fate of the Lodge-Gossett resolution is a long and complex one. An excellent, concise account can be found in Peirce, *The People's President*, pp. 166-71.
14 U.S., Congress, House, House Judiciary Committee, *Hearings on Electoral College Reform*, 91st Cong., 1st sess., February and March 1969, p. 528.
15 Appreciation is expressed to John H. Yunker for this argument.
16 Ruth C. Silva, "Reform of the Electoral System," *Review of Politics* 14 (July 1952): 397; and idem, "The Lodge-Gossett Resolution: A Critical Analysis," *American Political Science Review* 44 (March 1950): 92.
17 Silva, "The Lodge-Gossett Resolution," p. 93.
18 Ibid., pp. 94-96.
19 See House, *Hearings on Electoral College Reform*, pp. 973-99, and U.S., Congress, Senate, Subcommittee on Constitutional Amendments, Senate Judiciary Committee, *Hearings on Electing the President*, 91st Cong., 1st sess., January, March, April, and May 1969, pp. 867-93. Unfortunately, in the latter source, some of the most interesting tables are made almost unusable because of an inking error in the printing. The 1972 election data were supplied by the Library of Congress especially for this book.
20 This Nixon lead under the proportional plan would be due to quirks in the distribution of the two candidates' votes. For example, in 1960, Kennedy received 50.1 percent of Illinois's popular vote. Under the existing electoral college arrangement he consequently obtained all twenty-seven of that state's electoral votes. Under the proportional plan Kennedy would have received 13.577 electoral votes from Illinois, while Nixon would have received 13.471 electoral votes. Anthony Lewis, "The Case against Electoral Reform," *Reporter*, December 8, 1960, p. 31. The proportional plan results for all the states in 1960 can be found in House, *Hearings on Electoral College Reform*, pp. 980-81.
21 Sayre and Parris, *Voting for President*, p. 131.
22 Nelson W. Polsby and Aaron B. Wildavsky, *Presidential Elections: Strategies of American Electoral Politics*, 2nd ed. (New York: Scribner, 1968), pp. 247 and 242.
23 Theodore H. White, *The Making of the President: 1968* (New York: Atheneum, 1969), p. 409.
24 One must wonder what purpose electors, so bound, would serve. In lengthy 1966 testimony before the Senate Judiciary Subcommittee on Constitutional Amendments, Mundt appears to assume that the office of presidential elector must be retained, but offers no reasons for its retention. Senate, *Hearings on Election of the President*, pp. 48-69. It appears that the only plausible answer is that the electors would be retained for the sake of tradition.
25 Under the Mundt bill, these districts would not have to be the existing congressional districts, but could be special presidential

election districts. The opportunities for gerrymandering and political advantage are obvious here. The figure 480 is the total number of congressional districts smaller than a state, together with the fifty states and the District of Columbia.

26 Thus it can be seen that the political risks of Maine in switching, in 1969, to a district system for the 1972 election, were not very great—at worst, they might lose one of their 4 electoral votes as a bloc.

27 A full account of this activity can be found in Peirce, *The People's President*, pp. 157-60. The Daniels substitute of 1956 was to be the last electoral college reform plan to reach the floor of either house of Congress until the direct vote plan in 1969.

28 Michener, *Presidential Lottery*, p. 111, The California House of Representatives delegation elected at the same time was divided 21 to 17, Democratic. Ibid.

29 Library of Congress data, in House, *Hearings on Electoral College Reform*, p. 976.

30 See chapter 1.

31 Appreciation is expressed to Dorothy Kirie and Margaret McCulla for this and the following analysis.

32 Sayre and Parris, *Voting for President*, pp. 142 and 104-05. Sayre and Parris note that 430 of the 538 electoral votes would be, under the district plan, determined in areas smaller than states.

33 Peirce, *The People's President*, p. 181.

34 Only a few months earlier in 1966, Senator Bayh had denounced the direct vote plan because "it would inevitably take the nation down the path of splinter parties that have plagued so many European nations for so many years." In May, he recanted his earlier stand, saying "I hate to admit we were wrong, but I think we were." Quoted in ibid., p. 191. See chapter 5 for a fuller discussion of this and subsequent events.

35 ABA, *Electing the President: A Report of the Commission on Electoral College Reform* (Chicago: ABA, 1960), pp. 3-4.

36 Peirce, *The People's President*, chapter 8.

37 James, *American Political Parties*, p. 55.

38 Sayre and Parris, *Voting for President*, p. 131.

39 Conservative journalist James J. Kilpatrick has argued: "The proposal, if adopted, would tend to convert this Republic from a union of states into a consolidated form of democracy. Overnight, we would abandon our structure of federalism in one of its most important manifestations—the election of a President." Nationally syndicated column by James J. Kilpatrick, September 10, 1969.

40 Along this line, Myron P. Curzan argues that: "Presidential races marked by a proliferation of parties and a bargaining process, either to avoid a run-off or during a run-off, pose the distinct possibility of not only seriously weakening the two-party system but of tearing apart the fabric of society," Myron P. Curzan, "Voting for President," *New Republic*, April 18, 1970, p. 15.

41 This plan was advocated at the time in Ralph M. Goldman, "Hubert

Humphrey's S.J. Res. 152: A New Proposal for Electoral College Reform," *Midwest Journal of Political Science* 11 (February 1958): 89-96.

42 Peirce, *The People's President*, p. 196. Much of the above discussion of hybrid plans is drawn from pp. 194-96 of this work.

43 This plan apparently was conceived and developed by Myron P. Curzan, a young Washington lawyer in the very prestigious law firm of Arnold and Porter. Mr. Curzan expounded on this approach in his article, "Voting for President," pp. 14-16.

44 Sayre and Parris, *Voting for President*, p. 77.

45 Neal Peirce expressed this objection in his 1970 Senate testimony: "The Eagleton-Dole Amendment [the federal system plan] would be simply incomprehensible to all but a tiny handful of election law purists, and thus fails to meet the first requirement of any Presidential election system: simplicity that leads to acceptance by the people and legitimacy of the choice." U.S., Congress, Senate, Judiciary Committee, *Supplemental Hearings on Electoral College Reform*, 91st Cong., 2nd sess., April 15, 16, and 17, 1970, p. 230.

Chapter 4

1 Three particular attempts to identify reform criteria should be mentioned. The first of these resulted from a Brookings Institution conference of electoral reform experts in February 1969, at which there was an acceptance of four criteria as "components of an ideal system for electing the President and Vice President." These were: "the election procedure should guarantee, insofar as possible, a quick election decision with a clear-cut winner . . . , the system should be democratic . . . , the President should be 'legitimate' . . . , [and] the system should not undermine accepted norms of American politics, particularly the two-party system." Sayre and Parris, *Voting for President*, p. 153. Another set of goals was presented by Myron P. Curzan early in 1970. This was that an electoral system should provide a broad mandate, an effective party system, nationwide campaigning, and orderly, unconfusing elections. Curzan, "Voting for President," p. 15. Political scientist Allan P. Sindler, writing in 1962, identified three "customary criteria": voter equality, reduction of popular vote distortions, and minimization of the chance of minority presidents. To these, he then added seven or eight additional further criteria. Allan P. Sindler, "Presidential Election Methods and Urban-Ethnic Interests," *Law and Contemporary Problems* 27 (Spring 1962): 213.

2 Some of the following criteria were initially identified and summarized by John H. Yunker.

3 A similar criterion is identified by Max S. Power, who observes, "the movement for electoral college reform is motivated by the widespread belief that presidential elections ought to conform more closely to the norms of popular sovereignty and political equality." Power, "Analysis of the Electoral College," p. 220. Power utilizes

Robert A. Dahl's model of "populistic democracy" and his chain of definitions for majoritarian democracy in stating four definitions:

DEF. 1: An institution is democratic if and only if the process of selecting its personnel is compatible with the condition of popular sovereignty and the condition of political equality.
DEF. 2: The condition of popular sovereignty is satisfied if and only if it is the case that, whenever there is a contest for filling an office, the candidate selected is the candidate preferred by the members of the group or society.
DEF. 3: The condition of political equality is satisfied if and only if the preference of each member is assigned an equal value in settling contests for office.
DEF. 4: THE RULE: The principle of majority rule prescribes that in choosing between alternative candidates, the candidate preferred by the greater number is elected.

Ibid., pp. 15-16.

4 *Counting the Votes* was the original title of Sayre and Parris, one of the few scholarly works of recent years to totally reject all of the proposed reform plans—including the automatic plan—in favor of a basically unchanged present electoral college system. In this study, the authors approvingly quote, on page 1, Hamilton's statement "I ... hesitate not to affirm, that if the manner of it [the electoral college system] be not perfect, it is at least excellent. It unites in an eminent degree all the advantages; the union of which was to be desired." Sayre and Parris themselves conclude: "the electoral vote system, with the winner-take-all, state general-ticket system, is the best of the several methods." (*Voting for President*, p. 135.) They also express their belief that much of the electoral reform movement results from "a strong urge toward perfection, not just the 'excellence' Hamilton called for." (P. 1.)

5 See, especially, pp. 18-21 of chapter 1.

6 For data illustrating this point, see the analysis, by the Library of Congress, of possible election results under each of the major reform alternatives, for the presidential elections since 1948, chapter 3, figure 1.

7 The logic underlying the case for the direct vote plan is thoroughly and expertly examined in Max S. Power, "Logic and Legitimacy: On Understanding the Electoral College Controversy," in *Perspectives on Presidential Selection,* ed. Donald R. Matthews (Washington, D.C.: The Brookings Institution, 1973). Power sees the basis of the direct vote plan as a desire to make the presidential electoral process as democratic as possible—a goal that the direct vote plan only approximates.

In an example of a particularly relativistic view of the argument that the candidate with the most votes should win, one noted legal scholar recently wrote, "When some 70 million votes divide so closely [as in 1960 or 1968], only an immensely dogmatic majoritarianism would insist that the so-called winner has the sole legitimate claim to office." Alexander M. Bickel, *The New Age of Political Reform: The Electoral College, the Convention, and the Party System* (New York: Harper & Row, 1968), p. 17.

8 In this view, we are not entirely alone, for as Max S. Power notes, "A large body of politicians, commentators and political scientists, as well as voters at large clearly now do put these values [popular equality and popular sovereignty] forward as the exclusive, or nearly exclusive, basis on which presidential elections should be conducted." Power, "Analysis of the Electoral College," p. 221.

9 The "other regards" on which there is considerable disagreement include whether the direct vote plan: contributes to presidential legitimacy through providing a broad mandate (which is questioned because of the absence of any multiplier effect and the possible splintering of popular votes); ensures a quick and decisive verdict and avoids constitutional crises (because of the possibility of multiple parties forcing runoffs); maintains the existing two-party system (because of the "rewards" in counting votes given to all parties); preserves federalism (because of the elimination of the constant two); and avoids incentives for fraud (because of the inclusion of all votes in the national count). Those specific points are taken up in the next section under the four criticisms of a general nature.

10 Herbert Wechsler, "The Political Safeguards of Federalism: The Role of the States in the Composition and Selection of the National Government," in *Federalism: Mature and Emergent*, ed. Arthur W. MacMahon (Garden City, N.Y.: Doubleday, 1955), p. 99.

11 Interview with Senator Birch Bayh, *Congressional Quarterly Weekly Report*, April 17, 1970, p. 1026. We explicitly disagree that the electoral college system operates as described by author Theodore White: "What is right about the old system is the sense of identity it gives Americans. As they march to the polls, Bay Staters should feel Massachusetts is speaking; Hoosiers should feel Indiana is speaking, blacks and other minorities should feel their votes count, so, too, should Southerners from Tidewater to the Gulf." Theodore H. White, "Direct Elections: An Invitation to National Chaos," *Life*, January 30, 1970, p. 4.

12 Sayre and Parris, *Voting for President*, p. 54.

13 Mike Mansfield, quoted in Birch Bayh, "Electing a President: The Case for Direct Popular Election," *Harvard Journal on Legislation* 6 (1969): 138. Similarly, Herbert Wechsler argues, "If Congress, from its composition and the mode of its selection, tends to reflect the local spirit predicted by Madison, the prime organ of a compensating 'national spirit' is, of course, the President—both as the Chief Executive and as the leader of his party," Wechsler, "Political Safeguards of Federalism," p. 104.

14 Bickel, "Direct Election of the President," p. 9; White, "Direct Elections," p. 4.

15 See chapter 2, table 4. In addition, it should also be noted that a shift in 1960 of only 8,971 votes could have created an electoral college deadlock. See chapter 1, pp. 5-6, for a discussion of the

indeterminable character of the popular vote in 1960.

    In the 1968 election, a total of 73,211,562 votes were cast. A direct vote runoff would be necessary if and only if neither candidate received 40 percent of this total, which would be 31,785,480. The Republican candidate in fact received 2,300,855 votes above this figure, and the Democratic candidate had 1,990,540 votes above it. In order for there to be a runoff in the 1968 election, then, close to 4.5 million major party votes would have had to shift to minor party candidates without causing countervailing trends.

16 William Boyd points out that this is the percentage of the total electoral college that New York's electoral votes represented in the 1960s. William J. D. Boyd, *After the Electoral College?* (New York: National Municipal League, 1968), p. 27.

17 Peirce, *The People's President*, p. 239.

18 Alexander M. Bickel, "Wait a Minute!", *New Republic*, May 10, 1969, p. 13.

19 Editorial in the *New York Times*, September 29, 1970.

20 The question of whether campaign expenditures would greatly increase under the direct vote plan is a tricky question. To some degree, the need to wage campaigns nationally, in all states and areas, might have this result. Yet, it should be noted that today huge sums are expended in inefficient efforts to swing large, marginal states. Under the direct vote plan attention would focus on any centers of population that could be contacted efficiently and economically. It would seem, in fact, most plausible to argue that whatever increased expenditures result from the direct vote plan might well be due to increased involvement by state and local organizations throughout the nation in efforts to maximize the vote, not just carry the state. For a view somewhat along these lines, see Peirce, *The People's President*, p. 276; for an opposing view, see Kristol and Weaver, "A Bad Idea Whose Time Has Come," *New York Times Magazine*, November 23, 1969, p. 151.

21 William T. Gossett, "Direct Popular Election of the President," *ABA Journal* 56 (March 1970): 230.

22 Sayre and Parris, *Voting for President*, p. 154; Frank J. Sorauf, *Party Politics in America* (Boston: Little, Brown, 1968), p. 35.

23 Sorauf, *Party Politics in America*, pp. 35-37.

24 For an excellent review of the literature specifically on this point, see Feerick, "The Electoral College," pp. 37-38, as well as the 1969 testimony of Neal Peirce, House, *Hearings on Electoral College Reform*, pp. 523-24.

25 James MacGregor Burns, "A New Course for the Electoral College," *New York Times Magazine*, December 18, 1960, p. 28. Lucius Wilmerding similarly argues: "The sole way to destroy the two-party system is to offer multiple prizes distributable to the several factions in proportion to their relative strengths. But the presidency, being a single office, is not distributable." Lucius Wilmerding, "What to Watch Out For," *National Review*, January 28, 1969, p. 72.

26 See, in addition to the Sorauf study already mentioned, the classic works by Maurice Duverger, *Political Parties* (New York: Wiley, 1954), and E. E. Schattschneider, *Party Government* (New York: Holt, Rinehart, and Winston, 1942). In the latter work, Schattschneider makes no mention of the electoral college in his discussion of the causes of the two-party system. He terms the system the "Rock of Gibralter of American politics" and states that the "American two-party system is the direct consequence of the American election system, or system of representation." (p. 69.) Schattschneider's basic argument is that the two-party system derives its strength from the vast number of national, state, and local elections that are conducted in single-member districts under a plurality vote system. This system encourages parties to try to attract the broadest possible base of support in hopes of being assured of a victory by receiving a majority of the votes. Schattschneider noted that *"since parties are built around elections* it would be amazing if the form of the party system were not influenced profoundly by the nature of these elections." (Ibid.) A more recent study of state legislative systems, however, found that a considerable number of districts for the lower houses in state legislatures are multimember districts. See Maurice Klain, "A New Look at the Constituencies: The Need for a Recount and a Reappraisal," *American Political Science Review* 49 (December 1955): 1105-19. For a mathematical analysis of the effects of multimember districts, see John Banzhaf III, "Multi-member Electoral Districts: Do They Violate the 'One Man, One Vote' Principle?", *Yale Law Journal* 75 (1965): 1309-38.

27 As Robert G. Dixon puts it, "The essence of the direct vote idea for the presidency is that we are dealing with a *national* election for a single *national* office. Each voter has a right to expect that he will stand in the exact same relation to this national office as any other voter." Robert G. Dixon, Jr., *Democratic Representation: Reapportionment in Law and Politics* (New York: Oxford University Press, 1968), p. 571.

28 Interview with Senator Thomas F. Eagleton, *Congressional Quarterly Weekly Report*, April 17, 1970, p. 1029. Senator Eagleton also observed that the direct vote plan "could mean the death of the two-party system." (Ibid.)

29 Peirce, *The People's President*, p. 294.

30 As has been previously pointed out, only one election among the thirty-eight for which popular vote totals are available would have required a runoff election. In this election, that of 1860, the leading candidate was not on the ballot in several states—in other words, no popular votes at all were cast for him in these states—yet he still received 39.8 percent of the national popular vote.

31 In 1970 Senate testimony, a leading supporter of the direct vote plan swung to support of a simple plurality direct vote plan. Neal Peirce testimony, Senate, *Supplemental Hearings on Electoral College Reform*, pp. 228-29. Similar views favoring a simple plurality election of the president were expressed in a Washington interview

with Richard Scammon, Director of the Elections Research Center, September 15, 1970.

32 *Congressional Record*, September 18, 1969, p. H 8108, quoted in Power, "Analysis of the Electoral College," p. 174.

33 V. O. Key, Jr., in his classic study, *Southern Politics in State and Nation*, (New York: Vintage, 1949), esp. p. 417.

34 James, *American Political Parties*, p. 55. See also Key, *Southern Politics* pp. 416-23, especially p. 420.

35 Gossett, "Direct Popular Election," p. 231. Peirce, *The People's President*, p. 300.

36 Much of the material in this section is drawn from Lawrence D. Longley and John H. Yunker, "Who Is Really Advantaged by the Electoral College–and Who Just Thinks He Is?" (Paper delivered at the sixty-seventh Annual Meeting of the American Political Science Association, Chicago, Illinois, September 7-11, 1971); Yunker and Longley, "The Biases of the Electoral College," in *Perspectives on Presidential Selection*, ed. Matthews; Lawrence D. Longley and John H. Yunker, "The Changing Biases of the Electoral College" (Paper delivered at the Annual Meeting of the American Political Science Association, New Orleans, September 4-8, 1973) [also in U.S., Congress, Senate, Subcommittee on Constitutional Amendments, Judiciary Committee, *Hearings on Electoral College Reform*, 93d Cong., 1st sess., 26 and 27 September 1973, pp. 187-217]; and John H. Yunker and Lawrence D. Longley, "The Electoral College: Its Biases Newly Measured for the 1960's and 1970's, *Sage Professional Papers in American Politics* 3 (August 1975).

37 Bickel, *New Age of Political Reform*, p. 7; interview with Senator Carl T. Curtis (R., Nebr.), *Congressional Quarterly Weekly Report*, April 17, 1970, p. 1028.

38 See Peirce, *The People's President*, p. 137; Sindler, "Presidential Election Methods," p. 216; Joseph F. Kallenbach, "Our Electoral College Gerrymander," *Midwest Journal of Political Science* 4 (May 1960): 166; Dixon, *Democratic Representation*, pp. 565-66; and John D. Feerick, "The Electoral College–Its Defects and Dangers," *New York State Bar Journal* 40 (August 1968): 319-20.

39 Gossett, "Direct Popular Election," p. 227.

40 Albert J. Rosenthal, "The Constitution, Congress and Presidential Elections," *Michigan Law Review* 67 (November 1968): 3. Similar calls for the systematic evaluation of the consequences of the electoral college and of its reforms abound in the literature on the electoral college. See, for example, Richard N. Goodwin, "In Defense of the Electoral College," *Current* 113 (December 1969): 335; and Alexander M. Bickel, "The Case for the Electoral College," *New Republic*, January 28, 1967, pp. 15-16.

41 Joseph F. Kallenbach, "Recent Proposals to Reform the Electoral College System," *American Political Science Review* 30 (October 1936): 928; Wechsler, *Political Safeguards of Federalism*, p. 105; Edward S. Corwin and Louis W. Koenig, *The Presidency Today* (New York: New York University Press, 1956), p. 113.

42 Albert J. Rosenthal, "Some Doubts Concerning the Proposal to Elect the President by Direct Popular Vote," *Villanova Law Review* 14 (Fall 1968): 87.

43 Estes Kefauver, "The Electoral College: Old Reforms Take on a New Look," *Law and Contemporary Problems* 27 (Spring 1962): 196.

44 Dixon, *Democratic Representation*, p. 567.

45 Nelson W. Polsby and Aaron B. Wildavsky, *Presidential Elections*, especially chapter 5 of the second edition, p. 242. Further references will be to this edition. Polsby and Wildavsky viewed the proposal for direct vote as undermining slightly this advantage. The district plan, they wrote, would be "most extreme in its impact, which would be to confer an additional political bonus upon states already overrepresented in positions of Congressional power." (p. 242.) They dismissed the proportional plan, which would eliminate that feature favoring the large states (the unit rule) while retaining that favoring small states (the constant two) as "not a compromise, but the most extreme 'reform' of all." (P. 247.)

46 Interview by *Congressional Quarterly*, *Congressional Quarterly Weekly Report*, April 17, 1970, p. 1026.

47 Peirce, *The People's President*, p. 262. The great decisions in our nation's history, Peirce argues, have been along ideological, economic, or regional lines, not between large and small states.

48 Sindler, "Presidential Election Methods," p. 218.

49 This advantage, based on the solidarity of the regional vote, is compounded by the advantage of the South in having electoral votes based on census populations, rather than on actual votes.

50 If this is, in fact, the case, then it is truly ironic that southern representatives and senators were among the leaders of the successful congressional opposition to the abolition of the electoral college in 1969 and 1970. See chapter 5.

51 Harvey Zeidenstein, "The South Will Not Rise Again through Direct Election of the President, Polsby and Wildavsky Notwithstanding," *Journal of Politics* 31 (August 1969): 808-11.

52 Bickel, "Wait a Minute!", pp. 11-13; Rosenthal, "Some Doubts Concerning Direct Popular Vote," p. 90; Albert J. Rosenthal, "Rooting for the Electoral College," *New Leader*, October 21, 1968, p. 18.

53 Letter to the Editor from James Tobin, *New Republic*, October 11, 1969, p. 32.

54 As Max Power succinctly puts it: "There may be voters to whom 'liberal' appeals should be directed and whose needs ought to be given special recognition. But they are not likely to be 'self-conscious and cohesive,' nor are they necessarily the urban and minority groups identified by proponents of the argument." Power, "Analysis of the Electoral College," pp. 195-96. For a useful and comprehensive examination of the swing-vote theory as it applies to the electoral college and liberal interests, see pp. 194-205 of his study.

55 See Neal R. Peirce, "The Case against the Electoral College," *New Republic*, February 11, 1967, p. 12; idem, *The People's President*, pp. 282-83; and Sayre and Parris, *Voting for President*, pp. 47-48.

56 Sayre and Parris, *Voting for President*, p. 46.

57 Bayh, "Electing a President," p. 132.

58 Senate, *Supplemental Hearings on Electoral College Reform*, p. 230. See also *Hearings on Electoral College Reform*, p. 522.

59 Rosenthal, "Rooting for the Electoral College," p. 16. This analysis has been sharply contradicted by Carleton Sterling who, based on his analysis of actual voting distributional patterns, concludes: "The thesis that bloc voting in the Electoral College favors the urban liberal and ethnic groups is a myth. The system does not favor urban groups per se, has never consistently favored such groups, and is not especially likely to." Carleton W. Sterling, "The Failure of Bloc Voting in the Electoral College to Benefit Urban Liberal and Ethnic Groups" (Paper delivered at the Sixty-sixth Annual Meeting of the American Political Science Association, Los Angeles, September 1970), p. 12.

60 William J. D. Boyd, quoted in League of Women Voters of the United States, *Who Should Elect the President?*, p. 55.

61 House, *Hearings on Electoral College Reform*, p. 522.

62 Paul A. Freund, "Direct Election of the President: Issues and Answers," *ABA Journal* 56 (August 1970), p. 733.

63 For an examination of three representative but also unsatisfactory attempts to measure the influence of states, by Senator Harper in 1816, Senator John F. Kennedy in 1956, and Senator Holland in 1967, see Longley and Yunker, "Who Is Really Advantaged by the Electoral College?", pp. 7-9.

64 Irwin Mann and L. S. Shapley, "Values of Large Games VI: Evaluating the Electoral College Exactly," *Memorandum RM-3158-PR* (Santa Monica, Calif.: The RAND Corporation, 1962).

65 John F. Banzhaf III, "One Man, 3.312 Votes: A Mathematical Analysis of the Electoral College," *Villanova Law Review* 13 (Winter 1968): 303-46. The Banzhaf article was later reprinted in House, *Hearings on Electoral College Reform*, pp. 309-52, and Senate, *Hearings on Electing the President*, pp. 823-66. Banzhaf's technique measured the relative voting power of *citizen-voters*. This term is meant to indicate that his calculations were, of necessity, based on census figures, rather than on the number of actual voters. Banzhaf noted, however, that this method is very reasonable in light of the fact that electoral votes are also apportioned according to census figures. As such, neither Banzhaf's calculations nor the distribution of electoral votes takes into account such factors as the number of registered voters in a state, the number of voters who actually participate in a given election, or population changes between censuses.

66 William H. Riker and Lloyd S. Shapley, "Weighted Voting: A Mathematical Analysis for Instrumental Judgments," *Memorandum P-3318* (Santa Monica, Calif.: The RAND Corporation, 1966).

67 Irwin Mann and L. S. Shapley, "The A Priori Voting Strength of the Electoral College," in *Game Theory and Related Approaches to*

Social Behavior, ed. Martin Shubik (New York: Wiley, 1964), p. 154; Mann and Shapley, "Values of Large Games VI," p. 9.

68 Weighted voting in legislatures is an attempt to give equal representation to citizens of all districts without requiring all districts to be of equal population. Suppose that in a given legislature, there is one legislator for each ten thousand people. Now suppose there is one district with a population of twenty thousand while all other districts have ten thousand citizens. Rather than divide the larger district into two equal districts, a weighted voting plan would give the legislator from the larger district two votes, while all other legislators would have one vote. This system does not ensure equal representation, but gives a disproportionately greater influence to voters from the larger district. See John F. Banzhaf III, "Weighted Voting Doesn't Work: A Mathematical Analysis," *Rutgers Law Review* 19 (Winter 1965): 317-43.

69 Riker and Shapley, "Weighted Voting," p. 26.

70 Banzhaf, "One Man, 3.312 Votes." See also the literature cited in appendix B of this volume.

71 Ibid., p. 313. Banzhaf generalizes the effects of the present electoral college by saying: "[It] can be shown that the voting power of any member of a reasonable sized voting group will be proportional to the voting power of the group (which is roughly proportional to the number of votes cast) and inversely proportional to the square root of its population." (p. 316).

Banzhaf's analysis provides mathematical proof of Riker and Shapley's, as well as Mann and Shapley's, hypotheses concerning the results of such a multimillion person delegate model game. Banzhaf's conclusion indicates that in such a game there is a strong bias in favor of the large states. The two crucial differences between his analysis and the previous analyses are that Banzhaf uses citizen-voters within a state, instead of states themselves, as players in his model and that he assumes the voting power of an individual voter in an *n* person constituency is inversely proportional to the square root of *n*, not merely inversely proportional to *n*, as had been assumed in Mann and Shapley's analysis. If an individual's voting power was inversely proportional to his constituency's population, the big-state advantage would be outweighed by the small-state advantages from the "constant two"—as was earlier concluded concerning Nevada and New York in the Mann and Shapley analysis. For further discussion of the theoretical assumptions and methodology of the voting power approach, see Longley and Yunker, "Who Is Really Advantaged by the Electoral College?", pp. 7-17; Yunker and Longley, "The Biases of the Electoral College," pp. 174-78 and 195-203; and Yunker and Longley, "The Electoral College."

72 Longley and Yunker, "The Changing Biases of the Electoral College," and Yunker and Longley, "The Electoral College." Data for the 1960 apportionment of the electoral college, newly calculated and somewhat different from that reported by Banzhaf, are also presented in these studies, and some comparisons are made of how the patterns and biases have changed over a decade. These papers also develop

several different methods of determining voting power, including approaches utilizing vote turnout data instead of state population data and approaches based on alternative definitions of pivotal voting power. Technical appendices consider a number of special problems, including that posed by Maine's use of the district plan starting with the 1972 election and the mathematical complexities introduced by a three candidate election.

73 The Twenty-third Amendment grants the District of Columbia the "number of electors of President and Vice President equal to the whole number of Senators and Representatives in Congress to which the District would be entitled if it were a State, but in no event more than the least populous State." (U.S., *Constitution,* Amend. 23, sec. 1.) These voting power indices, as well as the statistical interpretations of these data, apply to the automatic plan of electoral college reform, as well as to the present system, since that reform would not affect the structural characteristics of the electoral college, but only abolish individual electors.

74 Banzhaf, "One Man, 3.312 Votes," p. 322.

75 Longley and Yunker, "The Changing Biases of the Electoral College," pp. 29-34; and Yunker and Longley, "The Electoral College."

76 The Mountain states are defined as the eight states of Arizona, Colorado, Idaho, Montana, Nevada, New Mexico, Utah, and Wyoming. The South is defined as the thirteen states of Alabama, Arkansas, Florida, Georgia, Kentucky, Louisiana, Mississippi, North Carolina, Oklahoma, South Carolina, Tennessee, Texas, and Virginia. The Midwest is defined as the twelve states of Illinois, Indiana, Iowa, Kansas, Michigan, Minnesota, Missouri, Nebraska, North Dakota, Ohio, South Dakota, and Wisconsin. The East is defined as the twelve states of Connecticut, Delaware, Maine, Maryland, Massachusetts, New Hampshire, New Jersey, New York, Pennsylvania, Rhode Island, Vermont, and West Virginia. Finally, the Far West is defined as the five states of Alaska, California, Hawaii, Oregon, and Washington.

77 State by state figures for these demographic groups for the 1970s are from the 1970 census, *General Population Characteristics,* table 16 ("Summary of General Characteristics: 1970") of each state volume, and table 60 ("Race of the Population for Regions, Divisions, and States: 1970") in the *United States Summary,* pp. 1–293 (for the black populations).

78 See Yunker and Longley, "The Biases of the Electoral College," pp. 195–202, and Yunker and Longley, "The Electoral College," for a consideration of these reservations.

79 Samuel Robinove, "The Electoral College Enigma," *Midstream* 15 (June-July 1969): 55.

Chapter 5

1 A further danger point lies in a possible conference committee between the two houses if plans passed by each differ. If these con-

ferees are unable to reach a mutual resolution of their differences, reform efforts may die at this point also.

2 Burns, "A New Course," p. 26.

3 In his foreword to Neal Peirce's 1968 book, Tom Wicker of the *New York Times* concluded about the direct vote plan, "the time of this particular idea has come." *The People's President*, p. 13. This idea was picked up the following year by Irving Kristol and Paul Weaver in the title of their article, "A Bad Idea Whose Time Has Come," pp. 43-44 ff.

4 See chapter 1.

5 See chapter 1, pp. 2-7.

6 U.S., Congress, Senate, Subcommittee on Constitutional Amendments, Senate Judiciary Committee, *Hearings on Nomination and Election of President and Vice President and Qualifications for Voting*, 87th Cong., 1st sess., May, June, and July 1961.

7 His testimony about his aims in his private plot about the presidency runs to almost one hundred pages.

8 U.S., Congress, Senate, Subcommittee on Constitutional Amendments, Senate Judiciary Committee, *Hearings on Nomination and Election of President and Vice President*, 88th Cong., 1st sess., June 1963.

9 Baker v. Carr, 369 U.S. 186 (1962).

10 Chamber of Commerce of the United States, *Electoral College Reform* (Washington, D.C.: Chamber of Commerce, 1963). Chamber of Commerce of the United States, *Referendum No. 98 on: Electoral College Reform*, (Washington, D.C.: Chamber of Commerce, 1965); this document is reprinted in most of the congressional hearings of 1967 to 1970.

11 Although it is only speculation, it is possible that President Johnson's interest in electoral college reform was assisted by the disappearance, in the preceding presidential election, of the solid Democratic South, which had traditionally supplied to Democratic candidates large blocs of regional electoral votes unmarred by signs of Republican votes.

12 The members of the ABA Commission on Electoral College Reform were: Robert G. Storey, Texas lawyer; Henry Bellmon, Oklahoma governor; Paul Freund, Harvard University law professor; E. Smythe Gambrell, Georgia lawyer; Ed Gossett, former representative from Texas; William T. Gossett, Michigan lawyer and president of the ABA; William J. Jameson, Montana lawyer; Kenneth B. Keating, former senator from New York; Otto Kerner, Illinois governor; James C. Kirby, Jr., Northwestern University law professor; James M. Nabrit, Jr., president of Howard University; Herman Phleger, California lawyer; C. Herman Pritchett, University of California political scientist; Walter P. Reuther, United Auto Workers president; and Whitney North Seymour, New York lawyer.

13 Senate, *Hearings on Election of the President*, pp. 22-23.

14 Birch Bayh, quoted in Peirce, *The People's President*, p. 190.
15 See *Congressional Quarterly Weekly Report*, December 16, 1966, p. 3030. Furthermore, Senator Burdick did not find any significant large-state–small-state differences concerning support for direct vote.
16 This legal action was initiated by a formidable foursome: David P. Buckson, attorney general of Delaware, John A. Gosnell, chief Washington representative of the National Small Business Association, James C. Kirby, Jr., former chief counsel for the Constitutional Amendments Subcommittee of the Senate Judiciary Committee during the 1961 hearings and currently a member of the ABA's Commission on Electoral College Reform, and Robert G. Dixon, Jr., professor of law at George Washington University and a recognized authority on reapportionment legal questions. For an excellent account of the activities that led to the suit, see Neal R. Peirce, "The Electoral College Goes to Court," *Reporter*, October 6, 1966, pp. 34-37. The broader legal questions are considered in Dixon, *Democratic Representation*, pp. 565-71. The text of the plaintiff's brief, along with other legal papers, are reprinted, among other places, in Senate, *Hearings on Election of the President*, pp. 807-903. It should be kept in mind that if the suit had been successful and the unit rule struck down while all other aspects of the electoral college system remained the same, the result would have been basically the proportional plan, with its greater voter inequities than the present electoral college (see chapter 4, pp. 107-18).
17 *Electing the President: A Report of the Commission on Electoral College Reform* (Chicago: ABA, 1967). This report is reprinted in most of the congressional hearings of 1967 to 1970.
18 Senate, *Hearings on Election of the President*.
19 League of Women Voters, *Who Should Elect the President?*, p. 76.
20 Kallenbach, "Our Electoral College Gerrymander," pp. 162-91.
21 Before the 1967-68 Senate hearings went to press, an advance copy of the entire Banzhaf article was made available and was reprinted on pp. 904-47 of these hearings.
22 The Banzhaf article was later reprinted in House, *Hearings on Electoral College Reform*, pp. 309-52; and Senate, *Hearings on Electing the President*, pp. 823-66. The original tables themselves were reprinted even more widely including in various Senate and House committee reports from 1969 on and in the appendices of several books of this period. Throughout this time, the findings of Mr. Banzhaf served as grist for the polemic arguments of both sides, some using his data to show the inequities of the present electoral college and most alternative plans, and others using his data to prove the necessity of retaining a defense for the large states or for other favored groups.
23 See chapter 4, section entitled "New Approaches and Avenues," Longley and Yunker, "Who Is Really Advantaged by the Electoral College?"; Yunker and Longley, "The Biases of the Electoral College"; Longley and Yunker, "The Changing Biases of the Electoral College"; and Yunker and Longley, "The Electoral College in the 1970's."

24 For valuable background information and specifics on this material, appreciation is expressed to the members of the House Judiciary Committee who completed a mail questionnaire, as well as to the following persons who were interviewed in Washington, D.C.: Donald Channell, director of the Washington Office of the ABA; Bess Dick, staff director, House Judiciary Committee; Joseph J. Fanelli, manager of Public Affiars Department of Chamber of Commerce of the United States; Representative Clark MacGregor (R., Minn.); and Benjamin L. Zelenko, general counsel of House Judiciary Committee (telephone interview).

25 Among the concerns of Dr. Bailey were Nixon's appointment of Dr. Henry Kissinger of Harvard as a foreign policy adviser and his request that Chief Justice Earl Warren remain in the Supreme Court for an additional six months while Nixon decided on a successor. Dr. Bailey's testimony to the Constitutional Amendments Subcommittee of the Senate Judiciary Committee about his actions can be found in Senate, *Hearings on Electing the President*, pp. 36-63.

26 The congressional debates on the challenge to Dr. Bailey's electoral vote are summarized in *Congressional Quarterly Weekly Report*, January 10, 1969, pp. 54-55: The House and Senate roll call votes can be found in ibid., p. 79.

27 The most delightful of this was the skillful little satire published early in 1968, Baker, *Our Next President*. A major examination of the very serious possibilities inherent in the electoral college system in light of current political developments was a widely cited (and even more widely used without citation) analysis, "Wallace Candidacy Raises Fears of Electoral Stalemate."

28 See, for example, Bickel, "Wait a Minute!"; "The Talk of the Town," *New Yorker*, February 8, 1969, pp. 25-26; Gossett, "Electing the President"; and Gaylord Nelson, "How Not to Elect a President," *Playboy* (November 1968), pp. 151 ff.

29 For example, by William T. Gossett, see "Electing the President: New Hope for an Old Ideal"; "Electing the President," *National Civic Review* 57 (June 1969): 241-47; and "Direct Popular Election." By John D. Feerick, see "The Electoral College: Why It Was Created," *ABA Journal* 54 (March 1968): 249 ff.; "The Electoral College—Its Defects and Dangers"; and "The Electoral College: Why It Ought to Be Abolished." By Ed Gossett, see "Will We Elect the President We Vote for in 1968?", *Reader's Digest* 91 (November 1967): 211-18. And by Paul Freund, see "Direct Election of the President."

30 The most elegantly stated claim by Professor Bickel for the present system was: "It simply happens that the electoral college can satisfy, at once, the symbolic aspirations and remote hopes of the small states, and the present, practical needs of the large ones. Not many human institutions work out quite as artistically as that." "Wait a Minute!", p. 13. Professor Bickel's major articles in *New Republic* included: "Case for the Electoral College"; "Wait a Minute!"; "Misreading Democracy," September 27, 1969, pp. 9-10; and "Direct Election of the President"; as well as a lengthy piece in

Commentary, "Is Electoral Reform the Answer?", 46 (December 1968): 41-51, later published as a brief book, *New Age of Political Reform*. A revised version of this last volume was published in 1971 under the title *Reform and Continuity*.

31 The text of President Nixon's statement can be found in *Congressional Quarterly Weekly Report*, February 28, 1969, p. 323. A summary of congressional reaction can be found in ibid., p. 308.

32 See chapter 3, pp. 57-58, where it is shown that the maximum division of electoral votes possible in this case is 3 to 1, or 75 percent to 25 percent.

33 In contrast, the comparable Senate hearings were held by an eleven-man subcommittee of the Senate Judiciary Committee, the Subcommittee on Constitutional Amendments. Although chaired by Senator Bayh, a direct vote advocate, this subcommittee proved to be hostile to the direct vote reform, and only subsequent action by the full Judiciary Committee, ironically chaired by direct vote opponent Senator James O. Eastland, saved the direct vote plan.

34 House, *Hearings on Electoral College Reform*, pp. 2-3.

35 Within the preceding month, both House Judiciary Committee Chairman Emanuel Celler and ranking minority member William M. McCulloch had publicly endorsed the direct vote plan.

36 House, *Hearings on Electoral College Reform*, pp. 615-16.

37 The latter point was made in a Washington interview with Donald Channell, director, Washington Office, ABA, on September 14, 1970.

38 Representative Charles E. Wiggins (R., Calif.), response to questionnaire. Much the same point was also made in a questionnaire response by Representative Tom Railsback (R., Ill.), in a Washington interview with Representative Clark MacGregor (R., Minn.), and in a telephone interview with Benjamin L. Zelenko, general counsel of the committee, on October 30, 1970. The Banzhaf findings subsequently made their way into the editorial columns of the *New York Times*. In an editorial of May 11, 1969, that newspaper observed: "Computer studies on the power of individual voters to affect Presidential elections recently confirmed what politicians have intuitively known. Voters in states like California and New York have more than twice as much chance to influence the outcome of Presidential elections as voters in smaller states. More voters go to the polls in the larger states, but they are able to influence the casting of many more electoral votes."

39 House, *Hearings on Electoral College Reform*, p. 2.

40 U.S., Congress, House, House Judiciary Committee, *Direct Popular Election of the President: Report on H. J. Res. 681*, 91st Cong., 1st sess., May 16, 1969.

41 *Congressional Record*, September 15, 1969, p. H 7883. Appreciation is expressed to Mark Roudane for pointing out this and the preceding two quotations.

42 David B. Truman, *The Governmental Process,: Political Interests and Public Opinion* (New York: Knopf, 1951), p. 265.

43 U.S., Congress, House, House Rules Committee, *Hearings on Proposing an Amendment to the Constitution of the United States Relating to the Election of the President and the Vice President*, 91st Cong., 1st sess., June and July 1969. During House floor debate, Representative William McCulloch similarly observed: "Although a good majority of the Republican members of the committee favored some reform other than the direct plan at the start of those hearings, 12 of the 15 Republican members were persuaded by the merits of the direct plan by the time the hearings had concluded. ... During those hearings we learned that the direct plan was supported by the ABA, the U.S. Chamber of Commerce, the National Federation of Independent Business, and the AFL-CIO." *Congressional Record*, September 10, 1969, p. H 7751.

44 Those opposed were three Republicans, Representatives David W. Dennis (Ind.), Edward Hutchinson (Mich.), and Richard H. Poff (Va.), and three southern Democrats, Representatives John Dowdy (Tex.), Walter W. Flowers (Ala.), and James R. Mann (S.C.).

45 Quoted in *New York Times*, April 30, 1969.

46 House, *Direct Popular Election of the President*.

47 Because of the nature of House procedure, a "special" rule is customary and even necessary for each piece of legislation. For a fuller discussion, see Lewis A. Froman, Jr., *The Congressional Process: Strategies, Rules, and Procedures* (Boston: Little, Brown, 1967).

48 House, *Hearings on Proposing an Amendment to the Constitution of the United States Relating to the Election of the President and the Vice President*, p. 14. Appreciation is expressed to Tom Hosmanek for pointing out this exchange.

49 Editorial, *New York Times*, June 2, 1969.

50 *Congressional Record*, September 10, 1969, p. H 7747. These points, arranged differently, are discussed in chapter 1, pp. 18-21.

51 Quoted in *New York Times*, September 11, 1969.

52 The Dowdy-Dennis-Poff substitute amendment lost on a teller vote of 159 to 192, and Representative Poff (but not Dowdy or Dennis) voted for House Joint Resolution 681 on final passage.

53 It is ironic that the House of Representatives should act first in eliminating its own unique powers and responsibilities for presidential selection in the case of electoral college deadlock.

54 Both House roll call votes can be found in *Congressional Quarterly Weekly Report*, September 26, 1969, p. 1830. The final House vote on passage of House Joint Resolution 681 was widely and erroneously reported at the time in wire service reports, as well as in the daily edition of the *Congressional Record*, to be *339* to 70. The actual roll call, as printed in the later bound *Congressional Record* and in the *Congressional Quarterly*, however, shows the correct affirmative vote to be 338.

55 These rankings can be found in *Congressional Quarterly Weekly Report*, February 20, 1970, pp. 570-71. The ADA scores were based on the percentage of the time each representative voted in accordance with the ADA position on fifteen selected votes of

1969. The percentages were compiled by ADA. Failure to vote lowered the scores. The ACA scores were based on the percentage of the time each representative voted in accordance with the ACA position on seventeen selected votes of 1969. Failure to vote did not lower the scores, which were compiled by ACA. Only the ACA included the motion to recommit in its selected votes of 1969. The ACA position was "Yes." On the other hand, neither the ACA nor the ADA included the final vote on House Joint Resolution 681 in their selected votes of 1969. Appreciation is expressed to John H. Yunker for the following analysis using the ADA and ACA scores.

56 To some degree, the moderate character of the recommittal opponents is also due to the large size of the group, which tends to have a centrist influence on any overall average.

57 This group opposed to direct vote on the final vote included three "maverick liberals" with ADA scores over 80 and ACA scores under 15. Excluding these three deviant cases from the sixty-seven other representatives results in an ADA average for direct vote opponents of 7.7, and an ACA average of 76.0. Two of these direct vote opponents were blacks: Representative Charles C. Diggs, Jr. (D., Mich.) and William Clay (D., Mo.). Of the other black congressmen five voted for direct vote, one was paired for it, and one was absent.

58 "News of the Week in Review," *New York Times*, September 21, 1969. It was also noted that the appointment of Senator Robert P. Griffin (R., Mich.) as a member of the Senate Judiciary Committee on September 19 might provide a crucially needed new vote for direct vote in that committee.

59 *New York Times*, September 21, 1969.

60 Max Lerner syndicated column, September 25, 1969. Max Lerner also expressed concern about the psychological loss of the electoral college, which provides a "sense of identity. By being part of the big-state vote in the popular states, the historic American minorities—Catholics, Jews, Negroes—have had some sort of psychological equalization for their minority position." Syndicated column, September 24, 1969.

61 See, for example, *New York Times*, editorial of September 21, 1969.

62 The complete text of President Nixon's statement can be found in *Congressional Quarterly Weekly Report*, October 3, 1969, p. 1880.

63 *New York Times*, October 1, 1969.

64 *New York Times*, October 7, 1969.

65 For valuable background information and specifics on this material, appreciation is expressed to the sixty-eight United States senators (thirty-six Democrats and thirty-two Republicans) who responded to requests during the summer of 1970 for information about their position on electoral reform, as well as to the following persons who were interviewed in Washington during 1970: Doug Bennet, Jr., administrative assistant to Senator Eagleton; Jason Berman, staff director, Subcommittee on Constitutional Amendments; Judy Campbell, League of Women Voters of the United States, Legisla-

tive Action Committee; Donald Channell, director of the Washington Office of the ABA; David Clanton, legislative assistant to Senator Griffin; Myron P. Curzan, member of Washington law firm of Arnold and Porter; Ken Davis, legislative assistant to Senator Scott; Joseph J. Fanelli, manager of Public Affairs Department of Chamber of Commerce of the United States; Charles Ferris, staff member, Democratic Policy Committee; Jack Lewis, legislative assistant to Senator Spong; David Osterhort, legislative assistant to Senator Nelson; Neal R. Peirce, associate editor of the Center for Political Research; Richard Scammon, director of Elections Research Center; Robert Smith, chief counsel of the Subcommittee on Revision and Codification of the Senate Judiciary Committee; and Dorothy Stimpson, staff director, Legislative Action Committee of the League of Women Voters of the United States.

66 *New York Times*, February 4, 1970.
67 It was reported that these hearings, and the witnesses for them, had been secretly arranged in advance by Senator Sam Ervin, Jr. (D., N.C.) and Senator Roman Hruska (R., Nebr.), both staunch opponents of direct vote.
68 *New York Times*, April 16, 1970.
69 See Senate, *Supplemental Hearings on Electoral College Reform.*
70 *New York Times*, April 19, 1970.
71 Those who voted for the proportional plan were Senators James O. Eastland (D., Miss.), John L. McClellan (D., Ark.), Sam J. Ervin, Jr. (D., N.C.), Robert C. Byrd (D., W.Va.), Roman L. Hruska (R., Nebr.), Hiram L. Fong (R., Hawaii), Hugh Scott (R., Pa.), and Strom Thurmond (R., S.C.). Those opposed to the proportional plan (and thus in favor of the direct vote plan) were Senators Thomas J. Dodd (D., Conn.), Philip A. Hart (D., Mich.), Edward M. Kennedy (D., Mass.), Birch Bayh (D., Ind.), Quentin N. Burdick (D., N.Dak.), Joseph D. Tydings (D., Md.), Robert D. Griffin (R., Mich.), Marlow W. Cook (R., Ky.), and Charles McC. Mathias, Jr. (R., Md.). On the final vote on passage of the direct vote plan, these latter nine senators were joined by Senators Byrd and Scott who had previously voted for the proportional plan, resulting in eleven votes for Senate Joint Res. 1.
72 *New York Times*, April 26, 1970. See also the discussion of this tactic earlier in this chapter.
73 Senate Joint Resolution 1 as approved by the Senate Judiciary Committee differed from the House-passed H. J. Resolution 681 in only one significant respect—the date when the proposed constitutional amendment would become effective after ratification by the states. While the House measure provided for a January 21 date, and the Senate bill for April 15, Senator Bayh noted that he had an agreement from the House leadership to accept the later date. *New York Times*, April 24, 1970.
74 Washington interviews with Jason Berman, September 17, 1970; and Malcolm Hawk, September 16, 1970. The benefits of delay to direct vote opponents were clear to all concerned. The reason for

such delay on the part of the minority is thus easily understood; however, the delays on the part of the committee majority are less comprehensible.

75 Telephone interview with Benjamin L. Zelenko, October 30, 1970. One of the chief Senate aides working for direct vote concluded that the delay in obtaining a committee vote and the delay in getting the bill to the floor were probably, in retrospect, what hurt electoral reform the most. Washington interview with Jason Berman, November 13, 1970.

76 During the intervening months, one significant external event had occurred, somewhat boosting electoral reform's chances. This was the June 2 narrow victory of George Wallace in the Alabama gubernatorial primary, which, in addition to giving him a base for the 1972 presidential election, revived speculation about the possibilities of an electoral college deadlock resulting from a three-way 1972 contest. Some news reports went as far as to suggest that the renewed Wallace threat might lead President Nixon to push electoral reform in the Senate and, subsequently, in the states. See, for example, *New York Times*, June 4, 1970.

77 U.S., Congress, Senate, Senate Judiciary Committee, *Direct Popular Election of the President: Report on Senate Joint Resolution 1*, 91st Cong., 2nd sess., August 14, 1970, pp. 1-14, 15-21.

78 Ibid., pp. 24-55, esp. pp. 24 and 51.

79 One interesting but basically unrelated event during this period was the widely publicized September 8 release, by the Center for the Study of Democratic Institutions of Santa Barbara, California, of a draft of a new Constitution of the United States, which provided for direct election of a president for a single, nine-year term (unless rejected after three years of his term), who would exercise broad political and policy-making, but no administrative, responsibilities. The League of Women Voters of the United States announced its support for direct election on January 15, 1970, following a poll showing 78 percent of its 160 thousand members favoring the recently passed H. J. Res. 681.

80 Washington interview with Joseph J. Fanelli, manager of Public Affairs Department of the Chamber of Commerce of the United States, September 14, 1970.

81 See *New York Times*, July 12, 1970, and *Congressional Quarterly Weekly Report*, May 15, 1970, p. 1314.

82 Washington interviews with Joseph J. Fanelli, September 14, 1970, and November 12, 1970. See also *New York Times*, September 10, 1970.

83 For example, a Rowland Evans and Robert Novak nationally syndicated column of April 7 reported that the Nixon administration had seemed to have lost all interest in electoral reform due to a view that direct vote might hurt Nixon's reelection prospects. A public repudiation of the 1969 endorsement, however, would be politically awkward; therefore, the administration strategy was one

of "nonresponse," together with a private hope that the direct vote plan would be defeated in the Senate.

84 *New York Times*, September 7, 1970.

85 Interestingly enough, this criticism of Congress for not acting faster on a matter on which he himself had been so long ambivalent, was contained in a statement entitled "A Call for Cooperation."

86 Washington interview with David Osterhort, September 15, 1970; Washington interview with Doug Bennet, Jr., September 16, 1970.

87 "Hardy College Spirit: Senate Debate," *Newsweek*, September 21, 1970, p. 42.

88 Fanelli interview, September 14, 1970.

89 Hawk interview, September 16, 1970. This general conclusion was also reached in Washington interviews with Berman, September 17, 1970; Dan Leach, September 15, 1970; and Dorothy Stimpson, September 14, 1970.

90 Tom Wicker, *New York Times*, September 17, 1970.

91 Bayh, quoted in *New York Times* Editorial, September 10, 1970.

92 *Congressional Quarterly Weekly Report*, September 11, 1970. p. 2212.

93 Ibid.

94 Comment on the floor of the U.S. Senate, September 17, 1970. An inspection of the *Congressional Record* of that day fails to find that observation remaining in the edited record.

95 See *New York Times*, September 14, 1970.

96 Bennet interview, September 16, 1970.

97 The preceding discussion of the nature of this issue is drawn from interviews with Bennet, September 16, 1970; Berman, September 17, 1970; Fanelli, September 14, 1970; and Hawk, September 16, 1970.

98 *New York Times*, September 10, 1970. This assessment so heartened direct vote opponent Senator Strom Thurmond that he reportedly began to feel that a filibuster might not be necessary.

99 *New York Times*, September 14, 1970. This article was resented by direct vote supporters who objected to its air of finality. One key legislative aide opposed to direct vote stresses the importance of this and other articles in the *New York Times* at this time: "I feel they signaled the death knell for S.J. Res. 1 and were perceived as such by several wavering Senators." Personal letter from Malcolm Hawk, legislative assistant to Senator Roman Hruska, July 1, 1971.

100 This senator was Eugene J. McCarthy (D., Minn.) who, on September 15, cosigned a letter with Senator Sam J. Ervin, Jr. (D., N.C.) strongly opposing direct vote, which was then sent to all members of the Senate. In spite of what was described by an Ervin aide as "a sexy angle," Senator McCarthy's position failed to sway any other senators. The quoted statement was made by Professor Charles Black of Yale Law School, and was quoted approvingly by Senators Ervin and McCarthy in their letter.

101 Osterhort interview, September 15, 1970.

102 Mr. Mode was chief counsel of the Subcommittee on Constitutional Amendments.

103 Interviews with Berman, September 17, 1970; Fanelli, September 18, 1970; and Hawk, September 16, 1970. During this time, the Bayh and Mansfield staff worked essentially independently on such important matters as counting votes, with, as one key aide put it, Mansfield clearly playing the role of majority leader, as opposed to proponent of the bill. Berman interview, September 17, 1970.

104 *New York Times*, September 15, 1970.

105 Ibid.

106 Leach interview, September 15, 1970. Such a cloture vote would also move the Senate along toward adjournment.

107 Berman interview, September 17, 1970; Hawk interview, September 16, 1970.

108 This observation, and much of the preceding paragraph, is drawn from a Washington interview with Robert Smith, September 16, 1970. Mr. Smith served, in effect, as a member of Senator Ervin's staff.

109 This observation, and much of the preceding paragraph, is drawn from the Hawk interview, September 16, 1970.

110 Dan Leach, of Senator Mansfield's staff, discussed, in an interview held on the morning of September 15, 1970, the meeting of southern direct vote opponents currently in progress.

111 *Congressional Record* (Daily Edition), September 15, 1970, p. S 15477.

112 This cloture petition had five signatures more than needed, for a total of twenty-one: fourteen Democrats and seven Republicans.

113 One key lobbyist working for direct vote criticized Mansfield's decision to push for cloture on September 15, because this move may have been unfortunately premature. Apparently, this lobbyist would have preferred to have seen the attempts to work out a unanimous consent agreement continued and the cloture motion held back a little. These goals, of course, would have been comparable with those of Senator Bayh, but somewhat incompatible with the goals of the majority leader. They were also, in the light of the southern caucus decision of September 15, quite impossible. Telephone interview with Fanelli, September 18, 1970.

114 *New York Times*, September 16, 1970. Only forty-four of these fifty-one motions came to an actual vote. With approval in only eight of these cases, cloture has enjoyed a success rate of about 18 percent of all motions voted on.

115 Editorial, *New York Times*, September 18, 1970; ibid., September 19, 1970; column by Tom Wicker, ibid., September 17, 1970.

116 This vote, as well as the next one, will be subject to more detailed analysis later.

117 *Congressional Quarterly Weekly Report*, September 18, 1970, p. 2239; and Associated Press report, September 18, 1970.

118 Berman interview, September 17, 1970.

119 See, for example, Froman, *The Congressional Process*.
120 Since it was an election year, adjournment or recess by October 15 was necessary to allow senators up for reelection some time to make an appearance in their states. The question was not really whether there would be adjournment by October 15, but whether it would be necessary to come back for a lame-duck congressional session after the election in November. It was.
121 *New York Times*, September 26, 1970; editorial in ibid., September 29, 1970; ibid., September 26, 1970.
122 Ibid., September 30, 1970.
123 Ibid.
124 Washington interviews with Berman, November 13, 1970, and Fanelli, November 12, 1970, and news story in *Milwaukee Sentinel*, October 6, 1971.
125 The Spong plan was introduced on September 16, 1970, as a possible compromise direct vote plan (Washington interview with Jack Lewis, legislative assistant to Senator Spong, November 13, 1970). It was among those presented to and rejected by direct vote opponents at the October 5 meeting in room S220. At that time, Senator Bayh said that the Spong plan was acceptable to him, although, as one of his chief aides later noted, it is not as good as one which would avoid the joint session of Congress procedure (Berman interview, November 13, 1970). During mid-November, the head of the Washington office of the ABA indicated that possibly his organization could live with such a plan (Washington interview with Donald Channell, director of the Washington Office of the ABA, November 13, 1970) and possible similar lukewarm endorsement by the League of Women Voters was hinted at on November 13 (Washington interview with Judy Campbell, League of Women Voters Legislative Action Committee, November 13, 1970). Later in the month, however, the National Board of the League decided to oppose the Spong plan on the grounds that it was itself insufficient and would head off more fundamental reform (personal letter from Judy Campbell, December 14, 1970). Regardless of support—lukewarm or enthusiastic—for the Spong plan, the fact remains, however, that no warmth was exhibited toward it by direct vote opponents, who equally opposed all electoral reform plans incorporating a direct vote for president.
126 Personal letter from Judy Campbell, December 14, 1970.
127 The roll call vote on the first cloture vote can be found in *Congressional Quarterly Weekly Report*, September 18, 1970, p. 2239.
128 The roll call vote on the second cloture vote can be found in *Congressional Quarterly Weekly Report*, October 2, 1970, p. 2296.
129 *Congressional Quarterly Weekly Report*, September 18, 1970, p. 2239, and October 2, 1970, p. 2296.
130 These rankings can be found in *Congressional Quarterly Weekly Report*, April 16, 1971, p. 865. The ADA score was based on the percentage of the time each senator voted in accordance with, was

paired for, or announced for the ADA position on 32 selected votes
from December 1969 to December 1970. The percentages were
compiled by ADA. Failure to vote lowered the scores. The ACA
score was based on the percentage of the time each senator voted in
accordance with the ACA position on 24 selected votes of 1970.
Failure to vote did not lower the scores, which were compiled by
ACA. Only the ADA included the second cloture motion among its
selected votes, while neither group included the first cloture motion. The ADA position on the second motion was "Yes." Appreciation is expressed to John H. Yunker for the following analysis
using the ADA and ACA scores.

131 The mean scores of the ten senators not voting were ADA 36.6,
ACA 33.6.

132 The mean scores of the thirteen senators not voting were ADA
34.9, ACA 44.3.

133 Little concerted effort toward reform of the electoral college has
been evident in the years immediately following the 1970 defeat.
Bills incorporating the direct vote plan in different variants have
regularly been introduced in the Senate and House, but little activity
has resulted from these perfunctory moves. The only formal congressional action during this period was the little-noticed *Hearings
on Electoral College Reform* by the Senate Judiciary Committee,
Subcommittee on Constitutional Amendments, of 26 and 27 September 1973. The printed record of these proceedings provides
useful information on the status of electoral college reform as of
1973. Another recent publication offers an overview of electoral
college reform circa 1974: see Lawrence D. Longley, "The Electoral
College," *Current History* 67 (August 1974): 64–69 ff.–this is a
special issue devoted to "American Political Reform."

Index

Adams, John: in election of 1796, 29; in election of 1824, 36–37
AFL–CIO, 145, 159
Agnew, Spiro T., 138
Alabama, 121; unpledged elector slates, 2, 4–5; popular votes, 5; in election of 1960, 35, 54, 132
Alaska, 118; in election of 1960, 46; constant two, 95
Albert, Carl, 154
Allen, James B., 138
Allott, Gordon, 171
American Bar Association (ABA), 145, 146, 159; endorses direct vote plan, 65, 133, 135; Commission on Electoral College Reform, 88, 134, 135, 136, 139, 142
American Farm Bureau Federation, 143
Americans for Constitutional Action (ACA), 153, 175
Americans for Democratic Action (ADA), 153, 175
American Good Government Society, 142–43
American Jewish Council, 143
Apportionment of electoral votes, 179, 182
Arizona, 96
Arkansas, 8
Automatic plan, 43–49, 79–80, 119, 128–57 passim; arguments for, 47–48; arguments against, 48–49; evaluation of, 76–78
Average voting power: per citizen-voter, 106; percent deviations from, 106–20

Bailey, Dr. Lloyd W., 11–12, 137–39
Baker, Howard H., Jr., 138, 162, 171
Baker, Russell, 186
Baker v. Carr, 132

Banzhaf, John F., III, 105, 106, 107, 118, 136, 142, 144
Bayh, Birch, 133, 138, 148, 156, 160, 162–63, 168, 170–72; supports automatic plan, 45, 134; supports direct vote plan, 64, 134, 136; on federalism, 84; on swing voters, 101; in 1967 hearings, 136; fights Nixon's Supreme Court nominees, 161; opposes cloture motion, 166; objects to unanimous consent requests, 167–68, 170; faces adjournment push, 168
Bellmon, Henry, 162
Benson, Mrs. Bruce, 159
Benton, Thomas Hart, 19
Berman, Jason, 167, 171
Bickel, Alexander M., 85, 142, 157; on party politics under direct vote plan, 86; supports automatic plan, 139
Biester, Edward, 142
Bischoff, Dr. Charles W., on multiplier effect, 3, 10–11
Blacks, voting power of: under electoral college, 100–03, 119–22; under proportional plan, 123, 125; under district plan, 124–25
Booth, Arch, 159
Boyd, Willian J. D., 102
Bradley, Justice, 34–35
Brookings Institution, 88–89
Brooks, Jack, 142
Bryan, William J.: in election of 1896, 51–52; in election of 1900, 52
Bucalew, Charles R., 70
Burdick, Quentin N., 134–35
Burns, James MacGregor: on two-party system, 90; on chances for electoral reform, 131
Burr, Aaron, 31–32
Byrd, Harry F., 4–6
Byrd, Robert C., 171

Cahill, William, 144
California, 96, 102, 107, 118
Carswell, G. Harold, 155, 161, 164
Celler, Emanuel, 140–46 passim; in proportional plan hearings, 51; on direct vote plan, 127; exchange with Mitchell, 143–44
Central city residents, voting power of: under electoral college, 121–22; under proportional plan, 123, 125; under district plan, 124, 125
Chamber of Commerce of the United States, 145, 159; referendum on electoral reform, 132, 133; endorses direct vote plan and district plan, 133
Clay, Henry, 36–37
Cleveland, Grover, 35, 52
Cloture motion, 166–68; introduced on S.J. Res. 1, 168; failed first time, 169; failed second time, 170; third petition withdrawn, 172; voting analysis, 172–75
Colmer, William M., 146–47
Colorado, 96
Committee of Eleven, 24–25
Compromise of 1877, 35
Congress, Joint Session: contingent election, 62, 64, 71–73, 77–78, 81, 92–93, 135–36, 158, 171, 188; counting electoral votes in 1968, 137–39. *See also* House contingent election; Senate
Congressional Quarterly, 5
Connecticut, 95
Connecticut Plan, 23, 27
Constant two, 18, 21, 47–48, 56, 63, 76, 78–79, 82, 95, 107, 118, 148; problem, 20; eliminated in direct vote plan, 64, 66, 68; and federalism, 84; effect on small states, 97–99
Constitutional amendments, 129. *See also* Twelfth Amendment; Twenty-fifth Amendment; Twenty-third Amendment
Constitutional Convention of 1787, 23–28 passim
Conyers, John, 142
Corwin, Edward, 97

Coudert, Frederic R., Jr., 57
Coughlin, R. Lawrence, 142
Curtis, Carl T., 162
Curtis, Kenneth M., 140

Daniels substitute, 58
David, Paul, 136
Davis, Jerrett, 70
Davis, John W., 95
Davis, Justice David, 34
Delaware, 95, 135
Delegate model, 104–05
Dennis, David, 142, 149–50
Dickenson, John, 23
Direct vote plan, xv, 43, 51, 64–69, 81–83, 100, 102–03, 114–15, 117, 118, 119, 120, 125, 127–76 passim; possible effect in past elections, 53, 65–66; arguments for, 66–68; arguments against, 68–69, 83–128; recommittal motion in House, 149–53
District of Columbia, 105, 106–07, 121, 186, 202
District plan, 43, 54, 57–64, 112–13, 117, 118, 119, 120, 124, 125, 128–76 passim; possible effect in past elections, 53, 58–59; arguments for, 61–62; arguments against, 62–64; evaluation of, 79–81
Dixon, Robert G., Jr., 98
Dole, Robert, 71, 171
Donohue, Harold, 142
Dowdy, John, 142, 149
Dreele, W. H. von, 127
Dualism, 88–89

Eagleton, Thomas F., 71
East, voting power of: under electoral college, 121–22; under proportional plan, 123, 125; under district plan, 124, 125
Eastland, James O., 133, 148, 155–57, 158
Edwards, Don, 142
Edwards, Edwin W., 142
Eilberg, Joshua, 142
Election Commission, in 1876 election, 34–35
Election of 1796, 29, 31

Election of 1800, 31–32, 36, 46
Election of 1820, 29
Election of 1824, 36–37, 46
Election of 1828, 40
Election of 1836, 40
Election of 1840, 40
Election of 1844, 38, 40
Election of 1848, 38, 40
Election of 1856, 38, 40
Election of 1860, 38, 40, 66
Election of 1864, 40
Election of 1868, 40
Election of 1876, 33–35, 37, 38, 40, 46, 51
Election of 1880, 38, 40, 51
Election of 1884, 38, 40
Election of 1888, 35, 37, 38, 40, 46–47, 51
Election of 1892, 38, 40
Election of 1896, 40, 51–52
Election of 1900, 40, 52
Election of 1908, 40
Election of 1912, 39
Election of 1916, 39, 40
Election of 1924, 95
Election of 1948, 29, 39, 40, 53–54, 58
Election of 1952, 53
Election of 1956, 53, 188–89
Election of 1960, 1–7, 35, 37, 46, 53–54, 70, 132; popular vote, 2, 3, 33, 39; electoral vote, 2, 33, 39; disadvantages of electoral college, 7; faithless elector, 29; hairbreadth election, 40
Election of 1964, 53
Election of 1968, 7–18, 53, 58, 91, 137, 189; tallies of votes, 11, 39; popular vote shifts, 11; faithless elector, 29; hairbreadth election, 40
Election of 1972, xiv, xv, 60, 106, 181; electoral vote, xiii; faithless elector, xiv, 29; results under various plans, 53
Election of 1976, xiv, 106, 175
Election of 1980, 106
Electoral college: empirical research on, xiv–xv, 96–126 passim, 179–80, 196, 200–02

Electoral reform: obstacles to, 43, 127–29; goals of, 74–76; not a "gut issue," 163; prospects, 175–76, 214
Electors. *See* Presidential electors
Ervin, Sam J., Jr. 138, 159, 168, 171; supports automatic plan, 45; urges vote against cloture, 170

Faithless elector, 18, 76–77, 137–39, 148; in election of 1972, xiv, 29; in election of 1968, 11–13; problem of, 17, 18–19; cause of, 28; in elections of 1796, 1820, 1848, 1960, 29; in election of 1956, 188–89
Far West, voting power of: under electoral college, 121–22, under proportional plan, 123, 125; under district plan, 124, 125
Federalism, 75, 77, 159; under proportional plan, 79; under district plan, 80; under direct vote plan, 83–85; under electoral college, 130
Federalist, The, 21
Federal system plan, 81; features of, 71; arguments for, 72–73; arguments against, 73
Feerick, John D., 28, 142
Feighan, Michael, 142
Ferguson, Homer, 45
Ferris, Charles, 165, 171
Filibuster, 163, 165, 167, 169
Fish, Hamilton, 142
Florida, 34, 96
Flowers, Walter, 142
Fong, Hiram L., 159
Fraud, 76–77, 159; charges of in 1960 election, 4; under proportional plan, 79; under district plan, 80–81; under direct vote plan, 83; evaluation of, 85–86
Free-agent model, 105
Freund, Paul, 20–21, 103

Gallup poll, on direct vote plan, 134, 154, 156
Garfield, James A., 51
Georgia, 121

Goldwater, Barry, 6
Goodwin, Richard N., 157
Gossett, Ed, 50
Gossett, William T., 141, 145
Gray v. *Sanders,* 74
Great Compromise. *See* Connecticut Plan
Griffin, Robert, 158, 171
Group biases; under proportional plan, 79, 123, 125; under district plan, 80, 124, 125; under direct vote plan, 83, under electoral college, 96–126, 131

Hairbreadth elections, 37, 40–41
Hamilton, Alexander, 21
Hancock, Winfield S., 51
Harris, Lea, 6
Harrison, Benjamin, 35, 52
Hawaii, 3
Hayes, Rutherford B., 34
Haynes, Charles, 44
Haynsworth, Clement, 155, 161, 164
Hillhouse, James, 69
Hillhouse plan, 70
Hospers, John, xiv, 189
House, contingent election, 14–18, 30, 37, 62, 71–72, 76–78, 82, 92–93, 148; possibilities in 1960, 7; possibilities in 1968, 14–17; likelihood of, 20; problems of, 20–21; result of large and small state compromise, 27–28; modification of, 44, 46; eliminated in direct vote plan, 64, 66; disenfranchisement of D.C., 186; fictional scenarios, 186
House Joint Resolution 681, 34, 149, 160; reported by Senate Judiciary Committee, 146; open rule on, 147; proposed amendments to, 148–49; recommittal motion, 149–53; passage of, 150–53
House Judiciary Committee, on direct vote plan, 128, 139–46
House of Representatives, 130; in amending process, 129; reapportionment of, 132; rejection of faithless elector challenge, 139

House Rules Committee, hearings on H.J. Res. 681, 146–47
Hruska, Roman L., 159, 162, 168, 171
Humphrey, Hubert H., 58, 70; in 1968 election, 8–17 passim, 91
Hungate, William, 142
Hutchinson, Edward, 142
Hybrid reform plans, 69–73, 81–82

Illinois, 3, 102; state legislalture in 1876 election, 34
Irwin, Henry D., 132; unpledged elector in 1960 election, 4, 6

Jackson, Andrew, 36–37
Jacobs, Andrew, 142
Jaffe, Michael D., 143
Jefferson, Thomas: in 1796 election, 29; in 1800 electoral college deadlock, 31–32; on House contingent election procedure, 37; supports automatic plan, 44
Johnson, Andrew, 70
Johnson, Lyndon B., 141; supports automatic plan, 45; 1966 address to Congress, 133
Joint Session of Congress; counting electoral votes in 1968, 137–39
Joint Session of Congress contingent election, 61–62, 65, 71–73, 77–78, 81, 92–93, 135–36, 158, 165; from top three contenders, 190

Kallenbach, Joseph F., 97, 136
Kastenmeier, Robert, 142
Katzenbach, Nicholas, 45
Kefauver, Estes, 98, 132–33
Kennedy, John F., 46, 54, 59, 70; in 1960 election, 2–7 passim; supports automatic plan, 45
Key, V. O., Jr., 93
Kirby, James C., Jr., 142
Koenig, Louis, 97
Kristol, Irving, 74
Krock, Arthur, 42

Lacock, Abner, 64
Large state bias, 94, 97–99, 104, 106–07, 131

Lawrence, William T., 50
Leach, Dan, 165
League of Women Voters of the
United States, 159
Lerner, Max, 154
Lewis, Anthony, 154
Liberty Lobby, 143
Lodge, Henry Cabot, 50
Lodge-Gossett plan, 45, 50, 58
Long, Russell, 171
Long ballot, 188
Louisiana, 34, 121
Lynn, John C., 143

MacBride, Roger, xiv, 189
McClellan, John L., 159
McClory, Robert, 142
McCulloch, William M., 92, 141–42
MacGregor, Clark, 142
McKinley, William, 52
Madden, Ray, 147
Madison, James, 24, 27
Maine, xiv, 140, 176, 187
Mann, Irwin, 104
Mann, James, 142
Mansfield, Mike, 165–66, 170, 171;
on federalism, 84–85; introduces
cloture motion on S.J. Res. 1,
168, 170–71
Mason, George, 27
Massachusetts, 30, 107
Mass media, 91
Meany, George, 142, 159
Meskill, Thomas, 142
Michener, James, 12–13
Michigan, 102, 140
Midwest, voting power of: under
electoral college, 121–22; under
proportional plan, 123, 125; under
district plan, 124, 125
Mikva, Abner, 142
Miles, Samuel, 29
Minhart, Thomas, 13
Minority presidents, 37, 187
Mississippi, 121; in 1960 election,
2, 4–5, 46, 54, 132
Missouri, 3, 59
Mitchell, Clarence, 142
Mitchell, John N., 143–44
Mode, P. J., 165, 171

Montgomery, Thomas, 70
Morley, Felix, 26
Morley, John, 49
Morris, Gouverneur, 24
Mountain States, voting power of:
under electoral college, 121–22;
under proportional plan, 123, 125;
under district plan, 124, 125
Multiplier effect, 55–56, 77–78; 182;
in 1972 election, xiii, xiv, 182; in
1960 election, 2–3, 181–82; in
election of minority presidents,
37; in 1968 election, 182
Mundt, Karl E., 57, 138
Mundt-Coudert plan, 57–58
Muskie, Edmund S., 138

NAACP, 142
National Cotton Council of America,
143
Nevada, 3
New Jersey Plan, 23
New Mexico, 3
New York, 30, 35, 86, 102, 118
New York Times, 169, 171; on
direct vote plan, 153–56
Nicholas, John, 57
Nixon, Richard M., xiv, 46, 54, 58–
59, 70, 137–39; on minority
presidents, 1; in 1960 election,
2–7 passim; in 1968 election, 8–17
passim, 91; on electoral reform,
139–41; on proportional plan,
146; on direct vote plan, 146, 154,
156, 159–61, 164, 210–11
Norris, George W., 44
North Carolina, 8

O'Hara, James G., 138
Ohio, 35, 102, 138
Orfield, Gary, 184

Parris, Judith, 84
Party competition, 75, 77
Peirce, Neal R., 5, 142; on 1960
election, 1; on electoral college,
18, 26, 99, 101–02; on electoral
reform, 42; on proportional plan,
51; on direct vote plan, 86; on

black voters, 103; his *The People's President*, 137
Pennsylvania, 35, 102
Plurality election, 92–93
Poff, Richard H., 142, 149, 151
Political parties, 28. *See also* Two-party system
Polsby, Nelson W., 98–100
Popular vote: shifts, 17, 182; reversals in electoral college, 18, 20–21
Powell, Lazarus W., 70
Presidential Disability Amendment, 135
P. dential effectiveness, 75; under automatic plan, 80; under district plan, 80; under proportional plan, 80; under hybrid plans, 81; under direct vote plan, 83
Presidential electors, 78, 82; anonymity, 2; number, 2; independence, 21; laws requiring pledges, 29; popular election of, 30–31; eliminated in direct vote plan, 64, 66; methods of choosing nominees, 181
Progressive Party, 9
Proportional plan, 43, 49–56, 79–80, 107, 110–11, 116, 117–19, 120, 123, 125, 128–57 passim; arguments for, 54–55; arguments against, 55–56

Railsback, Tom, 142
Reform plans: comparative results, 45, 53. *See also* Automatic plan; Direct vote plan; District plan; Federal system plan; Hybrid reform plans; Proportional plan
Regional parties, 17, 67, 87
Relative voting power: of citizen-voters, 104; of states under electoral college, 104; of citizen-voters under electoral college and automatic plan, 105–07, 108–09, 116, 120; of citizen-voters under proportional plan, 107, 110–11, 116, 117–19, 120; of citizen-voters under district plan, 112–

13, 117, 118, 119, 120; of citizen-voters under direct vote plan, 114–15, 117, 118, 119, 120
Riker, William, 104
Roche, John, 22, 26
Rodino, Peter, 142
Rogers, Byron, 142
Rosenthal, Albert, 96, 102
Runoff election, 82, 85, 87, 158, 162, 165, 167; under direct vote plan, 83, 135–36; evaluation of, 90–94; likelihood of, 91–92; alternatives to, 92; effect on minor parties, 93; endorsed by Nixon, 140
Rural areas, voting power of: under electoral college, 121–22; under proportional plan, 123, 125; under district plan, 124, 125
Russell, Richard, 167
Ryan, William, 142

St. Onge, William, 142
Sandman, Charles, 142
Sayre, Wallace, 84
Scammon, Richard M., 143
Senate: in amending process, 129; rejection of faithless elector challenge, 139; contingent election of vice-president, 185
Senate Joint Resolution, 1, 162; reported, 158; debate on, 162; opposition to, 164–65; pressure for adjournment, 165–66; cloture motion, 166, 169, 170, 172; filibuster, 167
Senate Judiciary Committee: on direct vote plan, 128, 155–56, 157–59; 1970 supplemental hearings, 156–57; rejects automatic plan, 157; rejects district plan, 157; rejects proportional plan, 157; Constitutional Amendments Subcommittee, xiv, 65, 98, 132, 133, 134, 139–40, 147–49, 214; 1973 hearings, xiv, 214
Separation of powers, 159
Shapley, Lloyd S., 104
Short ballot, 181, 188

Silva, Ruth, 52
Sindler, Allan, 99
Small state bias: under electoral college and direct vote plan, 94–95; under electoral college and automatic plan, 97–99, 106–07, 130–31, 144; under proportional plan, 117–18, 125; under district plan, 118, 125
Smith, Henry, 142
Smith, William L., 42
Sorauf, Frank, 89
South: under proportional plan, 52, 123, 125; under electoral college, 99–100, 121, 122; under direct vote plan, 99–100; under district plan, 124, 125; opposition to S.J. Res. 1, 164
South Carolina: in 1968 election, 8, 95; resisted popular election of electors, 31; in 1876 election, 34
Spong, William B., 71, 171
Spong plan, 81, 172; features of, 71–72; arguments for, 72–73; arguments against, 73
States' rights, 164
States' Rights Party, 9
Story, Robert G., 142
Supreme Court of the United States, 135, 138
Swing states, 85–86, 99
Swing voters, 101

Tennessee, 8
Texas, 96, 102
Third parties, xiii, 9, 17, 87, 130
Thurmond, Strom, 9, 159, 162
Tilden, Samuel J., 22, 33–34
Truman, David, 145
Twelfth Amendment, 15, 28, 32, 36, 42
Twenty-fifth Amendment, 135
Twenty-third Amendment, 115
Two-party system, 159; under proportional plan, 79; under direct vote plan, 83, 86–90; under electoral college, 88–90, 130; theories about, 89
Tydings, Joseph, 157–58

Tydings-Griffin plan, 81, 158, 165, 167; features of, 70–71; arguments for, 72–73; arguments against, 73; feared by opponents of direct vote plan, 167

United Auto Workers (UAW), 159–60
Unit rule, 18, 21, 76, 78–79, 82, 95, 99, 107, 148; in 1960 election, 3; in 1968 election, 8; effects of, 17, 19–20, 104; problem of, 19–20; development of, 31; eliminated in direct vote plan, 64, 66; under electoral college, 104; under proportional plan, 118; Delaware suit against, 135
Unpledged elector strategy, in 1960 election, 4–6
Urban areas, voting power of: under electoral college, 100–03, 121–22; under proportional plan, 123, 125; under district plan, 124, 125

Vallandigham, Clement L., 70
Virginia, xiv
Virginia plan, 23
Von Dreele, W. H., 127
Voter turnout: discouraged by the unit rule, 19; under direct vote plan, 83; under electoral college, 181

Waggonner, Joe D., 148
Waldie, Jerome, 142
Wallace, George, 58, 127–38, 164; in 1968 election, 8–17 passim, 91; on his electoral vote strategy, 185; victory in Alabama gubernatorial primary, 210
Wallace, Henry A., 9
Washington, George, 26
Watergate, xiii
Weaver, Paul, 74
Weaver, Warren, 157
Wechsler, Herbert, 84, 97
Wekselman, Martin I., 143
White, Theodore H., 85, 157
Wicker, Tom, 5–6, 161–62, 169

Wiggins, Charles, 142
Wildavsky, Aaron B., 98–100
Williams, Harvie, 142
Wilmerding, Lucius, 136
Wilson, James, 24
Winner-take-all feature, 48, 63. *See
    also* Unit rule

Woodcock, Leonard, 159–60
Wright, Edward L., 159

Young, J. Banks, 143

Zeidenstein, Harvey, 100
Zimbalist, Chaim H., 141